The Cowboy and the Canal

How Theodore Roosevelt Cheated Colombia, Stole Panama and Bamboozled America

J.M. Carlisle, PhD

Tangent Publishers
An Imprint of
Integral Publishers
Tucson, Arizona

© 2014 Tangent Publishers

an Imprint of
Integral Publishers
1418 N. Jefferson Ave.
Tucson AZ 85712
831 333-9200

ISBN: 978-0-9896827-9-4

Cover design by Q.T. Punque Arts
Tucxson, AZ

To Russ

John Barrett, Panama Canal: What It Is, What It Means. Washington, D.C.: Pan American Union, 1913

TABLE OF CONTENTS

"Roosevelt's Rough Diggers." Roosevelt leading workers armed with shovels to work on the Panama Canal. Image addresses the worker shortage on the Canal project. *Puck*, Library of Congress, 1906.

INTRODUCTION

THE LORDS OF PANAMA: THE COUNT AND THE COLONEL

*We came to assist the king of Darien, who was the true lord of
Panama, and all the country thereabouts: and that since we
were come so far, it was no reason but that we should have some
satisfaction–THE PIRATE RICHARD SAWKINS, 1679*

This is not a story about the building of the Panama Canal. This is a
story of greed, corruption, fraud, and hubris underlying the purchase
by the United States of the bankrupt Panama Canal Company from
a group of American investors, not from the French government, as
accepted history mistakenly entails. Brilliant historians have amply
documented the story of the American construction of the Panama
Canal with all its heroism, ingenuity, hardship, discrimination, and
gallantry. The story of its acquisition is another topic altogether. This
story has rarely been told and less often, well received. It places one
of America's most beloved icons, Theodore Roosevelt, squarely in
the frame of as a bully and a thug, a vengeful and malicious conniver,
and betrayer of America's trust. Most people will not tolerate
such notions, let alone suspend what they think they know about
Roosevelt to entertain evidence to the contrary. Understanding
the history of the Panama Canal requires piercing the cartoonish
characteristics of the cowboy Rough Rider, spectacles, spurs, and
boyish enthusiasm, to reveal that these affectations were part of
Roosevelt's political calculation designed to deflect analysis, dodge

responsibility, and disorient his critics. Roosevelt's reasons for insisting the U.S. purchase the Panama Canal were both cynically political and intensely personal. It was never about national pride or the progress of civilization.

Roosevelt's Calculation

Above all things on Heaven and Earth, Theodore Roosevelt yearned to become President of the United States. But, stepping into the office over the corpse of William McKinley in 1901 was the last thing he wanted to do. Roosevelt knew the history. No other Vice-President of a slain Commander-in-Chief had ever been elected to the office. Early in his tenure, Roosevelt's hunger to be elected President in his own right propelled him into making policy decisions that would unshackle him from McKinley's ghost. Choosing Panama over Nicaragua was one of a series of cynical political maneuvers that would accomplish this. Bottom line, Roosevelt believed his audacious decision to reject the McKinley endorsed Nicaragua site for the American interoceanic canal and "take Panama" would be good for his election campaign in 1904. His means to this end was peppered with political backstabbing, unprincipled alliances with unscrupulous men, conspiracies, and wresting authority away from Congress to enhance the power of the President and his own family's wealth.

With his 1902 decision to force the purchase of the expiring concession, inaccurate maps and surveys, rotting machinery, and dilapidated buildings from the bankrupt French Panama Canal Company, Roosevelt shocked a nation that was already emotionally and cognitively committed to Nicaragua as the site of America's interoceanic canal. The dirty tricks played by Roosevelt's administration, family, friends, and political allies in Panama's so-called revolt against Colombia rises to the surface in a brew of privilege, politics, determination, bombast, and sheer luck. The story weaves together the intricate historical threads of raw corporate greed with the unrestrained political ambition and gunboat diplomacy of Theodore Roosevelt that resulted in one of the greatest frauds ever perpetrated upon the American public.

There are many scoundrels and few heroes in this progressive era drama. As Americans, we are accustomed to viewing Theodore Roosevelt as the quintessential hero but in this story, Roosevelt is revealed not as the rugged, high-plains cattleman or the valiant leader of the Rough Riders, but a man flawed in character and in spirit. Challenged by the inexorable disintegration of his carefully crafted image as the determined, forceful, fearless, and chivalrous American Westerner, Roosevelt fell further into the cowboy dogma that might makes right. In other words, Roosevelt becomes truly human through the telling of this tale. We see his anxiety of being seen as a weakling, his fear of disability and aging, his insecurity about losing the admiration of a fickle public, and his bewilderment of a changing American ethos. Collectively, these factors drove Roosevelt to double-down on taking bold cowboy measures that reinforced his image as a real man—to himself and to America.

Following Roosevelt's participation in the unseemly and cynical deceptions required to actualize his personal and professional goals, we can more clearly see the disintegration that can occur when a determined and powerful man of fragile character is compelled to retain his dominance regardless of the costs to others. When the scandalous manner in which the property was obtained came to light in 1908, Roosevelt unleashed the prodigious power of the United States government to persecute journalists who asked a most proper question about the $40,000,000 taxpayers paid for Panama, "Who got the money?" The question outraged Roosevelt to the degree that he mobilized the mighty U.S. Government to prosecute those who dared ask, because his own family's involvement in the transaction.

THE CAST OF CHARACTERS

Often blinded by his overriding ambition, Roosevelt allied himself with men and women who used his power-seeking predisposition to advance their own causes. Together they created an unstoppable force that imposed its desire for the Panamanian interoceanic canal over the objections of the majority of Congress, most of the public, and a preponderance of the press. The atmosphere in which this force incubated was thick with Roosevelt intimates and allies. Individuals who facilitated Roosevelt's behind-the-scenes American syndicate's takeover of the French Panama Canal Company and Panama itself range all the way from his brother-in-law, Douglas Robinson, husband of his youngest sister Corrine; to the scheming would-be French aristocrat, Philippe Bunau-Varilla; a slick New York corporate lawyer, William Cromwell; and the venerable John Hay, Roosevelt's Secretary of State. Some of the most prominent industrialists and capitalists of the day, including financier J.P. Morgan; former president of the New York Stock Exchange, J. Edward Simmons; railroad magnate, George J. Gould; and C.P. Taft, multimillionaire older brother of soon to become United States President William Howard Taft, played major roles in this political theater. All of these men abetted the scheme, but the three men without whom the Panama purchase would never have happened are Theodore Roosevelt, William Nelson Cromwell, and Philippe Bunau-Varilla. A fourth man in this saga, without whom the scandal would have never been revealed, was Joseph Pulitzer. Without Pulitzer's fierce commitment to the freedom of the press, Roosevelt's impropriety would have only been heard in hushed whispers and guarded rumors in the ranks of Washington politicians and Wall Street insiders.

T.R., the Lawyer, and the Frenchman

Roosevelt, Cromwell, and Bunau-Varilla had more in common than an interest in the Panama Canal. William Nelson Cromwell was a dandy. Cromwell—as Theodore Roosevelt as a young New York legislator and Cromwell's French collaborator Philippe Bunau-Varilla—understood the impact of the visual in projecting and maintaining a perceived reality. Indeed for Roosevelt, Cromwell, and Bunau-Varilla, clothes did make the man. All three were fastidious in their appearance, often to the point of being the objects of mockery. Roosevelt, early in his career, learned the power of a physical representation of self when he appeared at a Republican party caucus in a top hat and tails, sporting a gold-headed cane. Afterwards, his peers derided the man who would later be called the epitome of American masculinity as "Jane-Dandy." Variously described as a "Punkin-Lilly," and "Oscar Wilde" by both Democrats and members of his own party, Roosevelt fumed at these effeminate references and began a counter narrative by grounding his masculinity in a series of manly studio portraits. He posed for the camera in 1885 as a frontiersman dressed in deerskin, aiming a rifle, with a Bowie knife tucked into his belt. Later, he costumed as a cowboy in the fashionable portrait studios in New York. Roosevelt struck a similar dashing pose for the camera thirteen years later as a "Rough Rider" wearing a uniform that was tailored for him by Brooks Brothers of New York. While never posing as a cowboy as did Roosevelt, William Nelson Cromwell also gave meticulous attention to the symbolism of attire. However, rather than the rough-hewn of Roosevelt's buckskin costume, Cromwell went for the conspicuities of wealth.

Nearly always seen in a glistening silk top hat and striped silk pants, the flawlessly attired Cromwell gave the impression of congenial, aristocratic gentility, concealing a childhood of destitution and need. A brilliant and resourceful attorney, Cromwell was seen outside his law offices most often in the chic saloons and elegant restaurants where he preferred to conduct business. Rarely was he seen without a glass of champagne in his hand. At a little more than five feet tall, Cromwell's thick, prematurely snow-white hair fell in longish curls dramatically framing his baby blue eyes. For the unsuspecting, these features of the pint-size accountant turned lawyer could disguise Cromwell's other assets—a silver-tongue and his wizardry in accounting. He could, according to some, "smile as sweetly as a society belle and at the same time deal a blow to a business foe that ties him in a hopeless tangle of business knots."[1]

Cromwell's French counterpart in the Panama Canal transaction, Philippe Bunau-Varilla, also presented an air of aristocracy that his birth did not confer upon him. Equally diminutive as Cromwell, the excessively formal Bunau-Varilla struck Americans as charmingly eccentric with his dramatic, waxed and precisely spiked moustache. The fastidiously attired Bunau-Varilla, with his high forehead and piercing dark eyes presented a stern, almost a stage version, of elegant French nobility. Bunau-Varilla's illegitimate birth created a similar experience as Cromwell's humble circumstances, both growing up fatherless.

Each of the three men—Cromwell, Bunau-Varilla, and Roosevelt—used the artifacts of the domain each wished to inhabit to shift perceptions away from his original condition. In the case of

Theodore Roosevelt, people grew to recognize him only as the rugged westerner he portrayed in the studio, losing sight of his patrician Knickerbocker birth. Bunau-Varilla, festooned and decorated as any prince of the realm, used his regal appearance to circumvent questions of his illegitimacy that might, as a result of the cultural conditions of the day, cause concern about his character. And with his presentation of self, William Cromwell ensured a distinctive, yet disarming, appearance that resulted in perplexing his prey.

Panama

One of the strongest characters in the *Cowboy and the Canal* is not an individual, but the country of Panama itself. The Panama Canal—the engineering and logistical wonder forged in the crucible of the heroism and tragedy of the ordinary workers that brought the project to completion—takes second billing against the personality of Panama itself. The country is revealed in the early chapters as an implacable, ruthless force of nature, an adversary against which the formidable weight of progress could not withstand. It is juxtaposed to Nicaragua, the geographic heir apparent to the American interoceanic enterprise and darling of powerful interests represented by Democratic Senator John Tyler Morgan, a scrappy former Confederate general determined to bring prosperity back to his beloved South through the commerce generated by the Nicaragua waterway. Morgan, who had served Alabama in the Senate since 1877, was committed to rebuilding the South. He knew that the Nicaragua canal would bring prosperity to the ports of Mobile, New Orleans, and Galveston, invigorating and restoring the region, and he would move heaven, earth, and even a few Republicans to insure its fruition. In 1902, a fierce battle between the Democrat Morgan and Panama Canal Company supporter, Republican Marcus Hanna, erupted in the Senate, with Roosevelt acting as the *deus ex machina*. Roosevelt's behind the scenes coercion of the Walker Interoceanic Canal Commission—chartered by slain President William McKinley to recommend the best location for America's interoceanic canal—to recant its previous pro-Nicaragua findings, ended the duel and paved the way for the scandal to follow.

The Confederates and the Mogul: Unlikely Heroes

Even before the defeat of the Nicaragua Bill, former Confederate general, Senator Morgan held hearings to unearth the corrupt connections between big corporations and their attempts to undermine the political process of locating the interoceanic canal in Nicaragua. The political improprieties and corporate slight-of-hand that Morgan exposed in hearings after the defeat of the Nicaragua Canal Bill did nothing to abate the dishonesty or recompense the nation of Colombia for its loss of Panama. Another powerful ex-Confederate also aired his suspicions of corruption. Owner of the Louisville *Courier-Journal*, "Colonel" Henry Watterson, publicly proclaimed the sale was a swindle from the outset. The outspoken Watterson was not necessarily a fan of Nicaragua, but he was a foe of political corruption. In years past, he had decried the enforcement of Monroe Doctrine that Roosevelt embraced, not wanting the United States to "protect every little mongrel country" in Central America. He would have preferred that, if he had the power, he would seize Panama and "blow out a canal a mile wide," but when he suspected corruption and collusion between the Senate and the Panama Canal Company, he spoke out.[2] However, the potent combination of the robust Roosevelt and the Cromwell publicity machines overwhelmed Morgan, Watterson, and all other public criticism of the deal.

When Morgan died in 1907, the drive to uncover the truth behind the Panama Canal sale died with him. Not until 1908, after Roosevelt left office, did an uncharacteristic clumsy misstep by the nimble William Nelson Cromwell ignite public controversy highlighting the nefarious details of the Panama Canal purchase. The New York *Evening World* owned by an aging Joseph Pulitzer and the *Indianapolis News'* editor Delavan Smith, amplified the quiet concerns many had only whispered for years. After they posed the question, "Who got the money?" the extent of the fraud in the purchase of the assets of the French Panama Canal Company became a sincere question in the minds of the public. The newsmen exposed Cromwell and Roosevelt's personal and social connections to the principles involved in the fraud, and examined the President's direct role in orchestrating what amounted to a takeover of Panama by an American-run corporation.

This revelation pitted the vigorous Knickerbocker scion, Theodore Roosevelt, against the unlikely hero of the frail and ailing Jewish immigrant, Joseph Pulitzer, in a public battle royal for the hearts and minds of Americans. Among his last acts in office, Roosevelt had the United States government charge both the *News* and the *World* with criminal libel and employed Civil War era laws against distributing libelous news about the government on United States military reservations to prosecute the men. Lower courts dismissed the charges, but Pulitzer's *World* editorial staff egged Roosevelt to appeal the ruling in the highest court in the land, and he finally took the bait. On June 3, 1911, the Supreme Court of the United States ruled against Roosevelt, upholding an earlier circuit court decision in favor of the *World*. Roosevelt never quite recovered his political footing or his public popularity.

A Word on Meaning and Method

The perspective of this book is atypical in that it is predominantly informed by a collection of writings by commentators, historians, editors, politicians, public figures, and newspaper reporters that were contemporaries of events—actually living through, alongside, and with the events—rather than a reliance upon reinterpretation of modern historians and thinkers comfortably removed from events by time. The intent of this approach is to listen to the members of the culture and society at the time of the Panama Canal acquisition whose comments over time have been excised from the collective historical memory and allow them to speak. In essence, the voices of the critics of Roosevelt—and there were many—have been filtered out through the traditional process of analysis and agreement with historians viewing the work of other historians. We are left then, with versions of Roosevelt that echo each other. Although the voices of opposition were viable and vital at the time, traditional approaches have rendered them subalterns—effectively disappeared—from the conversation.

Drawing directly from primary sources—newspaper accounts, political cartoons, Congressional records, books, photographs, and letters, the narrative ripens into a fully developed history of how Roosevelt's intolerance for opposition, his insatiable political ambitions, his hyper-masculine and racist imperialist perspective created the perfect ally for the unappeasable gluttony for riches of powerful industrialists and capitalist investors. Together, Roosevelt, his family, and the "Panama Lobby" created became an unstoppable force that imposed its will over the objections of most Congressmen, much of the public, and a preponderance of the press.

Leadership and the Cowboy Within

A leader misleading their followers for personal gain is not a Progressive Era phenomenon. The themes in *The Cowboy and the Canal* embroider all history and are woven into the tapestry of our political culture today. And, in some sense, all human collectives on some level in all times, require heroes and create fables to support and extend their influence. Yet, the characteristics ascribed to Theodore Roosevelt as an American hero simply do not measure up to the reality of the man. Lust for position and power, the abuse of power once attained, the misuse of its force, a callous disregard for the common good, and rapacious greed are not qualities usually associated with the American demigods carved into Mount Rushmore, let alone American's favorite president, Theodore Roosevelt. Yet, these characteristics were displayed and recorded and reflected in the writing of his time.

How do we reconcile these differences in the Roosevelt we have come to know simply as "Teddy" and the Roosevelt revealed in this contra narrative? *The Cowboy and the Canal* seeks to reveal that the absence of exploring this complexity, missing from many analyses of this great American icon, not only diminishes our understanding of Roosevelt, but also impoverishes the way we all think of heroes. Self-understanding is reflected in the intricacy of our relationships with our heroes, whom we as Americans often see as "Cowboys." Adopting a caricaturist value of one-dimensional icons encourages us to applaud when our heroes commit acts of dishonor and thievery, as when Roosevelt boasted he "took" the Panama. Instead of judging his acts on the merit of the action, we marvel at the vigor of Roosevelt's rhetoric and admire the swagger of his presentation while the profound implications of his actions drown in the sea of his charisma. Without the ability to hold the ambiguous and contradictory aspect of our heroes' lives, we are unable to entertain the fullness of our own.

THE FIRST PANAMA CANAL FRAUD

Count Ferdinand de Lesseps, 1812-1894

Count Ferdinand de Lesseps, the builder of the Suez Canal and progenitor of the Panama Canal, was no engineer. Instead, he was an ambitious promoter, a retired minor French diplomat, who never attained a post of any vital political significance. The source of his striking success in the construction of the desert waterway rested upon his natural talent to exploit his political and social relationship with the Khedive of Egypt, his dexterous maneuvering of the necessary political and financial support into place, a highly honed ability to overlook corruption and abuse, and the plain good luck of having a robust French engineering culture to provide the technical expertise crucial for the success of such a massive project. In 1859, his social and political capital converged and reached the critical mass necessary to launch the Suez Canal project, the greatest engineering feat of the time. Ten years later—in the greatest international fête of all time—at the official opening of the 100-mile-long, sea level Suez Canal, de Lesseps, the 64-year-old "hero of the Isthmus," was hailed as the world's preeminent engineer.[3]

The Foundations of Disaster: The Suez Canal, 1859-1869

In the midst of the Suez Canal construction, however, rumors of unethical—some suggested criminal—activities began to erode the glittering façade of de Lesseps' genius. Condemnation over an "unscrupulous potentate," the Khedive of Egypt, and conscription of thousands of Egyptians as forced labors on the canal began surfacing in the press. Supervision of the workers was as harsh as it was severe and the working conditions of the forced laborers were so gruesome that thousands died. Estimates of the death toll range from 30,000 to 120,000 during the construction from 1858 to 1869. Scandalized, by the reports in 1863 the British pressured the Khedive to abandon

16

his use of slave labor. Upon learning laborers would no longer be compelled to work on the canal, de Lesseps despaired that the canal could ever be built. Yet, the canal was built and according to Joseph J. O'Brien, a historian contemporary to de Lesseps, it was the talented group of French engineers that the Count cleverly surrounded himself with that saved the venture.

Young French engineer Alexandre Levalley saw the loss of slave labor as an opportunity to actually apply modern engineering theories. "Thank God you have no more labor," declared Levalley to the distraught de Lesseps, "At last you are going to be able to dig the canal."[4] An incredulous de Lesseps demanded to know what Levalley could possibly mean by such an outlandish statement. The youthful, but wise engineer replied that now, instead of hand digging the ditch and using human power to haul away the spoil in buckets, de Lesseps could use the vastly superior techniques of using dredges for excavating and barges for transporting the dirt.[5] De Lesseps' limited imagination and abundant self-interest had confined him to a ghastly and inefficient approach. De Lesseps did not see the human or engineering costs of the slave labor, because the Khedive absorbed its minimal cost and De Lesseps did not have to spend one sous on the digging.

Failure had dictated his decision," pronounced O'Brien, "not intelligent initiative… de Lesseps did not possess any original ideas about the mechanics of moving dirt, nor about the internal work of dirt in motion… the history of the Suez Canal show[s] the character of de Lesseps' inferior engineering ability."[6] He did not possess outstanding engineering ability nor was he a humanitarian of any kind, but de Lesseps was a mastermind of sorts. He was a genius of publicity. Even so, his lustrous reputation began to tarnish in the 1870s. The project had cost more than twenty times the sum estimated and the Suez Canal Company failed to pay dividends. Bankruptcy loomed before de Lesseps, but a new stock offering and an increase in toll rates saved the company for the moment.[7] Nevertheless, despite de Lesseps' known or merely suspected shortcomings as an engineer, he was the darling of the industrialized world. Not only did his own country, France, honor him with the Grand Cross of the Legion of Honor, but also a once hostile Great Britain awarded him the Star of

India for his efforts. In the maturity of his years, the once obscure minor diplomat reached unparalleled celebrity and prosperity.

The Panama Delusion

At the seasoned age of 74, de Lesseps looked about the globe for another project to surpass the grandeur of his Suez success. Obviously, now that joining the Mediterranean Sea with the Red Sea was accomplished, the next great commercial interoceanic canal opportunity would be joining the Atlantic and Pacific Oceans. Many possible sites in South and Central America had been explored over the decades but de Lesseps was looking for what was available, not for preeminent waterway potential. The most applauded route was through the massive lake system of Nicaragua, but the United States and Great Britain held dominion over that territory. He solved the location issue by sending a junior partner, Lucien Napoléon Bonaparte Wyse, to obtain a concession from Colombia to dig a canal through their territory of Panama. Having secured the pathway for a canal, Panama held the promise for a successful and even more lucrative iteration of his Suez triumph and de Lesseps would entertain no evidence to the contrary. In spite of the dreadful record of disease, the horrendous climatic events, and the geological evidence to the contrary, de Lesseps was fixed on Panama. It was not the climate, the season, or any feature of Panama other than the ability to acquire a concession from Colombia to which de Lesseps was drawn. For his scheme to work he needed to start with possessing a concession and since the United States and Great Britain had territorial claims in Nicaragua, all that was left was Panama.

De Lesseps' endorsement to the world of Wyse's eighteen-day survey project was essential before prospective founders would loan monies in anticipation of a huge return for their investment. As a promoter, de Lesseps was sensationally effective, but his lack of engineering expertise and his incompetency as a businessman trumped his promotional abilities. One great irony is that had de Lesseps listened to bona fide engineers and undertook the project on the terms the geography dictated, instead of forging ahead with a scheme that no engineering authority believed would work, he might have actually been successful. He neither acknowledged nor developed engineering solutions to address the three most formidable geological features of the Isthmus—Panama's Culebra mountain range, the uncontainable Chagres River, and the mismatched elevations of the two ocean coastlines. He claimed he could build a sea-level canal just as he had done in the Suez, and he would entertain no other approach. Because of his implacable insistence on a sea-level canal through the Isthmus over the better-researched and surveyed routes, the purchase of the concession from Colombia by one of his companies, the resale of the concession to his own canal company, there is more than enough reason to believe—just as in the Suez endeavor—that de Lesseps was motivated more by potential for raking in profits from investors than his idealized claim of passion for the project. [8]

Projecting Power—Protecting Privilege

Beyond his desire for tribute and prosperity, de Lesseps' conspicuous and complete public success that crowned his work on the Suez Canal bestowed upon him a definite conclusiveness of thought that tolerated no contradiction. Once de Lesseps made a decision, he would not waiver from his position. All opposing voices withered before de Lesseps' legendary tyrannical temper. He operated within a world where the most decisive data or the most valid appeals could not dissuade him. It was his publicly stated opinion that a canal across Panama would be easier to build than the Suez Canal. His decision to construct a sea level canal across the Isthmus of Panama, in spite of the questions of engineering experts raised to the feasibility and wisdom of such a plan, reveals more than the painful consequences of his blind, tenacious will, but also reinforces the notion of his pecuniary motivations. The conquest of an interoceanic canal would insure his eminence and perpetuate his prominence as the greatest citizen of France and silence any reputation sullying whispers that the Suez Canal overruns caused, and make him extremely wealthy.

De Lesseps, the most artful among promoters, convinced practically all of France and most of the world that he would succeed where others had failed in the 400-year-old quest begun by Spanish Conquistador Vasco Núñez de Balboa's 1513 penetration of the Isthmus. "Science has declared that the Panama Canal can be built, and I shall be the servant of that science," he boomed at his critics.[9] After the triumph of the initial stock offering, ineptitude ruled from the first delivery of the heavy machinery to Panama. One American on the scene reported that the dredging machines, excavators, and stationary engines were specifically built for sand removal along the Suez Canal and not designed for the mud, sludge, rocks, and undergrowth found at the Panama worksite. Even the new locomotives were worthless, according to the observer, because they were too long for the short curves of the railroad.[10] Beyond doubts of de Lesseps' practical ability to execute such an ambitious feat, doubts were cast about the legitimacy—both financial and moral—of the entire enterprise. Suspicions appeared in the American press. "There is little doubt that the success of M. de Lesseps in raising money for the Panama Canal in Europe was owing to a deception," wrote the Washington D.C. *Sunday Herald* Ernest Lambert would later surmise about the de Lesseps project that:

> His agents, already primed with assurances that the canal would be completed in 1888, dazzled timorous investors with excessive tonnage estimates. From the first, money that should have been spent on the work was used to suppress the truth about it. Lying circulars were issued. Paris and Panama newspapers were muzzled with gold.[12]

Besides questions of financial integrity, the rumors of the grim work conditions continued to emerge in the press. De Lesseps defended his company against the reports as vigorously as he defended his company's solvency. "At first the mortality was high," de Lesseps admitted, "but some of the workmen were so filthy in their habits (especially the Belgians) that this is not astonishing. Matters have improved since."[13] However, matters only got worse for the workers and for the shareholders of the *Compagnie Universelle Du Canal de Panama*.

By the end of 1888, $400 million had vanished— one-third of the money received was spent on the canal work, one-third wasted, and one-third stolen. In 1899—nine years and 22,000 deaths after the digging began—de Lesseps was forced to face the reality that no amount of bluster, showmanship, or French engineering genius could keep the illusion from dissolving. Meanwhile, the United States—which had never viewed the ambitions of de Lesseps in a friendly manner—chartered the Maritime Canal Company, backed by leading New York banking interests, to build a rival canal in Nicaragua. Sadly, the hundreds of thousands of ordinary French shopkeepers and janitors who would follow were lured into investing their few Francs based on their confidence in the Great Frenchman, had no clue of how their lives would be hopelessly ruined by a catastrophic reversal of fortune.[14]

Over 800,000 ordinary French investors—15,000 of them single women—lost their entire investment, one hundred and sixty-one French officials were charged with accepting bribes from de Lesseps' group—among whom was the future Prime Minister of France, George Clemenceau. George Eiffel, the creator of the Statue of Liberty and the Eiffel Tower was also charged. Another prominent French nobleman, Baron Reinach, the company's chief lobbyist, committed suicide rather than face the humiliation of arrest. A list of Paris and London newspapers that had received the Baron's checks in payment for influence was published with the exact amounts received. The charges of bribery of officials, misappropriation of funds, and fraud were too easily proved once the façade fell. It was against Panama that de Lesseps' invincible will was broken, sweeping away his fortune, his fame, and every scrap of his honor. Instead of reflecting the luster of glory, the name of de Lesseps smoldered across the swamps of Panama alongside the heaps of rusty iron and ruined machinery and the spirits of thousands who had died in their labors. The financial ruin, suicides, and worker deaths are among the "several reasons," as Frank Lydston wrote in his 1900 remembrance of Panama, "why de Lesspes should have been called the "Great Undertaker" instead of the Great Frenchman.[15]

De Lesseps' Dishonor

By 1893, the old man was wholly ruined. Trapped in a purgatory between senility and death that must have seemed preferable to the reality of his position, de Lesseps was rarely seen in public. The former toast of two continents, the alchemist of alliances and mastermind of the Suez Canal, the once unassailable Viscount Ferdinand de Lesseps, languished in a tapestry framed sitting room, swaddled in blankets before a fire blazing, "dragging out the agony" of his old age.[16] One three-syllable word toppled the Count from his position as the most exalted citizen in France to that of the sleaziest criminal con artist on the Continent: Panama. After the 1892 bankruptcy of his company, the *Compagnie Universelle Du Canal de Panama*, scandal pursued the Count like the hounds of hell. His inability to cope with the shame and disgrace of the disintegration of the *Compagnie Universelle* was compounded by the grief and regret he felt that his eldest son Charles—president of his father's company—was serving the first year of a five-year sentence for his part in "having swindled whole or part of the fortunes of others."[17]

Only respect for his former role in the Suez Canal construction and the tenuous space the old man occupied between life and death prevented the Count from serving his five-year prison sentence for malfeasance and fraud in the bankrupt Panama Canal Company he founded. The intoxicating vision of his venerable old age, the *Compagnie Universelle Du Canal Interoceanique* De Panama, had become for the Count a foul and bitter draft served up daily. The trophy wife of his middle age, Helene—her beauty now as exhausted by the scandal as was de Lesseps' sanity—and a remnant of the covey of their nine children padded softly around the rambling chateau of La Chesnaye, exorcising the dreaded word from any newspapers or letters that might find their way to his shawl covered lap. "Panama," as one visitor noted, "is never even whispered, lest any echo of it should reach the ears of him to whom this word has meant ruin and disgrace and a broken heart." [18]

As he sat in his remote desolation while staring into the fireplace, de Lesseps could not have imagined the remnants of his audacious venture would showcase the will-to-power of an American president, Theodore Roosevelt. A mere eight years after de Lesseps' death in 1894, Roosevelt—a man very much like de Lesseps in temperament and character—would pick up the rusted, mangled pieces of de Lesseps' failure, subdue the Culebra Mountains and Chagres River, and change the power dynamics of the Western hemisphere. At the end of the day, the American Panama Canal would also heap the glory and extraordinary wealth upon Roosevelt's friends and family that de Lesseps craved for himself. He, too, would become the centerpiece of his own Panamanian scandal, aspects of which that would plague him until his death.

Death waiting at the Panama Canal. Title "Waiting." Udo Klepper, **Puck,** *22 June 1904, Library of Congress.*

CHAPTER ONE

Panama: The Dismal Swamp, 1513-1894

If Ulysses . . . had attempted to cross the Isthmus of Panama . . . he would have told . . . he had found this isthmus guarded by a wicked dragon that exhaled poison with every breath, and that lay in wait, buried in its swamps and jungles, for sailors and travelers, who withered away and died as soon as they put foot upon the shore. But that he, warned in time by the sight of thousands of men's bones whitening on the beach, hoisted all sail and stood out to sea—RICHARD HARDING DAVIS, 1896

"It seems almost as though the isthmus were unholy ground," wrote the adventurer journalist Richard Harding Davis in 1896 as he viewed Panama for the first time.[1] There must be a curse upon Panama, the dashing correspondent wrote. If a myth did not already exist to account for its sinister atmosphere, he mused, "someone should invent a legend to explain . . . [the] manner in which this strip of mud and water has resisted the advance of man, as though there really were some evil genius of the place lurking in the morasses and brooding over the waters, throwing out its poison like a serpent."[2] Davis loved a good story and he was uniquely situated to actually create such a legend. Talented and articulate, the wildly popular war reporter proved his mythmaking prowess time and again, but none would be more impressive or longer lived than his almost single-handed creation of Theodore Roosevelt's Rough Rider heroic legend when he covered the Spanish-American War two years later. The intrepid and strikingly handsome writer must have sensed the

25

spectral presence of all those men "arrogant in health and hope and ambition," who lost their lives in the attempt to slice open the isthmus to interoceanic traffic.[3] The seemingly ravenous spirit of Panama began this wanton harvesting of human lives centuries before Davis' observation of the decaying relics left in the mud by the gigantic swindle of Ferdinand de Lesseps and his bankrupt *Universelle de Compagnie du Panama Canal.* The mission to achieve interoceanic communication across Panama began as a deadly enterprise with the bloodletting commencing in earnest in 1513 and there was no reason for the journalist to believe it was over. In thinking the Isthmus was cursed, Davis might have been on to something.

VASCO NÚÑEZ DE BALBOA, 1513

Vasco Núñez de Balboa, once a penniless stow-away fleeing his creditors, now led the hunt for "the other ocean" for his Spanish lord, King Ferdinand II. Balboa officially inaugurated the mayhem on September 1513, with the slaughter of six hundred indigenous men, women, and children in the Panamanian village of Cuarecuá. Although it mattered little to Balboa, the tangled bit of fetid jungle he was slashing his way through in pursuit of his goal was home to many native people ruled by a chief named Torecha. This slab of mud that Balboa and his men were stumbling through was all that knit North and South America together in a thin, but unyielding ribbon that blocked the torrent of treasures of the Far East and the New World from flowing unimpeded to his benefactor and King. If he succeeded in a unification of the oceans, his greatness would be assured and his future secure with his ambitious benefactor—or so he thought. Balboa's 190 harquebus firing, crossbow shooting, sword wielding *conquistadores* accompanied by a large pack of ferocious war-dogs had penetrated the narrow strip of land and hacked their way through the slender thread of land reaching Cuarecuá on the 25th of September.

The native people, in general, and Torecha in particular displayed—at least according to Balboa—an intolerable inhospitality to him and resisted his progress. To say the least, the natives were unimpressed with Balboa's mission and his manners and were

Theodor de Bry, "Balboa Throwing Indian Sodomites to the Dogs," 1594. University of Houston Digital Collection.

disobliging when he demanded gold and directions to the big water. They resisted and Balboa and his forces pacified the insurgents by brutally killing most of the villagers. Nothing—certainly not a group of hostile and, in his assessment, wicked sodomite savages—would get in Balboa's way.[4] Having smoothed away the obstacle of the native inhabitants in an orgy of Spanish ball-shot, steel, and vicious war-dogs, Balboa trudged and hacked his way to the Pacific Ocean. Four days after his Mastiffs ripped Torecha's head from his neck in a display of brutality soon to become a common occurrence between the natives and newcomers in the New World, Balboa thrust his sword into the Pacific and claimed it for his King. Since that day, the body count across Panama mounted.[5]

Balboa never found a natural waterway through the isthmus. The subsequent failure of other explorers led to calls for an artificial waterway in the 1600s. Yet, ambitions to swing wide the door that barred the flow of the Spanish commercial traffic were never realized, not from lack of physical courage or a deficiency of will, but from lack of vision and technology. In the 1700s, a proposition was made to the Court of Spain, "to open a canal from the bay of Panama, to communicate with the river Chagres at Cruz, and so with the Atlantic Ocean" was rejected on the belief that such an enterprise would drain the Pacific of so much water that the harbors on that side would all dry up.[6] Balboa failed both in his mission to discover a natural water passageway for the glory of Spain and to obtain riches, fame, and security for himself. For all his trouble, Balboa, along with four of his captains, was himself beheaded accused of planning to usurp territorial control from the King of Spain.

Nevertheless, his spectacular failure to find a waterway across the Isthmus did in no way deter hundreds of future freebooters, swashbuckling entrepreneurs—often called pirates—and explorers from Balboa's quest. The Spanish placed the Isthmus of Panama under the jurisdiction of the Viceroyalty of New Granada in 1713 and there it remained until New Granada, later known as Colombia, threw off the Spanish yoke in 1821. It is not possible to know precisely how many lives have been lost in the century's old search for a wormhole-like passage across the continents, but what is certain is that death reigned over the passage seekers with more vigor and authority than fortune smiled upon them. The six hundred who died in the village of Cuarecuá that late September day in 1531 were just a drop in the proverbial bloody bucket; however, an estimate of 100,000 lives spent to establish interoceanic intercourse across Panama would probably not be too high.

The Panama Railroad Company, 1859-1879

The next noteworthy overland assault of the Isthmus was led by the Panama Railway Company three centuries later in 1849. In its own way, it was as gruesome as Balboa's march—only the number of dead from disease, malnourishment, landslides, and explosions exceeded Balboa's butchery a thousand fold. When the enterprising American capitalists seized the opportunity to "mine the miners," and began to build a railroad across Panama to transport the thousands of eager

"Forty-Niners" swarming from the East Coast of the United States to the goldfields discovered in California, the company imported tens of thousands of laborers from every corner of the world including Ireland, the United States, China, and the West Indies to lay tracks. Thousands of laborers, both white and non-white, died under the most appalling conditions imaginable, men from the West Indies and China, however, died in far greater percentages than white labors. Dead West Indians and Chinese were hauled off by the wagon loads, dumped in mass graves, unrecorded and uncounted. News stories and memoirs about the macabre and tragic deaths of the workers on the Panama Railroad began to surface in the United States in the mid-1850s, convincing readers that Panama was a death trap.

Stories in the newspapers of the massive mortality were so startling that people demanded some explanation from the officers of the New Jersey incorporated entity. "Nearly every white person going there to work is attacked with the fever," declared the Washington D.C. *Daily Evening Star* in 1953.[7] This was a common understanding of what awaited in Panama. Panama Railroad president, David Hoadley, tried to rehabilitate the reputation of the railroad in an 1868 interview

David Hoadley, in Francis Bacon Trowbridge's **The Hoadley Geneology,** *1894.*

telling newspapers that since the early days of the reports of massive mortality among workers, his company had kept meticulous records of the deaths, but only, "among the white men employed by the company."[8] Even so, Hoadley admitted in the same interview that exactly "how many white men were connected with the work during the period cannot be accurately detailed."[9] Basically, he admitted that there was no official accounting of how many men had worked on the railroad, let alone how many of them died.

The contradiction between the claim of keeping strict records, but then having no accurate number of workers, is striking. He did say that he believed that the number of white dead was only about 6,000. "No record was kept of the mortality among other classes," he said offhandedly.[9] West Indians, Africans, and Chinese were obviously left out of the mortality rate calculation, however, it is likely that Eastern Europeans, Irish, Italians, and South Americans were counted "among the other classes," as non-white. There is no way to know with certainty how many workers died. Any claim of an accurate record of deaths of the only category the company recorded, white men, is highly suspect and as Hoadley admitted, no documentation was kept the number of the "other classes" of laborers the company employed, let alone their deaths.[10] There were, however, survivors and witnesses who began to come forward from whose testimonies, whose estimates can be extrapolated.

Acres and Acres of Cemeteries

There is little doubt that Panama Railroad workers died in droves. *Popular Science Monthly* magazine, like dozens of publications of the day alleged that the, "Panama Railway cost 81,000 human lives destroyed by malaria; this death-rate is equal to one man for every one death for every yard of track."[11] Its claim of one death for the forty-seven miles of track is a certainly a tawdry journalist appeal to sensationalism, but as startling as the estimate sounds, it could easily have been correct. Everything about the mortality rate is guesswork; educated guesses hobbled together by reports of journalists, eyewitnesses, and United States Congressional hearings. These estimates range from somewhere around 22,000 to 82,000 deaths. There were so many bodies to dispose of that the Railway officials began to treat them as a commodity. The Railroad pickled the corpses of the nameless dead in wooden barrels and sold them to medical schools in the United States and elsewhere. Income generated from the cadaver business was sufficient to maintain the Railroad's own gleaming new whites-only hospital.

Even after the company began to report the fatalities of white workers, people became suspicious that their deaths were under reported. The death rate of one "cargo" of Irish laborers was so great that the company shipped the survivors back to New York, where "most died from the fever of the Isthmus which was fermenting in their blood."[12] That way, the deaths did not add to the company's annual tally of dead workers. The Railroad Company was insidious, according to one news article, luring poor white workers to their doom. "It seems most unjustifiable for the Railway Company to persist in the effort to seduce ignorant laboring men from the United States or Ireland," the article charged, "to a spot where they cannot escape severe sickness and where death, even, is more probable than such an escape."[13]

Slowly, the accounts of those who survived the "stifling, fever-laden miasmas" of Panama began to steadily ooze into the popular press and in memoirs. "I never met with a wholesome looking person among all those engaged upon the railway," wrote Wolford Nelson in his frank and descriptive memoir, *Five Years at Panama: the Transisthmian Canal.*[14] "There was not one whose constitution had not been sapped by disease," he continued, "and all, without exception, are in the almost daily habit of taking medicine to drive away the ever-recurring fever and ague."[15] Description of the "barbarous" burial practices for the non-whites also percolated through the newspapers. "It seems there are more dead people in Colon than are living," one writer reported. He went on to describe the remains of anonymous West Indian workers—identified only by a number—carried by train in a group casket to "Monkey Island," dumped in a common grave and the casket returned for the next load. Mingled with reports of deaths in worker riots and native violence against the Railroad, the Isthmus of Panama seemed too many Americans to have earned the title *Sepultura de Vivos*, the "living grave" of Europeans, as it was named by the first Spanish settlers.[16]

The range of disease that stalked workers on the Isthmus was breathtaking. Smallpox, leprosy, pneumonia, typhoid, dysentery, the bubonic plague afflicted workers, but yellow fever was the most fearsome ailment, attacking the men both physically and mentally. Initial symptoms of "Yellow Jack" were headaches, fever, and muscle pain. As the disease progressed, the infected worker faced jaundice, thirst, and black vomit caused by internal hemorrhaging. As it ran its course, the disease often led to kidney failure, delirium, seizures, coma and, quite frequently, death. Still, as appalling as reports of West Indian deaths were, it was probably the horrific stories published about the deaths among the Chinese laborers that sparked the tale that "there was a dead man for every railway tie between Colon and Panama City." Most of the Chinese—those who did not die from malaria—committed suicide.

On All Things is the Pall of Death: Chinese Labors , 1852

When the first transport of one thousand Chinese labors arrived in 1852, the men almost immediately succumbed to malaria. The workers untouched by the onslaught of disease saw their compatriots fall victim to the fever, became despondent, refused to work and "let the pick and shovel fall from their hands."[17] To mitigate the effects of the fever and depression and get the Chinese survivors digging, clearing, and laying track, Railroad management devised an incentive plan. The Panama Railway Company acquired and distributed 15 grains of opium to each Chinese worker per day. The desired result was accomplished and the Chinese laborers shuffled off their depression, rose from their sickbeds, and began to work. However, officers of the company in Maine raised questions about the legality of acquiring and distributing such an allotment—not to mention the added 15-cent cost per worker per day—and the policy came to an end. Whether it was owing to the cruel symptoms of opium withdrawal, "or the malignant effects of the climate, or home-sickness, or disappointment ... the poor sufferers yielded to the agony of despair [and] gladly welcomed death, and impatiently awaited their turn in the ranks which were falling before the pestilence."[18] Hundreds chose death by their own hands, rather than wait their turn to die from disease. Tawdry accounts of the suicides splashed across the newspapers. The sheer number and the grotesque variety of the Chinese suicides left an indelible association between horror and the name Panama:

> Hundreds destroyed themselves, and showed, in their various modes of suicide, the characteristic Chinese ingenuity . . . Some hung themselves to the tall trees by the hair, and some twisted their queues about their necks, with a deliberate coil after coil, until their faces blackened, their eye-balls started out, their tongues protruded, and death relieved their agony. Some cut ugly crutchshaped [sic] sticks, sharpened the ends to a point, and thrust their necks upon them until they were pierced through and through, and thus mangled, yielded up life in a torrent of blood . . . Some impaled themselves upon their instruments of labor—and thus, in a few weeks after their arrival, there were scarce two hundred Chinese left of the whole number. This miserable remnant of poor heart-sick exiles, prostrate from the effects of the climate, and bent on death, being useless for labor were sent to Jamaica, where they have ever since lingered out a miserable beggar's life.[19]

The same year as the Chinese suicides, Panama also made an indelible impression as the most unforgiving, unwelcoming isthmus on the globe on a future President of the United States. Ulysses S. Grant would experience the reality of the *Sepultura de Vivos* firsthand.

THE DOOMED DETACHMENT: ULYSSES S. GRANT, PANAMA 1852

Ulysses. S. Grant, a young but seasoned lieutenant in the 4th U.S. Infantry, crossed the Isthmus of Panama en route to California, like

A young lieutenant Ulysses S. Grant, Cover photo on Hamlin Garland's, **Ulysses S. Grant; His Life and Character.** *1898.*

thousands of Forty-Niners before them. He and his regiment arrived at the starting point for the railroad—the rain-drenched, mud-puddle town known as Aspinwall by the American émigrés, but called Colon by the Panamanians—in July of 1852. Grant later recorded his first impression of Colon in his memoires. He wrote, the "streets of the town were eight or ten inches under water, and foot passengers passed from place to place on raised foot-walks . . . I wondered how any person could live many months in Aspinwall, and wondered still more why any one tried."[20] The regiment was split into two parties that took separate routes. Grant led one group of about three hundred and fifty people and boarded the train. Two years into the construction, the railroad was completed only from Colon to the Chagres River, leaving twenty-five miles for the soldiers and the attendant followers to negotiate. At the end of the line, Grant's group disembarked the train and he secured boats propelled by natives "not inconveniently burdened with clothing," that moved the Americans along against the current at a speed Grant estimated to be between one-and-a-half to one mile per hour. [21]

When they came ashore, Grant with "all the soldiers with families, all the tents, mess chests and camp kettles" trekked a few miles higher up the Chagres River to the town of Cruces.[22] Grant had arranged to have his troops transported from Cruces by mule train, but when they arrived, the transporter had no mules for the soldiers, their families, or their gear. It would be the next day before the beasts of burden would arrive and by that time Grant wrote, "The cholera had broken out, and men were dying every hour."[23]

The trip was a disaster. One third of his party died. In all, it took over six weeks for the United States' soldiers—those who survived the initial deadly cholera outbreak—to complete the passage. The remainder of the company lay "buried on the Isthmus of Panama or on Flamingo Island in Panama Bay."[24] Grant's resolute performance of his duty toward his men and the fate they suffered surfaced two years later in an article published in *The Edinburgh Medical and Surgical Journal* by tropical fever researcher, Dr. Archibald Smith. Smith, who had stopped in Panama on his way to Peru, recounted the tale of the American soldiers' grim transit, which by this time had become part of the local lore. A yellow fever expert, Smith believed it was yellow fever, not cholera, that was responsible for the soldiers' deaths in 1852. As tales change in the telling, the brave young lieutenant was promoted to captain in the version of the story told to Smith. Still, there is no doubt that the researcher was describing of the fate of Grant's miserable detachment:

> The captain [Grant] of the transport soon found that
> his voyage to California was arrested by the sudden

appearance among the troops of yellow fever, with its fatal attendant black vomit. The captain quietly shifted his position to another but lonely isle in the offing, where, unobserved, he buried his dead, sometimes, as I was told, to the number of twenty or thirty in one day.[25]

Later, as President, Grant recommended Nicaragua—not Panama—as the preferred site to construct an interoceanic canal, relying no doubt not merely on research of the experts he had commissioned, but also informed his decision with his own intimate understanding of the evils lurking in Panama.[26]

The French Connection, 1881-1902

The large number of deaths of Panama Railway workers eventually dropped off as the workforce was reduced due to the completion of the project in 1855. However, misery and death continued to reign on the Isthmus, this time it was French enterprise that was responsible for luring workers to a place where thousands of them would die, not the Americans. The *Compagnie Universelle du Canal Interocéanique* attempted to crack open the Isthmus and join the two great oceans with Ferdinand de Lesseps' sea-level canal, just as he had done in the Suez. From the time the *Compagnie Universelle* won its concession to dig the waterway from the Colombians in 1881 until bankruptcy and scandal ended the French period in 1889, approximately 22,000 men died. Most of the dead were West Indian laborers.

Workers were recruited from all the islands, but Jamaica supplied the lion's share of laborers. Getting workers to come to Panama was problematic, to say the least, and the worker shortage had to be approached in a creative, yet practical way. The task fell to Charles Gadpaille, an ingenious, enterprising, and callous agent for the *Compagnie Universelle*. Gadpaille began an advertising campaign in Jamaica by promoting what has since become known as the "Colon Man" operation in 1881, ensnaring thousands of naïve and trusting men to perish in a muddy deathtrap, far away from home and loved ones, in despair and anonymity. Gadpaille ran newspaper advertisements featuring a robust, well-dressed West Indian man that had returned from Panama, his pockets bursting with cash. The healthy, happy, and well-heeled Colon Man appeared in ads throughout Kingston, as well as on flyers sent to more remote parts of the island to reach the widest possible audience. This image fired the imagination and hopes of poverty stricken Jamaicans and drove thousands of them toward Panama. The advertisement offered wages much higher than average on the Caribbean island, free medical care, and abundant food. The image lured thousands of Jamaican and other Caribbean islanders onto overcrowded freighters to a world nothing like Gadpaille promised. It is safe to say that Gadpaille, who was paid for each worker he delivered to the *Compagnie Universelle*, was undisturbed about what happened to the men afterward. The promise of riches made in the advertisement was an empty one. In reality, West Indians earned ten cents an hour for performing dangerous work in hazardous conditions; received inferior and indifferent medical attention in contaminated and unhealthy conditions; and as far as the promise for hearty meals, malnutrition was rampant among the workers.

Sepultura de Vivos of Panama

In 1883, ten percent of the *Compagnie Universelle* workforce died from disease alone. A report by the United States War Department noted that from 1884—three years after the French period began—to 1903, one year before the American period, at least 18,000 corpses were "received into the new Roman Catholic cemetery." And that was just the Catholic dead.[27] While malaria, yellow fever, dysentery, typhoid, and dengue fever took many thousands over the years, death from accidents—train derailments, falls from trains, land slides, rocks hurled long distances by dynamite blasts, dismemberment, suffocation from noxious gases—all were as commonplace as disease. Then of course, there were the snakes. The impenetrable, untamed jungle that covered the fifty miles between coasts was overflowing with poisonous snakes. The bite of a coral snake killed by attacking the victim's nervous system, while venom from the ten-foot *mapana* snake caused internal bleeding, organ degeneration, and death.[28]

Also, greatly feared was "a most mischievous serpent called the flying snake . . . which . . . darted itself from the boughs of trees on either man or beast that came within its reach," whose sting led to inevitable death.[29]

Yellow fever and snakes were not the only bugaboo of Panama—the geography was a nightmare for construction. Impassable "deadly swamps," incessant flooding, impenetrable jungle, menacing mudslides, unrelenting rain, and the occasional earthquake, rendered Panama low on the list for a realizable interoceanic canal. Panama, to most observers, was a place, "where dark mountains scowled, and disease circulated in the fetid miasma that floated over the face of the country," a place of death.[30] Until Dr. William Gorgas waged an implacable campaign against the mosquito in the American Panama Canal period, fevers and disease reigned on the Isthmus. Many of the over 5,000 men who died in the 1904-1914 American period of canal building also succumbed to the panoply of Panamanian fevers, including yellow fever. The most ironic and tragic facet of the deaths under American rule in Panama was that in the last fifty years of the nineteenth century, Panama—while it was flirted with intermittently by the occasional promoter—was rarely seriously considered as suitable place to dig the great interoceanic ditch.

Yellow fever's grisly symptoms and high death rate were so horrifying to canal workers that even a hint of an outbreak sent boatloads of men to take flight. In 1902, during the transition of the Panama Canal from the French possession to American hands, the 650 new workers refused to leave their transport ship because of the rumor of yellow fever. Police, armed with guns and bayonets, went aboard and convinced 500 workers to disembark, but the presence of an armed force had no effect on 150 laborers who said they would rather die there than go ashore. After two hours of waiting, "the police then attacked the laborers with their batons, and scores of unfortunate men were felled to the deck, bleeding profusely. Many laborers took refuge in the rigging, and upwards of fifty jumped overboard into the sea to escape."[31]

Panama was seen as a death trap—a land of leprosy, stagnant water, noxious vapors, and ghastly fevers. Its uncontainable flooding that spread "decomposition of the profuse tropical vegetation must of course generate an intense miasmatic poison."[32] It was, most thought, a perverse act of nature beyond human remedy. Upon his return from Panama in 1892, Edward Hobart Seymore recounted the tedious dreariness of the only two seasons on the Isthmus that helped promote unhealthiness; the wet and the dry seasons. He wrote:

> The wet lasts about seven months, from May to December; the dry occupies the other five months. An average of 120 inches of rain fell during the rainy season swelling the wildly meandering Chagres River to Biblical proportions. Chagres has, in the rainy season, been known to rise forty feet in a few hours, flooding many square miles of country; as it rushes to the sea it carries with it an immense amount of detritus from the forests."[33]

Even the United States War Department's analysis by Captain H.C. Hale noted in a confidential report to the Chief of Staff—a year after Roosevelt strong-armed the Walker Commission to recommend Panama over Nicaragua—that "malarious affections are everywhere prevalent and yellow fever a frequent visitor."[34]

Decades later, former Panama Railway Roadmaster S.L. Plume gave a disturbingly graphic testimony before the Congress Committee on Interoceanic Canals. Plume, by then a man in his seventies, described the last macabre train ride of the hundreds of Jamaican laborers:

> When I went there we used to run one train—perhaps it would be a car or two box cars—in the morning out of Colon up to Monkey Hill . . . Over to Panama it was the same way—bury, bury, bury running two, three, and four trains a day with dead Jamaica[ns] . . . all the time. I never saw anything like it . . . to see the way they died there! They die[d] like animals."[35]

The future Dismal Swamp continued to lay claim to hundreds of lives, even through the American Era. If Theodore Roosevelt—

like Cornelius Vanderbilt, statesmen, entrepreneurs, and six other presidents—had endorsed the healthier Nicaragua location for the site of America's interoceanic canal, no doubt, fewer men would have suffered. It was not as though the Panama or Nicaragua were unknown quantities. Starting in the 1700s with Benjamin Franklin, Americans considered no less than nineteen different routes to establish an interoceanic canal.

AN EXCELLENT STATION FOR MEN-OF-WAR: U.S. AND NICARAGUA, 1835-1902

Of these nineteen routes investigated by Americans, only the Tehuantepec, Nicaragua, and Panama projects captured the imagination of visionaries, yet neither Panama nor Tehuantepec ever seriously rivaled Nicaragua in the minds of engineers. In 1835, President Andrew Jackson charged Henry Biddle "to visit the different routes on the Continent of America best adapted for interoceanic communication, and to report thereon, with reference to their value to the commercial interests of the United States." Biddle spent several months in Panama and then in Bogota as the guest of the Colombian government, and returned to Panama. He was thought to have believed Panama a superior route for a railroad, but Biddle died from a fever soon after his return from the Isthmus before he could file an official report.[36] In a report for Emperor Napoleon III in 1845, engineer Franc Castellon confirmed in favor of Nicaragua and against Panama:

> There are certain countries, which, from their geographical situation, are destined to a highly prosperous future: wealth, power, every national advantage flows into them, provided that where nature has done her utmost, man does not neglect to avail himself of her beneficent assistance . . . There exists in the New World a state as admirably situated as Constantinople, and we must say, up to the present time, as uselessly occupied; we allude to the state of Nicaragua.[37]

Castellon urged the Emperor to immediately negotiate with Nicaragua for the commission to build the *Canale Napoleone de Nicaragua* without delay. The report considered other routes including Panama, and disqualified it because unlike the healthy Nicaragua route, "such a Canal could only cross a country marshy, unwholesome, uninhabited, and uninhabitable . . . amidst stagnant waters and barren rocks, yielding no spot of ground fitted for the growth of a trading community, for sheltering fleets, or for the development and interchange of the produce of the soil."[38] From the 1840s onward, American leaders and legends like Cornelius Vanderbilt, Ulysses S. Grant, and William McKinley supported a Nicaragua site. European powers also came to the conclusion that Nicaragua, not Panama was the preeminent route for an interoceanic canal. With the exception of a brief flirtation, in 1880 with a novel approach to a Tehuantepec, Mexico passage called a ship railway; the United States government also favored Nicaragua over all other routes.

History of American Interest in a Nicaragua Canal

Any American conversant with the subject of interoceanic canals could hardly dispute the advantages possessed by Nicaragua over any rival. In an interesting twist, the man who was most critical in moving toward Panama for the route, Theodore Roosevelt, was an early supporter of a Nicaragua canal and he called in vigorous terms for swift construction of the waterway. In 1897 as Assistant Secretary of the Navy, Roosevelt wrote with some urgency to Captain Alfred Mahan, author of *The Influence of Sea Power upon History, 1660— 1783*, strongly avowing, "I believe we should build the Nicaraguan canal at once."[39] The next year, the 1898 Spanish American War drove home the necessity for the United States to possess a short cut for battleships as the theatre of war encompassed two oceans. America's second largest warship, the *USS Oregon* took sixty-seven days from the Pacific coast, 14,7000 miles around the Straights of Magellan to join the Atlantic fleet in the 1898 war with Spain. North Americans had been clamoring for Congress to move ahead with the Nicaragua Canal ever since. It was a matter of national security and national pride. Legendary shipping entrepreneur, Cornelius Vanderbilt had

Cornelius Vanderbilt. Engraving by W.G. Jackman for Hunt's Merchants Magazine, (before 1877), Wikimedia Commons.

proven to the world that Nicaragua was the best location to dig an interoceanic ditch before the Civil War, and the new war with Spain intensified the public's interest in building on Vanderbilt's success.

Commodore Vanderbilt and Nicaragua, 1851-1859

The history of interest and enterprise in Nicaragua ran deeply in the American experience. When celebrated shipping tycoon, Cornelius Vanderbilt, envisioned expanding his empire, he fixed his gaze on Nicaragua, not Panama. The same incentive for the Panama Railway construction—reaping outrageous profits by transporting the swarm of gold-crazed prospectors from the East coast to California—inspired Vanderbilt's interest in Nicaragua. In 1850, one year after the railroad company began its work in Panama, he formed the Accessory Transit Company to deliver gold rush prospectors across Nicaragua to the West Coast. Vanderbilt's transit company had a much easier job than had the Panama Railroad Company laying down track in Panama "through a deep morass, covered with the densest jungle, reeking with malaria, and abounding with almost every species of wild beasts, noxious reptiles, and venomous insects known in the tropics."[40] With over 160 miles of relatively open waterways in Nicaragua—up the San Juan River and across Lake Nicaragua—the remaining 12 miles of terra firma across the Rivas Isthmus to the Pacific Ocean could be crossed by mule-train until Vanderbilt's canal could be dug.

To demonstrate to skeptics—and to uphold his reputation as "the bravest, coolest, and in all points the best boatman around"—on January 1, 1851 with "Commodore" Cornelius Vanderbilt at the helm, the steamboat *The Director* set sail up the San Juan River carrying a load of gold seekers bound for California. Hammering the vessel over sand bars and slithering through the rapids, Vanderbilt piloted the little vessel in an astonishing display of seamanship and nerve. The passengers at one time had jumped over the side of *The Director* to push it over a particularly difficult sand bar. Once dislodged, Vanderbilt audaciously—at full steam ahead, with the safety valve tied down—throttled the little ship across the obstacle and into the foaming rapids that awaited. *The Director* became the first steam-powered vessel to travel the entire 120-mile distance of the San Juan River to reach Lake Nicaragua from the Caribbean Sea. Vanderbilt committed his energy to undercutting the Panama Railway by reducing the fares as well as the travel time for passengers and carrying mail for free, peeling away vast layers of the Panama Railway's business. By late 1851, a traveler could cross Nicaragua in less than twenty-four hours at a cost far less than the charge for the Panama Railway.[41] The enterprise was thriving, but before long the Accessory Transit Company ran into trouble.

It seemed that Vanderbilt could control a throttle of a steamboat better than he could his business partners. He finally managed to parry off the attempts of his unscrupulous partners—Charles

"General" William Walker, Library of Congress, circa 1855.

Morgan and Joseph L. White—to wrench control of the Accessory Transit Company out of his hands and the Nicaraguan route continued in profitable operation for four more years. But, Vanderbilt underestimated the lengths his partners would go to achieve their success. In a plan to take control of the Accessory Transit Company, his crooked associates struck a deal with the freebooter William Walker to steal the Commodore's Nicaragua business right from underneath him. Walker, the quintessential opportunist and slavery demagogue, was the kind of man Morgan and White could depend upon to implement an audacious play to seize Vanderbilt's property. He had a history of taking what he wanted.

Walker's Influence on the Nicaragua Canal

In 1853, Walker in command of his mercenary "First Independent Battalion of Lower California" succeeded in capturing La Paz in Baja California, Mexico, which he proclaimed the capital of the Republic of Lower California and declared himself its President.[42]

Walker—the darling of the Southern slave-holding class—then put the region under the laws of Louisiana, making slavery legal. After several months of skirmishes and more than a few relocations of his "capital" closer to the United States border, the Mexican military forced him to withdraw to California. Although Walker was tried in 1854 for conducting an illegal war under the Neutrality Act, he was acquitted and came away as something of a hero to both Manifest Destiny adherents and pro-slavery groups. Then in 1855, the filibustering, megalomaniacal Walker overthrew the Nicaraguan government, declared himself president, and seized Vanderbilt's transit company.

After the marauding Walker confiscated Vanderbilt's property, his transit privilege was awarded to Edmund Randolph, a San Francisco lawyer who had financed Walker in his earlier freebooting exploits in Mexico. It was literally payback time for Randolph who wished to recover his investment by acquiring Vanderbilt's profitable concession. Soon word leaked out that Vanderbilt's former partners Morgan and White, in collusion with Randolph, had supplied money and arms to Walker for his takeover of Nicaragua. The Commodore was furious, but United States President Franklin Pierce—who would later align himself with the Confederate cause—recognized Walker as the legitimate leader of Nicaragua. Pierce asserted that the new Nicaraguan dictator was good for the interests of the United States, this in spite of the fact that one of Walker's goals included, once again introducing slavery with a view of entering the Union as a slaveholding state. Pennsylvania's *Raftsman Journal* predicted that "General Walker . . . will be the first Senator elected from the state of Nicaragua."[43]

Pierce was wildly unpopular and his move to legitimize Walker's rule was met with stern resistance. Under pressure from Vanderbilt, the United States withdrew its recognition of the Walker government, and Vanderbilt organized a small, but professional army of his own soldiers, equipped them with the best weaponry and provision, and sent them and large sums of money to help an alliance of South American countries to oust Walker in 1857. But Walker—who by all accounts believed himself genuine monarch material—with the assistance of his slaveholding patrons, decided to continue his conquest of South America. In 1860, he planned an invasion of

Honduras, but did not count on England's interest in the territory to include arresting him and his men. After Walker took possession of the port city in Truxillo, Commander Norvell Salmon of the British steam sloop *Icarus* ordered Walker to lay down his arm and surrender.[44] It appeared to Salmon that in Walker's occupation of the port, he had taken money from the Custom House that belonged to Great Britain by a treaty between Honduras and Britain. Following his surrender to Salmon, Walker was turned over to the Honduras army. After a quick trial, the thirty-six year old Walker was put up against a wall and shot by a firing squad.[45]

Meanwhile, the restored Nicaraguan government, wary of American Manifest Destiny fervor and weary of corporate shenanigans, awarded the transit concession to French citizen, Felix Belly, to build a canal, but he was unable to secure the necessary funds, and his concession lapsed.[46] Vanderbilt never finished the canal that would completely pierce the Rivas Isthmus, yet, despite the withdrawal of Vanderbilt, American interest in Nicaragua only intensified. In a mood of Manifest Destiny mixed with equal portions of the Monroe Doctrine vigilance, President Grant implemented measures in 1872 designed to create a Nicaraguan interoceanic canal beyond the influence of filibustering renegades and shipping magnates.

President Grant and the Nicaragua Passage, 1879

Keen to establish an interoceanic canal, President Grant appointed a commission in 1872, presided over by Admiral Daniel Ammen, charged to, "consider the subject of communication by canal between the waters of the Atlantic and Pacific Oceans across, over, or near the isthmus connecting North and South America."[47] As a result, surveying parties headed by engineer, A.C. Menocal, were sent out under the command of officers of the United States Navy. A complete survey was made of every proposed course from Tehuantepec, Mexico through South America, resulting in Nicaragua as the preferred route. The advantages of Nicaragua were numerous and substantial. "Nature seems," Grant reflected, "to have made the route through Nicaragua . . . If we do not do it; our children will."[48] The Nicaragua route was nearer to the United States by 600 miles over

Ferdinand Marie Vicomte de Lesseps, 1880, Wilimedia Commons.

the Panama route. Although it was also a tropical climate, Nicaragua was reasonably free from the terror of the miasmatic conditions that promoted so many deadly diseases in Panama.

In addition, the engineering dilemmas presented by the Nicaragua route were conventional engineering problems, believed the experts, and as such had recognized solutions. Also distinct from Panama—where almost all commodities had to be imported—Nicaragua seemed to possess a boundless variety of resources and products—coffee, sugar, rice, corn, rubber, bananas, indigo, cocoa, vegetables, timber, and cattle—necessary for an enormous enterprise as the construction of an interoceanic canal.[49]And not inconsequentially, the Nicaragua route was historically free from catastrophic storms, unlike both the Atlantic and Pacific approaches to Panama. The choice of Nicaragua over Panama was eminently practicable.

Americans in Paris: The International Scientific Congress, 1879

In May of 1879, Grant sent Ammen and Menocal to Paris as delegates to a scientific interoceanic canal summit organized by Count Ferdinand de Lesseps. De Lesseps, hero of the Suez Canal, seeking an occasion to again stun the world by surpassing his staggering Suez triumph, summoned the International Scientific Congress to convene with a view to once and for all, settle the question of the best route for the interoceanic canal. The ostensible purpose of the Congress was to gather together 136 of the world's most brilliant scientists and talented engineers to solve the thorny problem of the best interoceanic canal route and agree on the most practical passage. In fact, its true purpose was to legitimize the route de Lesseps had already chosen—Panama—in the eyes of the French government and public, de Lesseps' biggest target for raising millions of francs for the project. Most of the attendees were French. Eleven delegates hailed from the United States, but the American Government officially commissioned only two of that number, Ammen and Menocal. The other men in the American delegation were friends and business associates of de Lesseps. During the two fractious weeks of the summit, de Lesseps demonstrated remarkable skill in maneuvering the various committees to endorse all his plans.

During the sessions, Ammen vehemently protested in vain of de Lesseps' hijacking of what was supposed to be an open and free exchange of scientific knowledge. Menocal barely had a chance to say anything.[47] When they could get the floor, Ammen and Menocal vigorously argued that it was impossible to construct a canal by the

Panama route; that the time and money required would be wasted; that there was but one proper, feasible route, and that was Nicaragua. Regardless of what scrupulously sound scientific evidence gathered from years of detailed and exhaustive surveys offered by the Americans and others, the Panama course—spawned by an eighteen-day incomplete survey based upon an 1857 map acquired from the Panama Railroad Company—was delivered by the midwifery of the International Scientific Congress into de Lesseps' waiting arms.

After the Congress ended—although it could not be proven—many of the attendees said that the fix was in. De Lesseps packed the participants with his friends and supporters; all favorably disposed toward his ideas.[46] De Lesseps needed the Scientific Congress to conclude that Panama was the most practicable route, because he and his friends had formed a company that had obtained a concession to dig a canal across Panama from the Colombian government, based upon the "so called survey by Lieut. Wyse."[50] Whether or not the Congress was a sham is a question that can probably never be known categorically, but what is obvious is that the Scientific Congress was neither a meeting of engineers nor of scientists.[51] It was an assembly of speculators. Of the 136 participants, only forty-two were engineers, geographers, or had any scientific or technical training. The rest were politicians, financiers, investors, and promoters looking for the next big thing.[48]

Ammen and Menocal were furious, and above all, frustrated. After his return to the U.S., Ammen publicly declared that "on account of the character of the Paris congress virtually nothing was accomplished," and he recommended that another summit be called to give the American perspective "proper consideration."[52] Grant—who could never completely accept the fact that a man of de Lesseps' stature would make such a grave misjudgment as to choose Panama over Nicaragua—prophesied the demise of the ill-fated French project. In wonderment and disbelief, Grant declared that he did not care "how much money de Lesseps may spend upon Panama, he never will be able to build a canal there, because it is a physical impossibility."[49] Nonetheless, the world and some Americans endorsed the result of the Scientific Congress, believing despite the objections of Ammen and others "the Paris convention

James Buchanan Eads concept of the Ship Railway illustrated in E. L.Corthell's **The Atlantic & Pacific Ship-Railway Across the Isthmus of Tehuantepec, in Mexico: Considered Commercially, Politically & Constructively**, *1886.*

will be productive of much good."[53] Grant died in 1885, three years before his prediction come true.

THE TEHAUNTEPEC FLIRTATION: EADS SHIP RAILWAY, 1880-1888

Although it may seem preposterous in retrospect, when the imminent engineer James Buchannan Eads, the designer of the diving bell, proposed a "ship railway," as a means to convey ships between the Pacific and Atlantic Oceans, Congressmen, capitalists, and promoters took notice.[54] Eads was convinced—and managed to persuade more than a few supporters—that the only practical solution of the problem of interoceanic communication was neither Panama nor Nicaragua, but the construction of a railway through Tehauntepec, Mexico that could carry ships from one coast to the other. Eads' method—designed to ease 600 ton ships onto giant cradles, haul them overland by rail, and then deposit them on the opposite coast—would be cheaper to build, save ship operators millions of dollars in tolls over time, and get goods to their destination quicker than canal systems in either Nicaragua or Panama. Six, 100-ton locomotives—three at the front and three at the rear—would provide the power to propel the ship over the rails.[55] For Eads and his followers, the problem was simply one of scale, not difficulty. There already existed a highly functioning example, Eads argued that examples for success of his plan existed citing a project only a few miles from Congress where:

> A railway upon which canal-boats, heavily laden with their cargoes, are daily transported up a steep grade from the Potomac River to the canal above… Surely if a railway can be constructed of sufficient strength to carry a canal-boat, there is no reason why one could not be constructed strong enough to carry an ocean vessel. The whole question is one of force, and whenever an engineer can bring a problem down to this, its solution is an easy one.[56]

In 1885, legislation was submitted to relating to the incorporation of the Isthmus Ship Railway. Sadly, Eads died in 1887 and the project—which attracted enthusiastic support in both Houses of the United States Congress—was eventually abandoned. Meanwhile, the French were attempting to plow through Panama and the Americans continued down a separate path toward a United States interoceanic canal in Nicaragua. Thirty years of eyewitness accounts of the misery and disease, swamps, snakes, the horrific loss of life on the Panama Railway construction, and widely publicized news of the French difficulties convinced most Americans of the futility and waste of digging an interoceanic canal through Panama. Ordinary citizens, social commentators, and politicians alike understood the commercial and strategic military benefits of an interoceanic thoroughfare, but they wanted it to be practical, profitable, and safe. Panama, they had learned, was neither practical nor safe and with the French spending $400,000,000 on the unfinished project, everyone could see that it was far from profitable.[57] The only viable asset of the *Universelle du Canal* was the Panama Railroad that it had been forced to purchase. The interest in the most unorthodox ideas like Eads' ship railway somehow had seemed infinitely more reasonable to most decision makers than digging a canal in Panama.

The Reality of Imaginary Enterprises: The Disintegration, 1898

When Ferdinand de Lesseps' house of cards finally collapsed, Americans continued the notion of carving a passage from the Atlantic to the Pacific through Nicaragua outlined by President Grant's commission on interoceanic canals. In 1890, just months after the *Compagnie Universelle du Canal Interoceanique du Panama* abandoned its machinery across the muddy and merciless swamps of the capricious Charges River, the private American company, the Nicaragua Maritime Canal Company, revamped its long, but rocky relationship with the United States Government by renewing its 1880 charter.[58] The venture's goal was completing the project in Nicaragua that Vanderbilt started. The revelation of the scandals of Panama, the consequent suicides and financial panics, had nearly derailed the French government and Americans wanted no part of the scandalous and dilapidated enterprise.

One hundred and sixty-one French legislators were indicted for taking bribes from the old company. One was the future President of France, Georges Clemenceau. In addition to the politicians and the Cross of the Legion of Honor recipient de Lesseps and his son, the famous architect Gustave Eiffel, employees from six banks, and editors and reporters from two newspapers were among the offenders hauled into court.[59] Numerous government officials were convicted, the young de Lesseps received a five-year prison sentence, and Eiffel received a two-year sentence. The Great Frenchman, Ferdinand de Lesseps, received a sentence of five years, but due to his health and age, he was not incarcerated. In the company of those named in the corruption charges were the largest banking business in the world, *Credit Lyonnais*; the second largest bank in the France, *Societe Generale;* and the principal owner of one the most influential newspapers of Paris, *Le Matin*, Philippe Bunau-Varilla.[60] It would be Bunau-Varilla who would later carry out, with missionary zeal, a successful effort to convert the Americans to the new religion of Panama away from their long held faith in Nicaragua.

Statesmen, contractors like Bunau-Varilla, and other "common swindlers," were designated as "penalized" stockholders by the French courts.[61] This category consisted of the major investors in the *Compagnie Universelle*—both those banks and individuals who were complicit in the corruption in the first place—and were forced to take the stock in the new business or risk criminal prosecution. Thus, in a move that ignored the old warning to not "leave a fox to guard the hen house," the French government placed the very men and institutions that participated in the collapse of the venture in the position to turn a profit or go to jail. A new company was put together from the ruins of the *Compagnie Universelle*. It would be reorganized as the *Compagnie Nouvelle du Canal de Panama*.

In the frantic effort to salvage some capital from the gargantuan financial ruin, the French began a campaign to woo the only group that had the means and resources to bail them out of their sinking ship, the Americans. Most people thought it was a "great swindling canal scheme" and the company tainted beyond redemption.[62]

At this point, the project to rehabilitate the reputation of Panama or the French company was totally doomed. Then in 1893 the *Compagnie Nouvelle du Canal* hired American lawyer, William Nelson Cromwell, as the counsel for the new company. From that time onward, Cromwell's influence over the Panama Canal was supreme and—except for Theodore Roosevelt and Philippe Bunau-Varilla—his control over events was exclusive. Thus, began a new scheme that would fleece the American people as surely as de Lesseps swindled the French peasants. The plans Cromwell constructed to the financial advantage of himself and his fraudulent and shady clients was conceived and carried out while he was simultaneously acting on behalf of the *Compagnie Nouvelle du Canal de Panama*, the Panama Railroad Company, the United States State Department, and the Panama Canal Company of America. Indeed, the master manipulator Cromwell would have complete control of the distribution of the millions of dollars paid by the United States to Panama when later he was appointed the financial director of the entire country of Panama.

As de Lesseps' bankrupt venture spiraled into a scandalous vortex of suicides, arrests, and convictions, Nicaragua canal interests in the United States enjoyed a strong and able ally in the redoubtable Democratic Senator John Tyler Morgan. The venerable, ex-Confederate general and longtime Senator from Alabama skillfully led the Congress into effusive endorsement of the Nicaragua venture with the same vigor with which he led a cavalry charge at Chickamauga.[63] At the same time, Morgan deftly fended off transportation tycoon, C.P. Huntington's transcontinental railroad influence to have no interoceanic canal at all, and deflected the incessant and increasingly bothersome efforts of the ruined French canal company to unload its Panama assets on the American public. Yet, Morgan underestimated Cromwell's clout as the "active agent that represented all interests," concerning the Panama Canal project, and he miscalculated the inventiveness of Philippe Bunau-Varilla, who acted in concert with Cromwell.[64] The French court appointed president of the reorganized canal company, engineer and businessman Maurice Hutin; he also misjudged the forcefulness and intensity of Cromwell and Bunau-Varilla. Hutin would become the first public victim of the Machiavellian machinations of the indefatigable Bunau-Varilla and the cunning Cromwell. As for Nicaragua supporter Senator Morgan, he wrongly believed he had nothing to fear from the Panama Lobby as long as he had the sound science, the Congress, and President William McKinley on his side.

"The Isthmian Canal Game." Illustration shows a railroad lobbyist with a puppet show; the puppets, labeled "Nicaragua Route" and "Panama Route" stand in opposition to each other. Caption: "Railroad Lobbyist The railroads won't have to compete with a canal so long as I can keep these figures fighting!" Udo Klepper. *Puck*, 23 April 1902, Library of Congress.

CHAPTER TWO

CROMWELL AND HIS GANG OF RICH AMERICANS, 1896-1900

Two questions always present themselves in connection with Mr. Roosevelt. One is, "What would we do without him?" The other, "What are we going to do with him?" —HARPER'S WEEKLY, 1897

———————

The trajectory of the Panama Canal purchase cannot be understood apart from an appreciation of the inclinations of its creator, Ferdinand de Lesseps, his Panama Railroad Company business associates, the character and inclination of the Railroad's powerful attorney, William Nelson Cromwell, and the business atmosphere in which they evolved. The *Universelle du Canal de Panama* began as a way for a small group of men to fleece thousands of ordinary French people out of millions of francs and ended with another elite group of its investors swindling $40,000,000 from ordinary American taxpayers. The lies, grand larcenies, and avarice of both entities compounded with the callous necessity of a market system predicated upon a vast disposable labor pool, brewed up success in many other instances as well. The chilling of an initial moral outrage about the use of slave-labor on the Suez Canal project illustrates an accepted principle that ruthlessness and audacity were necessary features of the nineteenth century businessman to be admired and emulated. The forced labor issue was minimized and finally forgotten because de Lesseps became a millionaire and a hero to the world. Similarly, Panama Railroad executives reaped millions, even though tens of thousands of men died in the most squalid working conditions imaginable. It was standard business practice economist, social critic—and perhaps one of America's most original thinkers—Thorsten Veblen described in 1899. The milieu that Panama Railroad president Trevor Park, Ferdinand de Lesseps, and William Nelson Cromwell thrived within, wrote Veblen, was one bounded by "the conventions of the business world have[ing] grown up under the . . . derivatives, more or less . . . of the ancient predatory culture."[1] The uniting of two such companies with such similar operating styles and shared interests on the same fifty-mile stretch of mud and jungle seemed quite natural, especially when de Lesseps burst on the scene, the Panama Railroad Company was struggling for survival.

In its heyday, before the transcontinental railroad connected the United States coasts and the Suez Canal altered world shipping routes, the Railroad was a staggering financial success, paying as much as 26% dividends to its shareholders in 1869. But, with the advent of American coast-to-coast rail transportation and the Suez Canal, its fortunes plummeted. It was common knowledge that the Panama Railroad was in decline. In 1877, "rumors had been flying about for some time" concerning the president of the Panama Railroad Trevor Park's solvency, sending panicky tremors through Wall Street. A "scene of tremendous excitement" ensued on the trading floor of the stock exchange after Railroad share prices dropped and Park could not be located in any of his "usual haunts."[2] Friends who might have commented on his disappearance were also "mysteriously absent."[3] Park's personal financial difficulties continued to play on the front page, thus, causing his company's stock to slide over 40% in value. Then in 1878, fortune revisited the struggling Isthmian railway enterprise in the form of de Lesseps' business partner, a handsome, twenty-nine year old French naval officer, Lieutenant Lucien Napoleon Bonaparte Wyse.

The Wyse Concession

In 1876, Ferdinand de Lesseps, along with engineer, Lieutenant Lucien Wyse and Hungarian-born General Etienne Turr formed a corporation, the *Societe Civile Internationale Du Canal Interoceanique De Darian*. The mission of the corporation was to win a concession from the Colombians to dig a sea-level interoceanic canal route along the route traveled by the Panama Railroad. Turr—once called the most romantic figures on the Continent and Wyse's brother-in-law—finagled a concession from the Colombians that permitted surveying the area. In 1877, de Lesseps and Turr dispatched Wyse, on leave from the French Navy, to Panama to accomplish the task.[4] Wyse returned to France with a finding that emphasized the improbability of building any waterway through the Panamanian route he surveyed, let alone building a sea-level canal.[5] The engineering challenges, reported the young Lieutenant Wyse, were simply too great.

De Lesseps was infuriated. Wyse failed to grasp the fact that the Great Frenchman was not interested in the feasibility of a route; he wanted survey results that he could promote at the International Scientific Congress he was planning to hold in 1879. Obtaining the endorsement of the Scientific Congress was the most critical part of his plan to get the backing of the French government and banks

Lucien N. B. Wyse, **Le Canal De Panama, L'isthme Américain: Explorations, Comparaison des Tracés Étudiés, Négociations, État des Travaux,** *1886.*

to form the *Compagnie Universelle du Canal de Panama*—one that he would control—then make a huge profit by purchasing the Wyse concession from his other company formed with Wyse and Turr, the *Societe Civile Internationale Du Canal Interoceanique De Darian*. The emphasis on a sea-level canal was almost as crucial for the plan to work, because his success with the sea-level Suez Canal is what de Lesseps built his reputation as a brilliant engineer upon, which would raise the confidence of the investing public. He could also claim it would cost less than a lock system, further enticing buyers of stock in the *Compagnie Universelle*.

In an unrestrained display of his legendary temper, de Lesseps pitilessly screamed at Wyse for his ineptitude and naivety. He sent the chastised lieutenant back to Panama the following year with unambiguous orders to return with an outcome more in line with his scheme.[6] This time, Wyse completely understood of the scope of his mission; the goal of acquiring a concession to dig along a certain route was more important than the feasibility of the route itself. Wyse evidently appreciated that the crucial element for his company to be financially successful was a concession to build a canal—not the canal itself. He began his second survey, but abruptly aborted it, and headed to Bogota to secure the right from Colombia to dig a canal through the area of his intended survey. After a swift and strenuous trek to Bogota, Wyse received the concession from the Colombian government to dig a canal along the Panama Railroad route.[7] However, the franchise he negotiated contained one fatal flaw; it gave the Panama Railroad, the project's "natural enemy and rival," the right to control access to its land.[8]

Colombia agreed to a canal route that would follow the railroad path, but under the terms of its concession, the Panama Railroad Company controlled access to its land, not the Colombian government. The Panama Railroad Company was now in the position to dictate terms to Wyse.[9] The Wyse Concession, as it became known, was therefore viable only upon the condition that it could come to an amicable agreement with the railroad company. Even though it was obvious that "without the unqualified consent of the Panama Railroad" de Lesseps' venture would disintegrate before the first dirt flew, there was every reason for de Lesseps to be confident that he could get the company, or at the very least the rights of access, for a song.[10] The entire world, including de Lesseps, knew the Railroad was struggling. Surely, Park would jump at the chance to do business with the Great Frenchman.

Wyse travelled to New York in 1879 to meet with Park and discuss terms for access to the railroad's territory. He came away with an agreement to purchase the fledgling company—but the price was steep. Park knew he had de Lesseps over the proverbial barrel and he dealt with Wyse from a stance of absolute power.[11] Realizing his superior bargaining position of not simply controlling access to the land, but also as the sole provider of the means to remove soil and deliver machinery to the dig site, Park demanded $14,000,000 for controlling shares in the Railroad. De Lesseps was outraged, calling the price banditry, but Park never flinched. He refused to haggle, barter, quibble, or negotiate terms with de Lesseps.

In fact, to emphasize the dominant position of the Railroad Company, Park's only response to the Count's tirades was to tell him that if he did not take the deal on the table, the price would go up $250 a share every six months. Men, mud, and machinery were piling up without any means to move them. De Lesseps' stubborn refusal to pay Park's price held the project in perfect limbo, and by 1881 de Lesseps relented, paying the Railroad Company $25,000,000 for 68,887 of 70,000 shares. The *Compagnie Universelle du Canal de Panama* at last owned a controlling interest in the railroad, but they never controlled its operation. Park, along with his counsel, William Nelson Cromwell, exemplifying the "predatory temperament and habits of thought" that defined the rule of business, had completely bamboozled de Lesseps.[12]

The Railroad's New York 1849 charter stated explicitly that "the Directors should be annually chosen in the city of New York and on such notice as shall be directed by the laws of said corporation." It must have incensed de Lesseps to discover that under the terms of the Railroad's charter, he could not simply sack the Americans and move the operation to Paris. Its counsel, William Nelson Cromwell, effectively ran the company. Cromwell had been retained in 1881 by the Railroad. The negotiations and the predatory nature of the transaction were covered with his fingerprints. Over a decade after de Lesseps' dishonor and the reorganization of the canal company, the Panama Railroad Company was still beating them at their own game. The new French Panama Canal Company, the *Nouvelle Compagnie du Canal de Panama*, and the United States of America would both have good reason to feel as fleeced by the Railroad as de Lesseps did in 1881. William Nelson Cromwell would see to it.

SELLING THE *COMPAGNIE NOUVELLE DU CANAL*, 1896-1899

In the restructuring of de Lesseps' the old Panama Railroad Company, the French receivers formed the *Nouvelle Compagnie du Canal de Panama*—the New French Panama Canal Company— October 20, 1894 from the ashes of the *Compagnie Nouvelle du Canal de Panama* and attempted to restore some of the wealth lost to investors. The New Company sent its president, Marcel Hutin, repeatedly to Washington to court American policy makers, but Hutin's appeal was always unclear. Americans never quite understood what it was that Hutin wanted from the United States government. At first it seemed that Hutin's many trips focused not on United States governmental interest, but on "enlisting private capital in the enterprise where it can secure it," as the Washington *Evening Star* characterized the nature of one of his visits.[13] Still, he was constantly seeking audiences with those in political power, or those who might become politically powerful. Later, it became obvious that Hutin was looking to Uncle Sam to buy its remnants of de Lesseps' folly. Although he haunted the halls of the White House and the State Department, in D.C., Hutin was an ineffective presence. As one State Department official was overheard saying by a newsreporter, that despite his constant lobbying and continual labors, when it came to selling the Panama Canal idea, Hutin "never gets anywhere."[14]

The *Evening Times* of Washington D.C., commenting on one of director Hutin's visits to the State Department wrote that it was "the advances made by M. Hutin . . . have been both hopeless to the speculators and distasteful to this Government."[15] Echoing the *Evening Times*, the *Minneapolis Journal* claimed that there was not "one chance in a hundred that the United States government would ever purchase the Panama company interest in the half completed ditch . . . If the officers of the company . . . believe they have a chance to sell out to the United States they either deceive their stockholders or themselves."[16]

The New Panama Canal Company
Plus ça change, plus c'est la même chose

In 1896, eight years after the *Compagnie Universelle du Canal de Panama* collapsed in disgrace and bankruptcy, it was still in the hands of the French receiver. The reorganized company was seriously undercapitalized, with a capital stock of just $13,000,000. Shares valued at just $20 each, and six hundred thousand shares were sold for cash—the greater part being taken by the receiver and the contractors. Shareholders and bondholders were reconciled to either seeing their holdings shrink or they had written them off as a total loss. With just 75% capitalized, the *Compagnie Nouvelle* could not afford to do any significant work on the canal, but they put considerable effort into making it appear that work was ongoing, so prospective investors would believe it was a viable enterprise now that the company was under new management. Yet, in spite of all their efforts, the French government would withdraw all assistance, the European governments were wary of provoking Monroe Doctrine repercussions, and no private investors had the wherewithal to support such a massive project.[17] As he made his way to the United States to plumb the depths of new capital investment, Hutin was intensely aware that his company's only hope resided in the energy and wealth of Americans. Still, the American public, and their representatives in Congress were loath to have anything to do with de Lesseps' Panama debacle.

In addition to strong commercial and political support for the rival Nicaragua interoceanic route, the *Compagnie Nouvelle Canal de Panama* also had severe image problems with the American public. Swindling peasants, clerks, and shop girls out of their entire savings was particularly repugnant to most folks. "The people of America were so incensed at the story of Panama crime," fumed author Alexander Bacon, "that its very name became a by-word and a hissing, and no man would be rash enough to suggest any route for the American Government except the Nicaraguan."[18] Positive public opinion, powerful Senate influence, fifty years of glowing engineering reports, the unanimous declaration in favor of the Nicaragua site by the Intercoastal Canal Commission, and now President McKinley's latest ringing endorsement signaled the death knell for any hope Panama interests had and everyone—but William Nelson Cromwell and Philippe Bunau-Varilla—knew it.

The fatal defects of the malodorous French scheme were obvious to most American citizens. It all seemed so "foreign" and once again the idea of turning the Panama Canal Company into a Unites States holding—not a French company *per se*—appeared to Hutin the best course of action. Desperate to make headway against a strong tide of anti-foreign sentiment, Hutin hired New York lawyer, William Nelson Cromwell, counsel to the American controlled Panama Railroad Company to advance the cause of an American branch of the *Compagnie Nouvelle*. Cromwell came highly recommended by the Railroad, which was technically owned—although not operated— by the *Compagnie Nouvelle Canal de Panama*.

Hutin wanted an influential American who knew the interworking of the American political machine to grease the skids of a seemingly immovable United States Congress and Cromwell had a reputation as a tenacious and effectual lobbyist for the Railroad. "Americanizing" the canal seemed a sensible strategy to convince a public wary of foreign influence in the Americas. Still, it did not seem likely to most observers that Cromwell would be more successful in promoting the French ditch than was Hutin. Little did they, or Marcel Hutin, understand about the complexity of the relationship between Cromwell and the Panama Railroad. To the unsuspecting world, Cromwell was simply an accomplished Wall Street attorney and the Panama Railroad was just one of his many powerful clients, but in reality, Cromwell was both serving as their lawyer and a powerful, decision-making member of the board.

The Fox of Wall Street

Hutin did not need much convincing by Cromwell that to circumvent the powerful patriotic sentiment held by a post Spanish-

William Nelson Cromwell, **Frank Leslie's Illustrated Newspaper,** *Vol. 58, May 1904, Wikimedia Commons.*

American War public, that the French needed to "remove the deadly reproach of a 'foreign' enterprise," by Americanizing the Panama project.[19] Implementing this stratagem would mean the New Canal Company would form an American company governed by American directors. And who was there better than Cromwell, known as the "fox of Wall Street," to spearhead the operation?[20] A contract establishing such a venture, dated 21 November 1899, exclusively empowered Cromwell to effect an American organization for the purpose of the "Americanization of the Panama Canal Company." The move at first encouraged French holders into thinking that they might recoup some of their losses. They would have been even less confident had they understood the implications of the terms of agreement and the level of virtuosoity Cromwell had achieved in legal banditry.

Among various stock transfers, the text of the agreement relating to the Panama Railroad gives unrestricted insight into Cromwell's inspiration for his tireless efforts to defeat the Nicaragua Canal proposal. Cromwell and his already wealthy American associates would become exceedingly rich men, indeed. Under the terms of the contract, the American company would receive:

> The Panama Canal and concessions (and all existing deposits under such concessions), including all the canal works, plant, machinery, buildings, and all other real and personal fixed and movable property upon the Isthmus of Panama belonging to the *Compagnie Nouvelle du Canal de Panama* . . . all plans, surveys, reports, data, and records pertaining to the canal; also all lands ceded gratuitously by the Colombian Government . . . The American company will also acquire the rights of every nature belonging to the French company in the 68,534 shares of stock (out of the total issue of 70,000) of the Panama Railroad Company, a New Jersey corporation created in 1849 under special act of the legislature of the State of New York. These railroad shares are to become the absolute property of the American company upon the completion of the canal, without any further payment whatever. In the meantime, they will continue to be held in trust (as at present is the case in respect to the French company) to abide the fulfillment of said condition.[21]

Had Hutin been less naïve, or perhaps just slightly more cynical, he may have realized that he had signed over any hope that the ordinary, defrauded shareholders in de Lesseps' corrupt enterprise would recoup any of their losses.[22] Cromwell urged Hutin to be aggressive, that the enemy of the *Compagnie Nouvelle* was no longer the specter of a bankrupt company, but he said, "It is the [United

66

States] nation itself. How to turn the nation away from this design becomes the new and serious problem."[23] Hutin was eager to remove the "fatal taunt" of French control of the project from echoing in the newspapers and in the halls of Congress.[24] Cromwell, Hutin believed, would deliver the investors of the Panama Canal from their losses.[25]

To help him fashion a counter narrative to the perceived threat of foreign influence and make the Panama route as patriotic at the Nicaragua route, the cunning attorney poached a sensationalist journalist from *The World*, Roger Farnham.[26] Farnham would miraculously rise in 1905 from Cromwell's lowly press agent to become a director of the Panama Railroad—to use his contacts to plant newspaper articles to influence the public and Republican leaders to rethink their views on Panama. Along with Farnham, Cromwell, true to his crafty reputation, hired the well-respected retired army Brigadier General and engineer, Henry Abbott, to act as an apologist for the Panama project. Through Cromwell, the following year the New Panama Canal Company created a Technical Committee to investigate the feasibility of continuing digging a sea-level waterway, and hired Abbott as one of its experts.[27] Abbott, a prodigious writer, authored over twenty articles and several studies that validated Cromwell's claim of Panamanian canal route superiority. Abbott created expert content and Farnham made sure his findings were well publicized.

Then, in the face of the superfluity of favorable publications about the Panama Canal that appeared from various sources and authorities, the American press began to run front-page stories by reporter James Creelman exposing an "abundant evidence of a widespread conspiracy" by the Panama Canal Company along with C.P. Huntington's great Pacific Railroad lobbies, the public's mood began to sour.[28] Numerous newspapers carried Creelman's story about a scheme concocted by the special interests to defeat the Nicaragua Canal bill introduced to the Senate by John Tyler Morgan. Those Congressmen who supported the Panama Canal, were gullible, Creelman wrote, and simply "did not recognize the sinister ends" of these two powerful lobbies.[29] He described in less charitable terms the French Panama Canal, with their "desperate attempt" to unload their worthless stock, while for his

"C.P. Huntington," William Keith, National Portrait Gallery, Smithsonian Institution, c. 1900.

part Huntington had from the beginning "fought every step of every effort to dig a canal" because did not want the competition.[30] It was not the first time that Huntington was suspected of surreptitiously funding opposition to interoceanic canal projects. In 1895, canal detractors began the heavy circulation of a pamphlet written by Joseph Nimmo—ex-Chief of the United States Bureau of Statistics—attacking on the Nicaragua Canal, questioning the logic of the project.[31] Nimmo declared in "that one transcontinental railroad is worth a dozen Isthmusian canals."[32]

Longtime Nicaragua Canal advocate and former United States Minister to Nicaragua and Costa Rico, Captain William Lawrence Merry, publicly and vigorously responded that he suspected some powerful and wealthy individual had a hand in Nimmo's sudden interest in the project. The statistician himself had "no personal interest in the canal," until he published the work, Merry asserted in the *San Francisco Call*, and he believed Nimmo must have been "paid for his trouble by some person or persons whose interests might be affected by it. There appears to be no doubt that Mr. Huntington was responsible." [33] Because of no prior interest in the project, his fifteen-year friendship with Huntington's Southern Pacific Company vice-president and general manager, A.N. Towne, "taken in connection with the fact that Mr. Huntington has uniformly opposed the canal project," Merry could only surmise that the railroad tycoon was at the bottom of the publication.[34] Five years later, according to Creelman, Huntington was still at it. As perceptive as Creelman was about the dangers presented by these two powerful lobbies, he did not understand the depth of the connection between them— Huntington's interest and the Panama Canal Company were bound together by the common thread of William Nelson Cromwell.

Cromwell's Web of Influence

The president of the rejuvenated Panama Railroad during Marcel Hutin's tenure as president of the New French Canal Company was J. Edward Simmons. Two years after the Panama Canal Company hired Cromwell, Simmons and Huntington signed a contract to end their clash about mail transportation concessions, bringing the Panama Railroad into Huntington's fold as a member of the Transcontinental Association.[35] Cromwell was at the center of the negotiations. In 1900, Simmons would be a major backer of the Panama Canal Company of America, ostensibly organized by Cromwell to Americanize the project.[36] During the same time Simmons was also the president of the most potent consortium of banks in the United States, the New York Clearing House, president of the Fourth National Bank of New York, and—not inconsequently to the success of Cromwell's ability to drive the United States Congress into discarding the

Nicaraguan route—the great friend and chief financial supporter of the influential Republican Senator Mark Hanna. It would be through Simmons' relationship with Hanna that Cromwell would solidify his control over the direction of Congress, in the State Department, and eventually of the White House.

President McKinley had dealt a "serious blow" with his delivery of his second annual address to Congress on December 5, 1898. His language toward an interoceanic canal through Nicaragua was tinged with urgency as he anticipated continuing friction with Spain over its Cuba policy and declared that the project to be even:

> More than ever indispensable to that intimate and ready intercommunication between our eastern and western seaboards demanded by the annexation of the Hawaiian Islands and the prospective expansion of our influence and commerce in the Pacific, and that our national policy now more imperatively than ever calls for its control by this Government, are propositions which I doubt not the Congress will duly appreciate and wisely act upon.[37]

Still, the "Panama Lobby," as it became known through the press, was patient, persistent, and prepared to confront the President's attitude toward Nicaragua through oblique means. However, even after the Cromwell influenced the language supporting the Nicaragua Canal in the 1900 Republican Party platform language changed, deleting the word Nicaragua and substituting the word "Isthmusian" in the declaration that afterward read "we favor the construction, ownership, control and protection of an Isthmian Canal by the Government of the United States," McKinley was first and foremost a Nicaragua man; something a rhetorical change would not alter. In his fourth annual address in 1900—nine months before his assassination—he all but drove a nail into the New Panama Canal Company's coffin by vigorously calling for the Senate "to facilitate the construction" of the Nicaragua waterway.[38]

The Confederate and the Fox

McKinley's string of endorsements for the Nicaragua route added to the mounting despair of the *Compagnie Nouvelle* stakeholders. If Morgan's Nicaragua Bill passed Congress, there would be little to no hope of recouping any of the losses suffered from the inglorious liquidation of the *Compagnie Universelle Du Canal Interoceanique De Panama* in 1889. But Cromwell continued to work methodically, relentlessly, and surreptitiously to undermine the Nicaraguan Canal Bill, the solitary obstruction to the success of his various clients' interest—which included the Panama Canal Company of America, the New Panama Canal Company, C.P. Huntington, the Panama Railroad Company, and of course, himself. But before he could ply the politicians, Cromwell had to get their attention. In that area, money worked its magic.

Muddying the Waters: Great Britain and Nicaragua

Cromwell was an imaginative and formable antagonist on his own. However all the opponents to the Nicaragua Canal project were not proponents of French Panamanian canal interests, but rather powerful enemies of the Nicaragua project for their own reasons. Great Britain's centuries long territorial claims along with the United States transcontinental railroad interests also came into to play. Great Britain, which had claimed the Mosquito Coast as a protectorate since 1655, was vocal about its discomfiture of the United States acquiring all privileges of the canal concession through Senator Morgan's bill funding of the Maritime Canal Company, leaving them out of the equation. Cromwell nimbly used the existing tensions between the UnitedStates and Great Britain over territorial claims and Americans' general fear of foreign powers establishing a foothold in the Americas to drum up doubts and apprehensions about Nicaragua's political stability. He used Farnam's newspaper contacts to publish stories accusing the Greater Republic of Central America—an association of Costa Rico, Nicaragua, and Honduras allegedly formed at the instigation of Great Britain for the purpose of enabling Nicaragua to "wriggle out of treaty concessions" with the United States—of "working against the United States" by offering the canal concession to Japan.[39] He also prompted the formal protest against continuation of the Maritime Canal Company concession lodged by the Greater Republic the following year.[40]

Under Cromwell's influence, the Nicaraguan minister to the United States and representative to the newly formed tri-nation association of Nicaragua, Honduras, and El Salvador, Jose de Rodriquez, also penned a letter to the Senate "In which a pointed protest to the State Department against the passage of the Morgan bill or any other Canal bill now pending in Congress on the ground that provisions in the bill would void the existing Nicaragua concession."[41] Moreover,

Senator John Tyler Morgan, Library of Congress, Library of Congress, 1880.

Rodriquez sent a copy of his note to the press. Senator Morgan immediately declared that Great Britain inspired Rodriquez' letter, as part of a plan to drive the United States out of Nicaragua by using Central American alliance as a catspaw."[42] The public was outraged that Rodriquez was interfering in United States government business and believed Morgan and other Nicaragua proponents' allegation that Rodriquez had never acted as an honest broker in discussions between the Greater Republic and the United States. Rodriquez was roundly criticized as unworthy to represent the Greater Republic in the U.S. his actions were seen as interference regarding the canal made him wholly objectionable to most political pundants. "Having performed his mission—that of preventing the Maritime Canal Company from receiving Congressional assistance—and seeing no further usefulness for himself in this field so long as certain Senators were unfriendly to him, Minister Rodriguez closed his legation and withdrew to Central America."[43]

The results of the various lobbying efforts unfolded in many instances and in many ways, but none more dramatic than the 1897 bipartisan attack on Morgan and the Maritime Canal Company. Republican Senator and avowed "railroad man" from Indiana, David Turple, issued an "antagonistic invective" that lasted for three days against the Maritime Canal Company and Morgan's bill on the Senate floor.[44] After Turple's harangue about Morgan and his canal bill in which he characterized the Maritime Canal Company as an "incorporated myth," his Democratic colleague William Freeman Vilas took over the assault.[45] He filibustered against the Nicaragua rider to the waterways bill for four days. When Vilas moved that the bill be sent back to committee for reconsideration, Morgan quite rightly decried the motion as a personal insult. In spite of the "vigorous and almost successful efforts" of the Nicaragua proponents, the bill had not reached a vote when the closure of Congress came on March 4, 1897.[46]

CROMWELL AND CONGRESS

Meanwhile, closer to home than any Mosquito Coast drama, powerful Congressional "friends and supporters of the great transcontinental interests," men upon whom railroad magnate, C.P. Huntington relied to promote his interests—which were not those of the friends of Nicaragua—were exerting pressure.[47] Not only did Huntington see the opening of an interoceanic waterway as a threat to his transcontinental earnings, but also his Southern Railroad virtually controlled the Panama Railroad Company. And by this time, William Nelson Cromwell was counsel for the Panama Railroad, served on its Board of Directors, and held shares in the company. It was long rumored that "the hand of Huntington"—and by default, Cromwell's hand—was guiding every obdurate and obstructive move retarding the culmination of Nicaragua canal legislation. By 1898, newspapers linked Huntington and the "Panama schemers" together in formidable "combine" that would "spare neither money nor expense to sidetrack the bill."[48]

Cromwell had a lot to lose if a Nicaragua waterway plan was followed. He was heavily invested in the Panama Railroad, his American Panama Canal Company had deployed confidential agents to secretly buy shares of the *Compagnie Nouvelle* throughout France, while his law firm was collecting hefty fees from the *Compagnie Nouvelle*. Cromwell's inspired and deeply cynical campaign for the hearts and minds of the politically influential members of the United States government took root as he relentlessly attacked the Nicaraguan Canal Bill, the only thing standing in the way of his success. Through proxies and in person, he fought the Nicaragua project in Congress and he battled public opinion in the newspapers. It would be the American company Cromwell created that would lead to the final demolition of Morgan's Nicaragua Canal venture, an international confrontation, a constitutional crisis, and prompt the greatest defrauding of the American people at the time. It is little wonder that William Nelson Cromwell would be assessed over a dozen years later as "the most dangerous man this country has produced since the days of Aaron Burr."[49]

Although President McKinley's response to Hutin's overtures and Cromwell's manipulation was anemic at best, Cromwell generated much more sanguine interest from members of Congress. Over a relatively short, but concentrated space of time, he garnered enough influence to redefine national policy. Needless to say, Cromwell's focus was on derailing the Nicaragua canal legislative process. "Keenly alive to the gravity of the situation," and not taking his influence on his associates in the House for granted, Cromwell continued to burrow through the wall of resistance against the Panama project using stealthier means.[50] He and his staff worked several weeks writing a pamphlet, "The New Panama Canal Co." Cromwell, testified that they distributed copies to:

> Each member of Congress, to all the higher officials of the Federal Government, to the governors and other high officials of all the States, to all the leading newspapers of the East (the number of which reaches several hundreds), to all the commercial bodies of the large cities, to the libraries, to the heads of educational establishments and other influential institutions, and generally wherever the influence of this pamphlet might have weight.[51]

While his publication was circulating, Cromwell looked toward moving the Executive branch toward favoring Panama. He sought from Secretary of State John Hay an official audience with William McKinley to try and persuade the President of Panama's advantage over Nicaragua. Cromwell and Marcel Hutin met with the President on December 2 of 1898. Hutin, a man who was never accused of being a savvy businessman, offered to sell the whole works to the United States for $130,000,000 and, as he would until the very end, reiterated threats to take his wares elsewhere—specifically, to Germany—if the President refused the offer.[52] McKinley was not impressed. After the meeting, an anonymous confident of the President told reporters that there was no possibility of McKinley paying any attention to the Panama Canal promoters.

More South American Intrigues

Two days after Cromwell's presentation to President McKinley on December 4, 1898, the State Department released a statement that the Colombian House of Representatives in Bogota had refused to grant another extension of its concessions to the *Compagnie Nouvelle*. "This," according to the *San Francisco Call*, "is considered a death blow to the Panama enterprise," and that New Panama Canal Company representatives who had just met with Hay and the President—Cromwell and Hutin—falsely claimed they had "ample time at their disposal" to complete the project.[53] Hutin and Cromwell beat a hasty retreat to New York that very day, but the diminutive lawyer fired a pointed letter to the State Department challenging the validity of the report from the American consul in Bogota.

On December 6, 1898, McKinley delivered the second of a series of stinging blows to Cromwell and his employers with his positive and earnest declaration in his message in favor of the Nicaragua Canal route. The President's plea for legislation in the present session to dig the canal at Nicaragua was unambiguous and emboldening to the friends of the Nicaragua Canal. If the Morgan Nicaragua bill should fail during the Congressional session as "nearly all the leaders expect," McKinley proposed assembling a Nicaragua Canal Commission "to secure direct and permanent control of the territory through which the canal is to be built."[54] McKinley tapped the retired Rear Admiral John Grimes Walker to head the Commission and invited Army engineer Colonel Peter C. Hines and eminent professor Lewis W. Haupt to fill out the team.

After McKinley's address in December of 1898, the Panama project looked doomed. Yet, in spite of everything that had happened, Cromwell demonstrated an unsinkable confidence. He immediately began lobbying the real political powerhouse in the Senate, Marcus Hanna, whose influence on McKinley through their close personal friendship was well known. Hanna was devoted to McKinley and McKinley regarded Hanna as a true friend and ally. His influence on McKinley cannot be underestimated. Hanna, a wealthy businessman before his political career, left his iron and coal firm to work full time on McKinley's nomination in 1895. By then, the two men had known each other almost twenty years. They had met when as a young lawyer McKinley represented striking miners that Hanna's company was accused of exploiting. The unlikely friendship for the Ohioans formed in opposition and came into full flower with each succeeding year.

Nicaragua Canal Commission Chairman, Admiral John Grimes Walker,
Library of Congress, 1904.

Ever the faithful McKinley ally and enthusiast, Hanna once again was promoting his friend's presidential aspirations, as the chair of McKinley's reelection campaign for the 1900 campaign. Cromwell, who knew Hanna through his ties with Panama Railroad president, J. Edward Simmons, offered the huge contribution to Hanna. Cromwell knew it would be the donation that would provide access to the one man who had the power to determine the fate of the Panama Canal, the next likely President of the United States, William McKinley. There was reason to believe that McKinley was someone with whom Cromwell could "do business." McKinley was a man to whom an "informal empire" of commercial hegemony held great appeal, and Cromwell could offer him an opportunity to fulfill his mandate.

On behalf of the *Compagnie Nouvelle,* Cromwell gave Hanna $60,000 for McKinley's 1900 reelection campaign—$1,620,000 in today's currency—and with the donation, he purchased from Hanna the one small and inconspicuous thing he needed to deflect the trajectory of the Nicaragua Canal. Through his financial influence on Hanna, the crafty lawyer had the word "Nicaragua" changed to "Isthmus" in the 1900 Republican platform. This was by no means a minor victory for Cromwell. The cash donation, which he would later charge back to the *Compagnie Nouvelle* as "a necessary expense," bought the lawyer a change in the language of the Republican platform on an interoceanic canal: It was with $60,000 the ambiguous word "Isthmus" replaced the geographically specific "Nicaragua" in the 1900 Republican platform. After his generous contribution, Cromwell acquired considerable access to the man himself, McKinley.

The Veneer of Diplomacy—House Rules

On 21 January 1899—by a resounding majority of forty-eight to six—the Senate passed Morgan's bill to appropriate $140,000,000 for the Nicaragua canal project. Even "the most sanguine advocates of the bill" were surprised at the margin of victory. Morgan, understanding the value of compromise, had hammered out an agreement with the committee that incorporated several changes and through the amendment process produced a bill that virtually sailed through. However, although Morgan suspected the House would offer some resistance to the bill as written, he completely underestimated the potency of Cromwell's aged brew of interference and obstruction that was seeping into the legislative process of the House of Representatives. The indefatigable, inventive *Compagnie Nouvelle* counsel merely adjusted to the new reality.

"An examination of the situation convinced us," Cromwell said when asked to recount the period, "that the Senate bill ... would ... certainly be adopted. We, therefore, concentrated our attention on the House and planned a new measure of defense."[55] Before the new defensive ploy, no one in America thought the session of Congress could pass without the ratification of a law for the construction of the Nicaragua Canal; no one that is, except William Nelson Cromwell.[56] Cromwell entirely understood that "an enthusiastic and large majority of the House" openly supported Nicaragua, and if the bill went forward immediately, the result would be "absolutely certain." If the vote could not be stalled, the fate of the *Compagnie Nouvelle*—and more importantly to Cromwell's American Panama Canal Company—was sealed. Thus, how to prevent a vote became an imperative, crucial in deciding of the fate of the Panama Canal.

In his own words, Cromwell moved in an "audacious and aggressive" manner to secure the attention of the House Committee on Interstate and Foreign Commerce, responsible for creating legislation on the isthmus canal project.[57] Other influences came into play that Cromwell astutely capitalized on, such as the inborn and long-running suspicion and jealousy simmering between Hepburn and Morgan over the authorship of the canal legislation. Panama sympathizers made certain that Hepburn knew that unless something happened to radically change the course of events, the most monumental legislation of the century would enshrine John Tyler Morgan's name and herald a victory for the Democrats. William Hepburn, although a Nicaragua supporter, bristled at the thought, and Cromwell knew it.

Tension in the House: Hepburn Committee

On 10 January 1899, the House Committee on Interstate and Foreign Commerce took up four bills on the Nicaragua Canal offered by Representatives Corliss, Hawley, Hepburn—the Committee Chair—and Hanley. Despite the fact that only two of the measures— the Hanley and the Hepburn bills—had much traction, all the bills would be deliberated and as it was, the session was a short one. The Hanley Bill was considered at the previous session and was practically identical to the Morgan Bill, which was at this time being considered in the Senate. The private-public partnership aspect of the Morgan Bill appealed to many Representatives, because using the Maritime Canal Company to build the canal would deftly evade the provisions of the Clayton-Bulwer Treaty with Great Britain that prohibited either government from controlling the waterway. Congress wanted—just as President Grant had said in 1879—an American canal under American control. The idea that Great Britain could enforce the so-called neutrality of the interoceanic canal conjured up all sorts of patriotic, Monroe Doctrinaire distemper which either the Morgan or the Hanley bill would soothe.

The other significant legislative proposal was the Republican Hepburn Bill providing for the outright government ownership of the canal, and was generally understood to be McKinley's preferred approach to possession of the Nicaragua Canal project.[58] Sixteen of the seventeen-member committee were in favor of a Nicaragua Canal and would vote for some kind of bill. Nevertheless, they were not in agreement about which plan. A plan that was not being considered, according to the popular press and did not "have a ghost of a show is the revival of the Panama Canal. This plan . . . exists chiefly among those interests which are shrewdly suspected of being inimical to all canals and is accepted as merely a means to stave off action, if possible, for a year or two longer."[59] As for Senator Morgan, he was on record saying that he "wasn't wedded to his bill" and that he would support any Nicaragua bill that both Houses would pass.

Cromwell was hard at work on the House side of the equation. An astute observer of human nature, he had rightly gauged that he could influence events through a dexterous manipulation of the committee chair. He used William Peters Hepburn's ego and his partisan allegiance to buy the Panama project what it needed the most—time. It was from this "desperate position" Cromwell conceived the plan of recommending the disbanding of the Nicaragua Canal Commission and appointing a new canal commission—Isthmusian Canal Commission—ostensibly for the examination of alternative routes, including the Panama route. The practical effect of such a commission, however, was simply to "prevent the United States from deciding in favor of Nicaragua before the presentation to Congress of an official report on Panama."[60] At first, this proposal was met with vigorous opposition, but "by personal interviews," and persistence, Cromwell convinced several important members of the House including the Speaker Thomas Brackett Reed, who was also chair of the powerful Committee on Ways and Means, and Joseph Cannon, the obstreperous leader of the Republican Party in the House and—most importantly to Cromwell—the chairman of the Committee on Rivers and Harbors.

Four days later the Washington, D.C. newspaper, *The Times*, warned the American public that the Nicaragua Canal Bill was in danger of "being smothered to death in the House."[61] The committee was moving slowly and there were so many bills bearing upon the same question, time to pass Morgan's Bill would surely be squandered, projected the reporter. In addition, the already overburdened committee, for reasons that were unclear, agreed to hear from the new Panama Canal Company even though "no one had any faith in the Panama scheme."[62] Cromwell used his influence with committee members—one of which was Marcus Hanna—to grant a series of public hearings about a Panama route with the committee held on January 17, 18, and 19. In the hearings, he stated that the New Panama Canal Company—he never used the French name of the company, *Compagnie Nouvelle*—was in no way seeking and did not request any financial aid from the Government of the United States in the completion of the canal. "But," he modestly explained, "I am authorized by the company to state that . . . it places its canal works on the Isthmus subject to the personal examination of this committee, or any special commission through whom it may be desired to make such examination, and that it will be a pleasure to facilitate in every possible way, with all its resources, any such desire of the committee or the Government."[63] Cromwell, it seemed, was simply performing his patriotic duty by insuring that the committee had all the facts before reporting out a bill on Nicaragua. While the committee hearings were going on in the Senate, two Republican giants in the House of Representatives, Henry Hepburn and Joe Cannon, locked horns over Nicaragua.

Clashes in the House over the various bills were extreme. Hepburn and fellow Republican "Uncle Joe" Cannon—a Cromwell devotee—were particularly nasty. Over one month into the process, on February 13, the Committee on Interstate and Foreign Commerce reported in favor of substituting the text of the Hepburn Bill for the Senate bill. Hepburn's canal bill was referred to the Committee of the

Joseph Gurney Cannon, Library of Congress, 1903.

Whole—which precluded any possibility of consideration except by unanimous consent or a special order from the Committee on Rules. The possibility of canal legislation seemed rather dim. Furthermore, every minute of the remainder of the session was needed for the consideration of five major appropriation bills.

Time was ticking away. In this predicament, Hepburn decided to offer his bill as an amendment to the miscellaneous civil appropriation bill that Cannon was marshalling through the House.

Cannon declared that Hepburn's amendment was out of order and asked for a ruling from the Chair. The amendment, according to Cannon, was not germane,"obnoxious" to House rules in that it appropriated money not authorized by existing law, and lastly, the amendment appropriated money for work that was not in process. Cannon was in a sound position, yet Hepburn hoped that even if the point of order were sustained, proponents of the canal bill would be numerous enough to overrule the decision. Still the deck was stacked against Hepburn: not only was Cannon an ally of Cromwell's associates and the railroad interests, but the Speaker of the House was a strong Cannon ally. Nevertheless, according to Hepburn's biographer a dozen years later, Cannon was on his guard and with the "full sympathy of the Speaker he mustered every influence to prevent the contemplated coup."[64]

After an extended quarrel on the floor, the Speaker sustained the point of order ruled that the canal amendment was not in order. Hepburn appealed the verdict, but his petition was defeated; thus, ended the prospect of the Fifty-fifth Congress authorizing the construction of an Isthmian canal. Public reaction was swift, insightful, and scathing. The Washington D.C. *Times* denounced the legislators who derailed Hepburn's bill as "idiotically penurious and submissive to the purposes of the anti-expansion and anti-canal elements." The article singled out Speaker Thomas Reed, a Huntington supporter and a Cromwell man, writing "It suited the interests represented by Reed to defeat the will of the people in the canal matter." Those who voted down the amendment, the tirade continued, voted "against the future prosperity, glory, and safety of the United States." The session would be remembered, according to the *Wilmar Tribune* as "nothing less than a base betrayal of the people's interests, and this for the benefit of the grimy-handed agents of the Panama Canal scheme."[65]

From the time the Fifty-fifth Congress adjourned in March until the beginning of the Fifty-sixth Congress, the battle against the Nicaragua canal project never subsided. Huntington and the railroad interests continued to use their influence against any plan that even gave the impression it was likely to succeed and the *Compagnie Nouvelle*—terrified of losing potential rescue from the

United States—continued to pay Cromwell to maintain a potent lobby in Washington, entertaining about sixty Congressmen at the expense of the company, and employing powerful publicity techniques to influence public opinion in favor of the Panama route.[66] Cromwell experienced scores of successes throughout the Fifty-forth Congressional session, the most significant of which was his strategy of ambushing Morgan's bill by delaying a House canal bill. This was all accomplished to fulfill the next phase of his desperate and inspired drive against Nicaragua: the establishment of a new Isthmusian canal commission and infiltrating its ranks with men of his choosing.

Through the access purchased by his donation to McKinley's re-election campaign, Cromwell convinced McKinley to choose members for the new commission from a list of candidates that included three men strongly aligned with the Panama lobby. On 3 March 1899, a bill conceived to support the commission Cromwell desired was passed to appropriate $1,000,000 for the creation and support of the commission. Cromwell' lobbying of the President paid off and three engineers over whom he exercised great clout, including engineer George S. Morrison, were placed on the commission. In due course, Morrison's appointment would act as a catalyst for the impending *coup d'état* within the commission— all according to Cromwell's master plan. Yet, at least one member of the new committee saw beyond the procedural subterfuge of the Harbor and Rivers' Bill calling for a neutral commission seeking unbiased information to best serve the country's need for an interoceanic waterway. Isthmusian Canal Commission professor, Lewis Muhlenberg Haupt, saw the commission as one more ruse to derail the Nicaragua project.

Lewis Haupt, who formally served on the newly disbanded Nicaragua Canal commission with Admiral Walker, believed the Isthmusian Canal Commission was just one of many orchestrated delaying tactics deployed by those opposed to the Nicaragua project. "The appointment of this commission," Haupt told the *San Francisco Call*, "is simply another game of procrastination brought about by the allied opposition to the United States getting possession of a short route to the Far East. This opposition is powerful and active. It never rests, and when you come to analyze it, it is enough to make one despair."[67] In the article, Haupt described the opposition as the English capitalist, transcontinental railroads, and the Panama Canal. Haupt energetically criticized the French project saying that the millions squandered on the scheme and the general impracticability of it was a matter of common knowledge.

The West Point educated and Harvard trained engineer had a fundamental and correct understanding of the organizational structure and the goals of the *Compagnie Nouvelle* revealing facts to which Congressmen seemed indifferent and of which newspapers seemed unaware. "No Frenchman can be found to invest a penny in it, [and] the company which now controls it bought it for a song and wiped out all former obligations . . . The great game," Haupt revealed, "is to saddle the Panama Canal onto the United States."[68] Cromwell would later substantiate Haupt's claims, rightfully boasting that but for his indefatigable work "this new commission would not have been formed, and the Nicaragua bill would have been adopted."[69]

Summer in Paris, 1899

Once establishing a grip on the commission, Cromwell used his access to the McKinley administration to leverage the proposal that a sub-committee of the Commission should visit Paris to assess the advantages of the Panama route, not Panama, the actual site of the project. A summer trip to France to judge the feasibility of a project already in progress in Panama since 1881 may seem out of the ordinary, but this tactic showed Cromwell's unparalleled brilliance at understanding human nature. He would seduce them with Paris. He would surround the committee with the elaborate trappings of sophistication and wealth, convincing them of the solidity of the *Compagnie Nouvelle* and of its project in Panama. In August of 1899, the perceptive and cunning attorney invited the commissioners— including their wives—for an elegant Parisian summer vacation. Cromwell sailed to France in advance of the party to ensure everything—from menus to maps—reflected the refinement, verve, and swagger that only the conspicuous consumption of the dominant class could provide.

He had to convince this group of skeptical American engineers that the Panama Canal was not a waterlogged, rusted-out boondoggle that cash-strapped investors wanted to off-load, but an enterprise that was exceptionally lucrative as well as beneficial, that the greatest men of the United States would clamor to join the endeavor. The conference oozed success. Cleverly, the little giant had already been busy for months preparing elaborate presentations of over 4,000 maps, engineers' reports, geologic profiles, projected dam and lock sites, hydrographic studies, excavation expenses, and inventories of equipment, which he presented with great confidence and panache.[70]

It seemed to those at the Paris conference that Cromwell, in addition to a corporate attorney of the highest caliber, had also become a consummate engineer. He impressed his audience with his vast understanding of challenging and complex engineering issues and explained with the casual confidence of a professional engineer, elegant solutions to those issues. As a result of Cromwell's lavish attention to every comfort, pleasure, and detail of the American visit, the sub-committee gained a positive impression of the Panama route. It was a major public relations coup for Cromwell. Altogether, newspaper reporters that were following the committee's activities with interest reported that the committee spent one month in Paris and two weeks touring the great canals of England and on the Continent.[71] Intriguingly, in the commission report about the Paris excursion, no mention was made of the event's master of ceremonies, Cromwell. In an allusion to Cromwell, however, the same report stated that representatives of the *Compagnie Nouvelle*, received "the commissioners with great courtesy and were ready at all times to assist them in making a study of this [Panama] route in all its aspects."[72]

Thanks to Cromwell's stagecraft, what the Walker commission heard and saw in Paris, as reported in the *San Francisco Call*, was truly "a revelation to them."[73] On the other hand—even though Cromwell's flamboyant presentation of the grimy miasmatic mess that the Panama Canal project in an opulent Parisian setting captivated the commissioners—the hesitancy of the company's president with the tragic negotiating style, Marcel Hutin, to set a realistic price for the *Compagnie Nouvelle* holdings annoyed

86

Admiral Walker. He simply did not believe that the $130,000,000 asking price for the works, plus the cost of actual execution of the staggering engineering tasks demanded by the endeavor added up to a good buy for Uncle Sam. Fortunately for Cromwell and his associates, by the time that Walker had come to the end of his rope with Hutin's noncommittal and nebulous sales approach in Paris, another energetic influencer emerged who would fortify Cromwell in his efforts to persuade the sub-committee of Panama's superiority from another angle. It was during the meetings in Paris that Philippe Bunau-Varilla—the man who would become Cromwell's most potent ally and eventually one of his greatest detractors—first involved himself directly with lobbying efforts against the Nicaragua Canal.

The Evangelist of Panama, Philippe Bunau-Varilla

As a young man of twenty-six, Philippe Bunau-Varilla worked as an engineer for Ferdinand de Lesseps in Panama. He resigned a year ahead of the bankruptcy, but stayed in Panama to work as an independent contractor for the project and became wealthy bilking money out of the company. He was one of the "penalized" stockholders whom the French courts judged to have earned obscene profits from the company while ordinary stockholders lost their entire life's savings. His shares in the reorganized Panama Canal, forced upon him by the courts, were at grave risk of evaporating if the Nicaragua Canal were constructed. The hemisphere simply did not need two interoceanic canals. Bunau-Varilla, who elevated social networking to a new level of effectiveness, masterfully mined each friendship for any profitable connection he or she could provide. For example, he parlayed his friendship with the powerful American elder Statesman, John Bigelow, into viable contacts Bunau-Varilla used in his mission to resurrect the Panama Canal.

Up until 1899, Bunau-Varilla limited his involvement to acting through "intermediaries," through whom, he claimed, instigated the formation of the Isthmusian Canal Commission. In years to come, he publicly diminished Cromwell's role in the game-changing events related to the Panama Canal such as the formation of the

Commission—as Cromwell would do with Bunau-Varilla's role—and both would claim that neither collaborated with the other. But at this point in Paris, Bunau-Varilla efforts were obviously highly coordinated with Cromwell despite what the two would later claim

It stretched the imagination, however, to believe that Cromwell—a man who left no stone unturned, no enemy unchecked, or ally uncultivated—would not have been aware that three of the Americans attending the conference he so meticulously planned were having what amounted to secret meetings with Bunau-Varilla. It is equally hard to believe that Bunau-Varilla—a man who exploited every connection possible to get access to United States decision makers—would not have made his introductions to the renowned Wall Street attorney, the man at the epicenter of American corporate and political influence. For example, it would be through Bigelow's

Philippe Bunau-Varilla, **Panama, Its Destruction and Creation,** *1914.*

daughter, Grace, and her friendship with Corrine Roosevelt Robinson—Theodore Roosevelt's youngest sister—that Bunau-Varilla would be introduced to Roosevelt the following year. Also, Bigelow's letters of introduction led to the prolonged and private discussions between Bunau-Varilla with American commisioners Morrison, Ernst, and Burr at the Paris Panama Canal meeting. After sustained argument, the men "gradually turned away from Error," becoming—according to Bunau-Varilla—champions for Panama.[74] Cromwell played the cold and calculating lawyer to Bunau-Varilla's impassioned zealotry, obsessed by the same goal, but if the accounts are to be believed, in Paris each was a stranger to the other.

Meanwhile in Nicaragua: Fall 1899

By the end of September of 1899, rumors began to spread in the press that the Commission was prepared to offer Nicaragua as the "most practicable" route between the oceans. In October, Marcel Hutin trekked once more from Paris to Washington to meet with Walker. This time his message to the Admiral was one of desperation; the Panama Canal Company was prepared to meet any conditions laid down by the Commission. Ironically, at the time, the contract of the Maritime Canal Company was declared forfeited by the Nicaraguan government in October on the grounds of non-fulfillment of the terms of its concession. The company protested that any lack of progress was due to political instability, therefore, they were exempted by a clause in the concession relating to "extraordinary difficulties." The Nicaraguans did not concur: since 1893, the company had done very little work and Nicaragua was loath to continue the relationship. But conveniently for Nicaragua supporters, another syndicate was ready to slide into the vacuum and take over the concession. In fact, it was a carefully orchestrated coup by a rival company.

The Cragin-Eyre-Grace Syndicate, headed by the formidable former New York City mayor, William Grace secured the concession from Nicaragua for $400,000 in gold, and the United States accepted the syndicate as a substitute for the Maritime Canal Company. Some wondered if Grace, rumored to have played a role in the "wrecking" of other corporations, had a hand in the Maritime Canal Company losing their concession, but at this point, Senators wanted a canal and they were not overly concerned with who would do the job.[75] Besides, the syndicate also included other highly respected "very substantial gentlemen" and all of them men of very large means, including John J. Astor, George Westinghouse, and others. They had been angling for months to take over the concessions from the Maritime Canal Company, and as in most of their financial transactions, they were triumphant. A bonus for the Senators was that the syndicate was not interested in having the government as a business partner, as was the Maritime Canal Company. Grace's partner, Cragin, claimed that the group was "strongly opposed to the building of the Interoceanic canal by the Government and is an earnest advocate of constructing it by private capital."[76] The terms were quite favorable, according to the syndicate's attorney, David McClure, who described the agreement with Nicaragua in a Congressional hearing as a contract in perpetuity. "There is no determination to it. It goes on forever, with all of the value which comes from continued use . . . It gives the power to the canal company which shall be formed—the Inter-Oceanic Canal Company [under the Cragin-Eyre-Grace Syndicate]," explained McClure. "It is not a concession; it is only a contract for a concession to commence in October, 1899."[77]

This episode invigorated Hutin and Cromwell and gave those few politicians sitting on the fence about the two competing project sites pause. In November, Representative William Hepburn admitted that even he did not believe any legislation could be obtained in the remainder of the session after all the delays, but, declared the feisty Nicaragua supporter, he would reintroduce his bill at the beginning of the next session. Chiefly due to Cromwell's effective machinations and delft manipulations, it was impossible to obtain a discussion on the matter of the Nicaragua Canal Bill during the first session of the Fifty-sixth Congress. Late in December 1899, in a lengthy article one news commentator reported the purposes of the delays and predicted the fate of the Nicaragua project for the upcoming session of Congress:

> The [purpose] of the French syndicate it is to unload
> a very unfortunate and impracticable enterprise on
> the United States at a figure twenty times less than the

amount of French capital supposed to have been squandered in the Isthmus by the de Lesseps crowd. The other alleged purpose is the defeat of any attempt that may be made by this Congress to legislate in favor of the Nicaragua route. To this end, it is confidently expected that a powerful lobby will soon be organized here ostensibly in favor of the "Americanized" Panama Canal. The first effort, it is said, the lobby will make will be either to prevent the Walker Commission from making a report this year or to discredit the work of the Commission . . . It is known that the Walker Commission has made a preliminary report in favor of Nicaragua, but in view of the withholding of the report from publication . . . it is evident that the whole question will be held in abeyance for many months.[78]

The perceptive reporter outlined the issue with force and insight. The only variable the journalist did not take into consideration was that of the President of the United States.

If the Nicaragua Bill could get through Congress, McKinley would sign it, regardless of the potent intrigues of the Panama Lobby. Still, Cromwell had done well. He managed to penetrate Congressional Canal Committee circles and obtained a hearing to reconsider Panama. By lobbying members of the House of Representative to vote against the Nicaragua Canal authorization he successfully undermined the Nicaragua Canal Bill passed by the Senate, and most importantly, he engineered the appointment of the new canal commission to consider the Panama route. He created international pressures by inducing Colombia to enter a protest against the construction of the Nicaragua route until the international interests involved at Panama could be thoroughly studied. His tenacious and shrewd campaign paid off. Had the powerful Congressional champions of Nicaragua, Representatives Hepburn, and Senator Morgan not underestimated the extent of Cromwell's influence, they may have been better prepared to fend off his attacks. As it was, the two politicians felt poised for victory in 1900.

On a bitterly cold and snowy January 18, 1900 in Washington D.C., the House Committee on Interstate and Foreign Commerce issued a favorable report of the Hepburn Bill, essentially the same bill defeated in the previous session. On January 19, Senator John Tyler Morgan presented the report of the Interoceanic Committee to the Senate, recommending to no one's surprise, the Nicaragua route. "We have reached a point in the discussion of a ship canal through the Isthmus of Darien," declared the relentless elder statesman, "where the necessity for the canal and its advantages to our country are no longer debated in Congress or among the people . . . [a]s a highway for our war ships and merchantmen . . . is now a national necessity."[79] Nothing seemed to bar the bill. Negotiations abrogating the terms of the 1850 Clayton-Bulwer treaty between the United States and Great Britain that locked the United States into an unpopular position disallowing either country from fortifying the Nicaraguan Canal were drawing to a close. With the new understanding of territorial oversight ratified, Great Britain's Envoy Extraordinary and Minister Plenipotentiary to the United States, Sir Julian Pauncefote, and Secretary of State John Hay would have eliminated the most salient impediment that anti-Nicaragua canal forces exploited, the inability of the United States government to protect the canal.

By February of 1900, the *San Francisco Call* seeing "an evident disposition in both [H]ouses to waste no more time," confidently declared that the canal bill would pass in the new session. The Nicaragua Bill was one of the most popular in the House, the report went on to claim, "evidenced by the applause that greeted the report, when Hepburn arose and asked for its consideration on March 6."[80] By May 2, Hepburn's bill, only slightly modified from the one he offered in the Fifth-fifth Congress, overwhelmingly passed with 225 in favor with only 35 opposed. But once again just as in 1899, the two Republican pit bulls, Representatives Joseph Cannon and William Hepburn, were at each other's throats during the debate on the bill. The *Hartford Republican* reported the fracas:

> The House was in riotous confusion during the quarrel. Members crowded the aisles and the situation

at one time was so threatening that Mr. Wheeler Dem of Kentucky sought to pour oil on the waters by raising a point of order, but he was not upheld and the two irate members carried their war to the very hilt. There was a show of peace at the close of the incident, but the feeling between the two men ran so high that the mutual retractions with which such incidents generally end were but the cloaks for the keenest and most cutting sarcasm.[81]

Despite the dramatic and triumphant finish for the Hepburn Bill in the House, Senator Morgan would have little to celebrate in the upper chamber of Congress. Republican "managers" in the Senate, Morgan stated in a May 26 interview, were "afraid to allow the [Hepburn] bill to pass for the reason that they might offend powerful corporations, thus, materially affect the Republican campaign fund."[82] Morgan indicted the railroad interests and the New Panama Canal Company for being instrumental in preventing the passage of the Nicaragua Canal Bill in the previous session as well. Morgan considered the Panama Canal Company's offer to sell its assets to the United States was "a huge conspiracy to inveigle the United States into its crimes and robbery."[83] Morgan furiously, but elegantly warned that although "much money has been used to delay action on the Canal Bill… the American people will not be robbed by a foreign or New Jersey power."[84] Morgan was right about the delaying tactics of the Republican, but sadly wrong about the American people's unwillingness to allow corporate money to rob them of their "American Nicaraguan Canal." Debate on the Philippine Islands consumed the remainder of the session. On June 7, 1900, the first session of the Fifty-sixth Congress closed without passing a Nicaragua Canal Bill. The beginning of the second session on December 3, 1900, however, held more promise for the beleaguered champion of the Nicaragua Canal.

On the second day of the second session of the Fifty-sixth Congress, President McKinley submitted the final report of the Isthmian Canal Commission. It was the unanimous conclusion of the Commission that the most feasible route for the Isthmian Canal was through Nicaragua. This announcement sent the Panama lobby into a panic. It was at this juncture, penalized stockholder Philippe Bunau-Varilla could no longer afford to work through intermediaries, and came off the sidelines. [85] "American public opinion was jubilantly confident of the triumph of the Nicaragua scheme," Bunau-Varilla wrote later about this bleak period, "It was now the proper moment for me to intervene to combat that impression . . . by creating a current of opinion outside of it." He began to lay the groundwork for his American assault on Nicaragua.

1901- THE FRENCH INVASION

With the zeal of a missionary, Bunau-Varilla sailed for America on January 3 1901. Friends of friends—including Hadley Thomas Proctor of Procter and Gamble fortune—had invited him to Cincinnati. During his passage, in ways that more aptly showed the Frenchman's finesse than "Providence" —a term Bunau-Varilla liberally used to describe divine intervention on behalf of his crusade—he met a fellow traveler whom he immediately proselytized into his growing congregation of Panama Canal converts, the Monsignor Schmitz Didier. The well-connected Didier, who for twenty years was "more intimately connected with the Vatican at Rome than any other Catholic prelate," enthusiastically embraced Bunau-Varilla's message of Panamanian resurrection and offered to introduce the diminutive Panama evangelist to his friend, Colonel Myron T. Herrick, who had powerful friends in Washington and could help Bunau-Varilla get the attention of the right people.[86] Indeed, Herrick was associated with powerful government decision makers. Not only did he enjoy a close personal relationship with President McKinley, but Herrick also "knew intimately a man far more important" for Bunau-Varilla's purposes, Senator Marcus Alonzo Hanna."[87] Bunau-Varilla had a good start on achieving his "improbable" goal before he set foot on the shores of American.

Although Bunau-Varilla was met with success at every juncture, he knew he would have to work hard and smart to accomplish the impossible. His first speech was delivered to the Commercial Club of Cincinnati on January 16, 1901 to an august crowd of civic leaders and millionaires. He did not come to America, Bunau-Varilla would tell his audience, "as the representative of any private interest; I came to defend a grand and noble conception which gave me several happy years of struggle and danger, and for which I suffered many years of anxiety, during which I do not remember one hour of despair."[88] His listeners were both charmed by his accent and his engineering expertise and alarmed by his warnings of the dangerous seismic conditions in Nicaragua. All phases of the project where threatened by both earthquake and volcanic activity, cautioned the Frenchman. In the construction phase:

> The continual earthquakes may have a fatal influence on the definitive transformation from half-liquid mud into hard stone, of the concrete, which will during eight years be continually poured in the great Boca San Carlos dam; these violent shocks, interfering every month or more with the gradual crystallization of the elements of concrete, may destroy their reciprocal adherence, and ruin the perfect homogeneity of the solid mass which is imperatively necessary for the part it has to play. [89]

But that was not the worst of it, Bunau-Varilla alerted his audience. After the project was completed, the "unlimited disaster" like that caused by the eruption of Krakatau in 1883, loomed in Nicaragua's future:

> Outside of the impending and terrible danger of seeing ruined the dam or the locks by a great seismic commotion . . . there is great probability of seeing formed in the sea of Nicaragua . . . one of those terrible tidal waves . . . It must be borne in mind that these terrible menaces would mean, if realized, not only the destruction of that costly Canal, but the ruin of the immense interests of both sides of America, which will have been developed by the great waterway and receive a death blow by its paralyzation. Nothing similar can be feared in Panama.[90]

He repeated this speech in at least six major United States cities to enthusiastic listeners before he met the one person who had the power and influence to help him change the American view of the French Panama Canal project, Senator Marcus Hanna.

When Bunau-Varilla finally met Hanna in New York toward the end of his whirlwind speaking tour, the Frenchman described the encounter, as "decisive." Afterward, Bunau-Varilla believed he had convinced Hanna and, through him, the President and the Senate would realize the worthiness of his cause. By late March, Bunau-Varilla believed that all he needed to do now was to enlighten the sizeable pro-Nicaragua Canal masses about Panama, not just the elite members of the Commercial Clubs, Chamber of Commences, and the Engineer Clubs. Bunau-Varilla sensed that the American public's patience with Congress' seeming inability to undertake this vital work was beginning to wear thin, and the Frenchman could use the sentiment to work to his advantage. He needed Americans to see his campaign as a balanced one—the effort of an honest man simply seeking to help prevent the United States from making a major mistake, not as the penalized stockholder that he was trying to gain financially from his lobbying activities. He went to Washington hoping to find a way to co-opt or at least neutralize the leader of the opposition, Senator John Tyler Morgan. The French engineer later stated, "[I] needed to surround myself with precautions and guarantees."[91]

Bunau-Varilla later recorded that when he finally finagled an introduction to Morgan, he was elated. "Now I had the key to the Lion's cage," he wrote excitedly, but afterward, he realized that he did not have the weapons to deal with what he would encounter in the cage.[92] Bunau-Varilla had his audiences spellbound in Cincinnati, Chicago, Cleveland, Boston, Philadelphia, Princeton, and New York. However, his audience of one in Washington D.C. was far from impressed. To Morgan, his visitor was a lackey for the Panama lobby and he treated him as such. First, Morgan insulted the Frenchman when he dismissed his concern about volcanoes, then implied that he was a "foreign adventurer" in the pay of the Panama Canal Company. Bunau-Varilla was so enraged by this attack on his character that he raised his hand to slap the old Senator's face. But subduing the impulse, he lowered his hand, and left the Lion's den. As he left he vowed, "to be avenged for this insult," and swore "to beat Morgan in the Senate on this very question of volcanoes."[93]

The theatrical Frenchman had used vivid and dramatic language to impress upon his audiences the geologic dangers that lurked in Nicaragua, and had Morgan listened to him, he might have recognized the dangers Bunau-Varilla himself represented. In the coming months, the Frenchman would get his revenge on Morgan by conjuring fears in the imagination of the news reading public images that would loosen the grip the "American Nicaraguan Canal" had on Americans and dramatically change the course of events. Still at the close of summer, Bunau-Varilla and Cromwell, as powerful, inventive, passionate, and well-funded as they were, would have never changed the outcome of the interoceanic canal debates without the unimaginable, unplanned, and uncontrollable occurrence in September of 1901: the assassination of William McKinley.

Illustration shows Theodore Roosevelt taking over the duties of president following the assassination of President McKinley. He is standing in an office, holding a paper labeled "McKinley's Policy"; his rough rider uniform hangs on the wall behind him. Louis Dalrymple. Title: A New Uniform and New Responsibilities," **Puck**, *Library of Congress, 2 October 1901.*

CHAPTER THREE

The Accidental President, 1901

The Quaker City Journal is satisfied that Roosevelt will not be happy in the vice-presidency ... The Philadelphia Ledger, in the innocence of its heart, thinks that the President should invite Roosevelt to join his cabinet. The Ledger does not know Roosevelt, evidently. Certainly it does not know McKinley. Roosevelt will simply have to grin and bear it. That he can grin we all know; perhaps, also, he can bear with us as we for two or more have borne with him.
—The Washington Post, 1900

———————————————

The date was ominous—Friday, September the 13th 1901. President William McKinley lay in a borrowed bed in Buffalo, New York, dying from a gunshot wound while his Vice-President, Theodore Roosevelt, was nowhere to be found. Seven days earlier on September 6, on the second day of the President's tour of the Pan American Exposition, self-proclaimed anarchist Leon Czolgosz shot McKinley in the abdomen at point-blank range. The shooter had managed to squeeze off two rounds from his .32 caliber Iver-Johnson revolver before being wrestled to the ground by African-American waiter James F. Parker. At six-foot six, weighing over 200 pounds, Parker was standing directly behind the shooter in the reception line at the Temple of Music, waiting his turn to shake McKinley's hand.[1] Before the assassin could fire a third shot, the "strapping big" Parker tackled him and disarmed him. A dozen officers and militiamen savagely fell upon the downed shooter along with Parker, pounding him mercilessly.[2] Frenzied onlookers joined the guards and pounced upon Czolgosz in an attempt to "rend [the] assassin limb from limb."[3] Had not the wounded McKinley intervened by uttering the words, "Go easy on him, boys," it is likely that Czolgosz would have been beaten to death on the spot.

To hold back the furious throng while the bloodied Czolgosz was hustled to a police carriage, the Marines and Artillerymen assigned to McKinley's security detail "dropped their guns till the bayonets were at charge," threatening to shoot if the mob came any closer.[4] It was a scene of utter bedlam, fear, and rage. One observer recalled that the "roar of the crowd was never to be forgotten . . . It had the intense growl, the bloodthirsty shriek and the savage note that is only heard in the voices of a frenzied mob."[5] Almost certainly, the angry swarm would have lynched Czolgosz that day had it not been for the military, the Buffalo police, and Secret Service guards.[6]

The horrified witnesses to the violent assault on the President took some comfort that at least McKinley would receive world-class treatment in the Exposition's medical faculty. According to popular reports it "provided well-equipped operating rooms, sleeping rooms, etc., such as are in any up-to-date hospital."[7] The hospital that received the President was, according to the official Exposition guidebook, the equal of any modern twentieth century medical center in the country. The President, assumed the anxious crowd, would get the best medical care modern twentieth century technology could provide at the Exposition Hospital.

McKinley arrived at the Exposition hospital at 4:18 in the afternoon, rushed to emergency treatment in a state-of-the-art electric ambulance. The Pan American Exposition was an orgy of a new century of technological achievements; an exercise in excess; a self-congratulatory homage to American progress. Yet ironically, the facility to which McKinley was rushed did not even have one functioning electric light bulb. By 4:40—before McKinley went under the knife—communication breakthroughs in telephone switchboards and telegraphs and transportation allowed newspaper extra editions to hit the streets quickly, spreading the news like wildfire. Within a surprising brief space of time, large crowds of distressed citizens were gathered on streets across the nation, waiting for the latest updates to be nailed to community newspaper bulletin boards. A gratified and relieved public learned from the newspapers that one of the most eminent surgeons in the world, Roswell Park, was currently on the scene to render service at the President's bedside. People were also comforted by the idea that modernization had improved McKinley's odds of recovery. "This is not 1881," said one prominent Buffalo surgeon to news reporters, "Great strides have been made in surgery in the last twenty years [since Garfield's assassination] . . . Everything that science can suggest is being done for him."[8] Innovations in communications and print technology assured people that in this critical time for the nation, the public could depend upon timely and reliable delivery of information and many Americans slept better that night because of their confidence in technology.

Electricity, Expansion and Nicaragua: America's Manifest Economic Destiny

It was technological and engineering achievements like the electric ambulance, breakthroughs in medical science, and advances in mass communication—made possible through the United States' command of electric technology that was celebrated at the Pan American Exposition—that reassured Americans their President would recover. The public's confidence in McKinley's recovery was as certain as its conviction of the United State's growing dominance over the Western hemisphere and, as many Americans believed was theirs for the picking, the entire globe. From the Wake Islands to Guantanamo Bay, America's manifest destiny expansionists successes pushed its boundaries ever outward. It was not unwarranted for most Americans to feel that their nation's reach was unlimited and in the new century the power of the stars could be plucked from the heavens as easily as the Philippines was taken from Spain.

As President, William McKinley was perhaps even more committed to an informal empire of commercial hegemony, as he was invested in military conquest. Since the Spanish American War ended in 1898, he focused on expanding the American Empire by acquiring extraterritorial dominance though public-private ventures like the one with the Maritime Nicaragua Canal Company. The company was organized to carve a watery passageway through Lake Nicaragua, etch an opening in the tiny split of land that divided it from the Pacific, and marry the two oceans in a near seamless union. They would do the heavy lifting; the United States would pay the bills. McKinley believed that with Maritime's expertise and financial backing of the United States, Americans would have and control the first interoceanic canal on the planet. Yet, the affiliation between the United States government and the private canal enterprise had been long and somewhat problematic. And as in most relationships, there were complications, but the long-range strategic and commercial importance of the canal kept the two sides together.

In 1889, the United States Congress had granted a charter to the Maritime Canal Company—officers of the company included Theodore Roosevelt's uncle, James Roosevelt, along with other gentlemen of great commercial and social import—and in June the company began the preliminary work of construction at Greytown. Over a decade later, the nature of the nature of the partnership changed, evolving into a relationship of financial dependency on the U.S. for the Maritime Company. Even so, through mismanagement of their assets, the Maritime Canal Company went bankrupt in 1898. Although many believed that the bankruptcy proved the project needed to be fully in the hands of the government, the United States stepped in to appropriate money for the stricken canal company because the prize was too dear to risk losing.

Echoing President Hayes reflection in an 1880 diary entry that, "The true policy of the United States as to a canal across any part of the Isthmus . . . is either a canal under American control, or no canal," McKinley—and so, his 1900 running mate, Theodore Roosevelt—assumed Hayes' philosophy and vigorously campaigned in 1900 on a platform in favor of "the construction of the Nicaragua canal under Government control."[9] The spectacular failure of private enterprise—of both the Maritime Canal Company and the French *Compagnie Universelle Du Canal Interoceanique De Panama*—to handle the job of interoceanic canal building convinced many Americans that only the United States government had the will and resources to complete the Herculean task of cleaving a continent and joining the oceans, and the idea of a Nicaragua Canal remained hugely popular. "The Nicaragua Canal has thus come, as it were," wrote scholar Lindley Miller Keasby, "to be identified in the people's mind with the manifest economic destiny of their country."[10] The *San Diego News* reflected Keasby's sentiment in an article entitled, "The People Want the Nicaragua Canal Built."[11] Cornelius Vanderbilt proved the feasibility and profitability of the passage decades before, and as far as McKinley, the independent Nicaragua Canal Commission he appointed, the influential bipartisan Senate Committee on Interoceanic Canals, and great swath of the American public were concerned, a muscular, sinewy Uncle Sam in his prime would dig its interoceanic canal across Nicaragua.

Nicaragua in the American Mind

From the time United States' "confidential agent" J.L. Stephens returned from his secret 1838 mission to Nicaragua and endorsed the British survey for a canal route there, America policy makers favored a Nicaraguan canal. Every President since Ulysses S. Grant worked toward establishing an American controlled Nicaragua Canal and now in 1901 McKinley was poised to actualize his predecessor's interoceanic canal ambitions. Nevertheless, the "Panama Lobby," seeing no room in the Western Hemisphere for two interoceanic canals, steadily pushed against Nicaragua canal interests, even when it was in the hands of the most "Famous Frenchman," Count Ferdinand de Lesseps. In 1880, as the French *Compagnie Universelle* began its fundraising *tour de force* across two continents, its creator and top promoter de Lesseps sought to divert American interest away from Nicaragua and generate financial and political support for a Panama Canal by seducing them with the first "Americanizing" of the project. De Lesseps poached United States Secretary of the Navy Richard Thompson to serve as chairman of something called the American Commission—a United States appendage of the *Compagnie Universelle Du Canal de Panama*—right from under the nose of President Hayes. De Lesseps thought Thompson brought the right credentials to the project. Thompson's high-ranking military panache and his reputation as an Americanism patriot would play very well to the potential American investors. Befriended by such an upstanding American as Thompson, Americans would trust any investments they made in the French company, thought de Lesseps.

President Hayes was flabbergasted. He knew de Lesseps was aggravated after he flatly shunned the French entrepreneur's attempts to Americanize his canal project by securing the blessings from the President, but de Lesseps' end-run around him made him furious. Hayes neither expected that de Lesseps would rustle his Cabinet members after the rebuff, nor did he imagine Thompson would be so eager to leave. Thompson was publicly lambasted for allowing his name "to be used by forwarding an enterprise regarded by the administration as not friendly to American interests."[12] Interviewed during the Thompson-Panama uproar, former President Ulysses Grant told a newspaper reporter that while de Lesseps' momentarily seduced a few Americans with his audacious plan, "the transient glory of Panama was unable to shake them in their faith" in Nicaragua.[13] Any subsequent attempts by the French to foist the bankrupt Panama Canal Company's assets on Washington policymakers in 1898 were considered laughable; a mere distraction at best.

When de Lesseps was charged in 1893 for fraud and bribery, Americans were appalled. People could barely wrap their minds around the fact that the famous builder of the Suez Canal was a scoundrel, but after all he was French and that explained a lot to Americans who were suspicious of foreigners to begin with. To ordinary folks, the Panama Canal was entirely a French debacle. De Lesseps' attempts to Americanize the project failed as completely as the canal project itself. With the public parading of the French catastrophe, the news dissolved any delusions the American public might have held about the feasibility of a Panamanian interoceanic canal, an enterprise fraught with so many "insuperable obstacles" that even the great maestro de Lesseps failed.[14] So, when the newly reorganized company, the *Novell Compagnie du Canal de Panama,* came calling on the United States government, naturally American citizens were skeptical. Most politicians—especially the scrappy Senator from Alabama, John Tyler Morgan, and a preponderance of the press—saw the move as a transparent play to salvage a remnant of the 1.8 billion gold Francs—$270,000,000 dollars—lost in the doomed project by flogging it on a gullible American public.

American's confidence in Nicaragua was firmly situated in a long established series of positive interactions. The Nicaraguan Canal Commission thoroughly investigated the question of whether picking up the remnants of the failed *Compagnie Universelle* offered any advantage over developing the Nicaragua route Vanderbilt previously established. They unanimously concluded that the engineering unknowns were too great in Panama, the known risks too high, and not inconsequentially—except for the Panama Railroad Company —the French Panama Company, was "practically without assets."[15] There had been some pressure of late from the Panama Lobby hoping to liquidate the French company's remaining assets, but the effort only further convinced decision makers that Nicaragua was "the most practical and feasible route for a canal to be under the control, management, and ownership of the United States."[16] The Senate Committee agreed and legislation was put forward for a government financed and excavated Nicaragua canal. The Panama Lobby had been active, persistent, inventive, and almost ubiquitous in Washington, but McKinley was certain that within weeks the Senate would adopt the Nicaragua bill and soon the dredging would begin. The American Empire that now covered two oceans, and with the interoceanic canal the United States Navy could rapidly deploy warships to protect American expanding interests across the globe.

A youthful, vigorous, and wealthy United States was in the process of subduing the world with sheer American grit and know-how, and it was this outlook that was flaunted in gaudy patriotic fervor every evening at the 1901 Pan American Exposition in Buffalo, New York. The Expo provided an exciting tableau for the two-day visit by the leader who guided the country into the new era of Empire, President McKinley. However, on day two of McKinley's appearance at what should have been a venue for highlighting the past success of his administration would transform into a place of national lamentation. One of the greatest ironies of the shooting of McKinley at an event that revered American triumph over natural elements and political enemies was the failure of that very technology to save his life. Until the shooting, the Pan—shorthand given to the Exposition by travel and culture writers of the time—was the place for Americans to revel in the glory of their imperial potency and celebrate McKinley, the "Chief" of their empire.[17]

McKinley's last public address at the Pan American Exposition the day before the shooting. C.D.Arnold, photographer, Library of Congress, 5 September 1901.

Doing the Pan: Buffalo, N.Y., 1901

The night before the shooting, in homage of McKinley's first day at the Exposition, a patriotic fireworks extravaganza designed as a tribute to "The American Empire" flashed across the Buffalo night. Outlines of America's territorial possessions exploded one by one, blossoming from the center of a dazzling American flag. The final burst displayed a gigantic pyrotechnic portrait of William McKinley emblazoned against the night sky with the words, "Welcome President McKinley, Chief of our Nation and our Empire," sparkling above his head. The claim of one Expo observer that "the eagle will scream louder than ever before at Buffalo and the Pan-American Exposition," was in no way an exaggeration.[18] The patriotic pyrotechnic display boasted a new and militant sense of American political prowess. "With the splendid prizes of the recent Spanish-American War, the United States had at last become a world power, complete with an overseas empire," and America's military, technological, and commercial prowess were celebrated nightly by thousands of visitors "doing the Pan."[19]

Before the first plaster dried for the Spanish Renaissance style buildings, the Pan-American Exposition heralded itself as the "electric exposition." The cover art on its promotional brochure depicted a winged creature as the once Free Spirit of Niagara Falls — the source of all the electric power for the Exposition. She was bound fast by the electric circles formed in the fierce cascade of the falls. The goddess, suspended directly over the spot where the exposition would take place, pointed to the electric stars as the cause of her defeat. Beneath her, "the globe is held by dark wings suggestive of the flight of time, and the change that lies between the ancient and the modern."[20] The ensnared spirit, her wings tipped into the raging Niagara, struggled mightily and yet failed to free herself from the control of the electric bonds. Bittersweet resignation filled her face. She was subdued by human will.

The figure embodied the theme of the Pan American Exposition: American ingenuity and determination had wrestled the control of the power of electricity from the hands of the gods and made it a slave

*Cover art, Pan American Exposition promotional pamphlet, **Pan-American Exposition: Its Plan and Purpose**, Buffalo, 1901.*

to human desire. Modern twentieth century American electrical technology—certainly not the Old World Europeans—enfeebled the ancient gods. Months earlier, on May 20, Vice-President Theodore Roosevelt opened the Exposition with a rousing speech glorifying the "enterprise, the shrewd daring, the business energy and capacity, and above all, the wonderful mechanical skill and inventiveness" of the American people.[21] The Pan-American Exposition intended to "eclipse all other expositions in the electrical features," and by all accounts, it succeeded.[22] Millions of visitors marveled over displays of thousands of astonishing scientific feats like the electrograph, a machine that transmitted images by wire, the teleautograph, which transmitted a handwritten signature over tremendous physical distances, or the newly invented X-Ray machine that allowed a view into the deep recesses of the human body without drawing one drop of blood.[23] From the marvelous to the mundane, like the electric ambulance that whisked the stricken President to the hospital, the Pan American Exposition reveled in American know-how, ingenuity, and Manifest Destiny.

Throughout the Exposition, American technological prowess was displayed, but it was the Electric Tower that was the "most emblematical feature" of the American Empire.[24] Soaring 409 feet into the air, the Electric Tower boasted restaurants, a roof garden, observation towers, and a 70-foot tall waterfall. A majestic spiral stairway in the center of the tower gracefully curled up to a domed cupola where a sculpture of the Goddess of Light stood "overlooking and dominating the entire Exposition." However, it was the Electric Tower's searchlights, designed by the General Electric Company atop the tower, effused writer Mark Bennitt, which presented the "most magnificent spectacle of the kind ever beheld."[25]

Terror in the Temple of Music, September 13, 1901

Like most of the Exposition attendees, the "crowning feature of the Exposition," the Electric Tower, fascinated McKinley. The night before the shooting, as he strolled along the balcony at the home of his host, Exposition president John Milburn, McKinley had been transfixed by the sight of the luminous splendor of the Electric Tower soaring into the night sky, its searchlights penetrating the night sky. The Tower's two 30-inch projectors formed a "crown of light" that demonstrated to all "the prosperity, the influence and the greatness of the American people."[26] A fierce proponent of American technological superiority, McKinley looked forward to visiting the incandescent edifice following a public reception in the Temple of

Music the next day. Unhappily for the President, the limitations of the technology he so firmly believed in, combined with human fallibility, would intrude upon the collective sense of American invulnerability cast by the Pan American Exposition.

The next morning, McKinley toured the Niagara Falls Power House then returned to the Exposition at 3:30 for an organ recital in the Temple of Music. The public reception to follow the recital made McKinley's personal secretary, George Cortelyou, particularly nervous. Anarchists had assassinated Italy's King Umberto while he was attending at a public event in the summer of 1900 and Cortelyou feared McKinley's aggressive expansionist policies could place him in equal danger. He urged McKinley to forego the open reception, but McKinley optimistically dismissed Cortelyou's concern. He had no enemies, McKinley informed his secretary; therefore, he had no reason to fear.[27] He would attend the reception. Other close aides had expressed similar concerns, which were greeted in the same dismissive manner. John William Griggs, McKinley's Attorney General in his first administration, has often warned his former boss "time and time again," about his vulnerability at public events, only to have McKinley laugh off his suggestion that he need bodyguards.[28] Despite McKinley's nonchalant attitude toward his security, Cortelyou had Secret Service Agents, additional Buffalo police detectives, and compliment military officers on high alert for "suspicious looking" characters. The jubilant public crowding into the Temple of Music to shake the hand of the Chief Executive, however, was as relaxed about the President's security as was McKinley. After all, newspaper accounts confidently reassured readers that "no other president had been so well guarded as is McKinley."[29]

An Innocent Looking Man with a Gun

Ironically, it was not the tall, clean-shaven Czolgosz waiting in line to greet the President—a handkerchief wrapped loosely around his right hand—that concerned Cortelyou. It was the short, dark man in front of the man with the handkerchief that fit the stereotype of the "murderous, fanatical dregs of Europe" who were infecting the American working class with their diabolical anarchist beliefs

Last photo of McKinley. Taken as he was ascending the steps of the Temple of Music, September 6, 1901. E. Benjamin Andrews, **History of the United States***, Vol. 5, 1912.*

that worried him. He called the attention of the guards to a swarthy man in line standing behind a woman and a young girl and just in front of the "innocent looking" Czolgosz.[30] The sinister-looking man troubled the Secret Service guards. He looked suspiciously Italian to the President's security detachment, keenly aware of King Umberto's fate. They watched as the girl said something to McKinley who bent down to better hear the twelve-year-old Myrtle Ledger. Myrtle abandoned language and pointed shyly to the red carnation in his lapel. He seemed to hesitate for a moment and then, with a sparkle in his eyes, McKinley removed his traditional good-luck boutonniere, bent down again and smiled as he presented the flower to the girl. A cheery Mrs. Ledger then moved past McKinley with Myrtle in tow. Smiling sweetly, Myrtle turned, twirling her bright red trophy with her fingers and gave McKinley a wave good-bye. The swarthy man that rattled the nerves of McKinley's guards was next to take the President's hand.

Just as the agents moved forward to break the clasp of what they considered a suspiciously long handshake between the mustached man and McKinley, the foreign-looking man smiled and moved on. In a collective sigh of relief, the agents relaxed and took no particular notice of the man next in line to meet McKinley—a tall, young man with a handkerchief in his right hand. The President smiled and extended his hand to the man who reached out to McKinley with his left hand and pulled the President toward him. With less than two feet between them, as their hands touched, Czolgosz fired the weapon hidden under the handkerchief. The first shot lifted McKinley "on his toes with something of a gasp."[31] With the second shot the President doubled slightly forward and then sank back into the arms of Buffalo detective John Geary, attached to the Secret Service guard. Looking calmly at Geary, McKinley asked, "Am I shot?" Geary unbuttoned the President's vest and seeing blood, answered, "I fear you are, Mr. President."[32]

Sunset at the Hospital

The electric ambulance attendants, young medical students, raced McKinley to an operating room that was not wired for electric lighting. The only source of light in the room where McKinley laid on the operating table was the sunlight—now beginning to fade—that filtered through skylights overhead. Over two million light bulbs outlined every building in the Exposition in resplendent relief, yet physicians attending the President of the United States had to hold up a mirror to capture the retreating sunlight for the surgeon to examine their patient. Among the many ironies swirling about

McKinley's shooting was the absurdity of McKinley being at the mercy of daylight in "an electric exhibition." Once the sun went down, the surgeon was literally "operating at the darkened end of a big hole." [33]

The first bullet deflected by McKinley's sternum did little damage; the second one bored deeply into his body. The surgeon, gynecologist, and obstetrician Matthew Mann, made ever-widening incisions into the bullet's path trying to find the missile in the darkness stalking the operating room. Roswell Park, the world famous surgeon rumored to be attending McKinley was not at the Exposition that day. Mann probed, poked, and explored McKinley's wounds, but he could not locate the second bullet. Almost as ironic as the scarceness of light in midst of the riot of incandesces illuminating the Buffalo night sky, doctors chose not to use the X-Ray machine before Mann carved the tortuous path through McKinley's body, hunting for the elusive lead projectile.

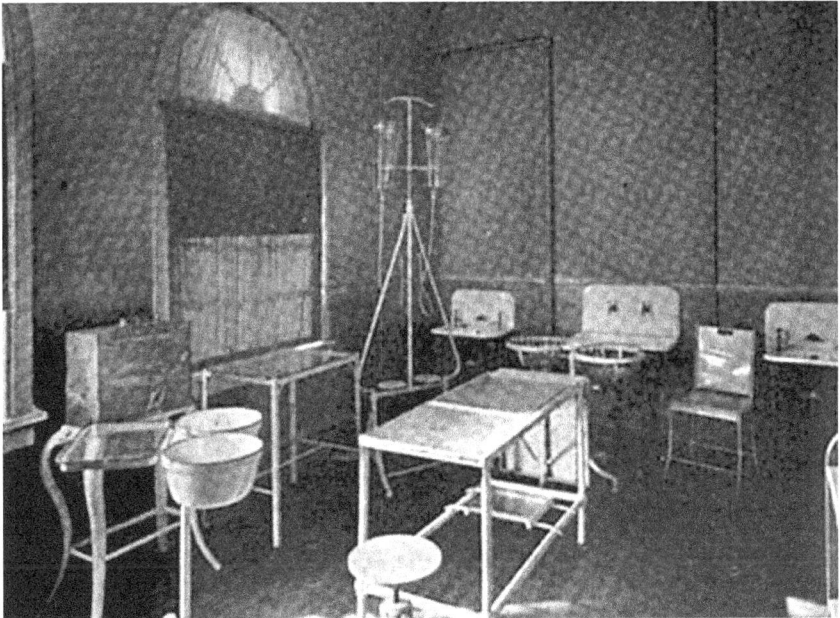

"State of the art" operating room where doctors preformed McKinley's was surgery. C.D. Arnold. The Trained Nurse and Hospital Review, Vol. 27, No. 1 July 1901.

The consensus among the physicians was that it would be too traumatic for McKinley to undergo something as radical as the X-ray procedure. Over an hour after he began the operation, Mann determined that since he had discovered no damage to any vital organ as he plowed through McKinley's body, the bullet must be lodged safely in the lumbar muscles. He repaired the stomach wound and Mann—who had never treated a gunshot wound before—stitched up his patient and sent him to the Milburn house to recuperate. The physician was confident as he closed the incision. "A bullet," Mann explained to reporters later, "once it ceases to move does little harm."[34]

McKinley's Death

After Mann operated, McKinley was transported to the Milburn house, home of the Exposition president, in the same electric ambulance that rocketed him to the Exposition hostital hours earlier. Over the next days, Roosevelt, cabinet members, McKinley's great friend Senator Marcus Hanna, and a raft of medical experts padded through the darkened room where the President lay. He had a constant fever, ranging for 100.2 to 102.8 and his respiration rate never registered within the normal range. Hourly, doctors and attendants steadily administered doses of strychnine, digitalis, morphine, and brandy intravenously along with various combinations of egg, whisky, soap, water, saline, and oil enemas to the suffering McKinley. His wound was dressed with balsam of Peru, a substance that is used today primarily in insect repellants and toothpaste. Post operatively, the President never showed any real signs that he was recovering, but the public was told otherwise.

With dexterous phrasing the phyhsicians issued upbeat press releases suggesting that McKinley was improving and the press excitedly printed glaring headlines that the President would surely survive. McKinley's physicians were lauded in the press. The eminent New York surgeon, Charles McBurney, joined the President's treatment team, proclaiming the surgery performed at the Exposition hospital portrayed "the climax of human skill. You have reached the supreme limit of science," McBurney gushed to Mann and McKinley's other physicians. "No greater victory has ever been won. If this wound had been inflicted upon a European sovereign, he would surely have died. I congratulate you."[35] Inside the Milburn house, however, the hourly account of the president's condition revealed his teneous grasp on life.

The official report of McKinley's symptoms and his hourly ordeal of treatments makes it clear that once the decision to operate on him in a poorly equipped, dimly lit setting by a surgeon more familiar with delivering babies than dealing with gunshot wounds, McKinley never had a chance to recover. On September 12, the physicians released the first public communique revealing that "the President's condition is not quite so favorable" as it had been earlier. Privately, those near the wounded man knew his condition was more than simply "unfavorable," but dire. Still, in spite of reports that McKinley had spent a restless night, Roosevelt—brimming with confidence that modern medicine would produce a full restoration of McKinley's health—announced that he was leaving the President's bedside for his home in Oyster Bay. He did not, however, have any intention of going to Oyster Bay. Instead, the man next in line to become President of the United States disappeared to the remote Adirondack resort, the Tahawus Club, for a little rest and relaxation with his family and friends.

ROOSEVELT'S RAMBLE, SEPTEMBER 13, 1901

Early Friday the 13th, about the time the Roosevelt party began their ramble up Marcy Mountain, newspapers broke the story of McKinley's condition to an astonished nation. "President McKinley is Dying," exploded in four-inch text across the front page of *The San Francisco Call*.[36] Houstonians awoke to "Condition Critical: President McKinley is Liable to Die at any Moment." In the capital, the evening *Star* prepared its readers for the worse: the President's "Life Hangs by a Thread."[37] Anxiety spread through the country. In far-flung locations from Honolulu to Red Cloud, Nebraska, the public longed for reassurance about their country's welfare and naturally looked toward the second in command to provide security and stability at this crucial moment in American history. As far as most Americans knew, Roosevelt was in Oyster Bay, but as the day wore on, it was clear that the whereabouts of Theodore Roosevelt was unknown. Unless they happened to read a two-sentence special notice in the Sarasota *Inquirer* announcing the Vice-President passed through the city on his way to the Adirondacks, the public believed the Vice-President was only a telephone call away should the unthinkable happen. And as a nation waited, the hunt began, while Mr. McKinley's successor, not dreaming that he was needed, was "lost in the woods."[38]

The Hunt for Roosevelt

A family vacation and hunting trip while President McKinley had been shot just seven days earlier seemed odd—or at the very least imprudent—for the man a heartbeat away from the Presidency. The rationale, according to Roosevelt supporters, was that the Cabinet had encouraged Roosevelt, as well as other high-ranking officials, to leave the bedside of their fallen chieftain, as their departure would be a strong public gesture of their confidence in McKinley's recovery. The President's Cabinet placed their full faith in McKinley's "magnificent constitution, his present excellent physical condition and the tremendous strides that have been made since Garfield's time in surgery," and did not want Roosevelt to assume the Presidency as the Constitution provided for under such circumstances.[39] They declared that "there will be no occasion to resort to the constitutional provisions made to meet the demise of a President in office" and advised Roosevelt to "hold himself in readiness to do whatever is necessary and to meet the obligations imposed upon the Vice-President by the Constitution of the United States," should the occasion arise.

Privately, Roosevelt felt he had played his role as the faithful second-in-command and since he had been in Buffalo long enough. More to the point, Roosevelt did not want to loiter helplessly around McKinley's tormented family and friends. Roosevelt did not mind the concept of suffering—in fact, in many ways he saw it as an ennobling vehicle toward character building—but, he did not want to witness the emotional pain of others. As his daughter Alice would later say, Roosevelt wanted to be the "bride at every wedding, the corpse at every funeral," and President McKinley's dramatic deathbed scenes of an American hero further diluted any attention Roosevelt might receive. Furthermore, the shooting frayed Roosevelt's nerves and he was anxious for a respite in the wilds of the Adirondacks. Although any mature, responsible second-in-command should have known differently, Roosevelt felt fully justified in disappearing into the Adirondacks. However, above and beyond all other personal reasons, Roosevelt—despite newspaper articles heaping praise upon him for his dignified, uncharacteristically non-ambitious demeanor after the assassination attempt—was especially thin-skinned about whispers overheard from some that his lingering in Buffalo was reminiscent of a circling vulture, waiting for its prey to die. Roosevelt did not want to appear eager to step into the White House over the body of William McKinley.[40]

Beyond a few basic facts, the story of finding Roosevelt to inform him of McKinley's dire condition, and his subsequent hair-raising ride to McKinley's deathbed becomes a tangled confusion of contradictory details. Even the number of messages, the form of the messages, the text of the message or messages, and what Roosevelt actually did in response to receiving the message or messages is unclear.[41] The tale has been told and retold with such contradictory detail, that most historians simply retell the narrative that upholds the view of Roosevelt as hero rushing to the side of his fallen comrade, and abandon sorting out the murky details. The details, however, add facets to the one-dimensional caricatured that has become the historical standard. The details add the complexity and dimensionality necessary to see to Roosevelt, the man and the politician. Every effort should be taken to sort through and piece together the fragments of the incomplete picture that the conventional historical approach offers which disallows considering the unflattering aspects of Roosevelt character in any analysis of his myth.

The telling, retelling, and shaping of a romantic narrative surrounding Roosevelt's "wild race with death and of his hazardous ride down the mountain side as he hurried to the bedside of the dying President," by far outnumber the reports that suggest a somewhat more human story of the event.[42] The conventional report is that Roosevelt was out for a ramble in the remote Adirondack wilderness along with fellow hikers; he was tracked down by one of the Lodge's hunting guides.[43] Harrison Hall, the guide who first reached Roosevelt, is said to have handed him the message that McKinley was dying and the Vice-President immediately left for Buffalo at a break-neck speed. However, enough contra-narratives exist that it is reasonable to doubt the standard, simplified story. A more detailed picture is difficult to paint because of the great variety and inconsistencies in the reports, but it is necessary to untangle the jumble in order to add texture and realism to the one-dimensional cartoonish saga that parallels the legend of Roosevelt's charge up San Juan Hill.

Among the variations in the accounts reported are about the number of telegrams sent to Roosevelt at Tahawus Lodge. Another is whether the messenger, Harrison Hall, was clutching a yellow Western Union telegram or white envelope when he finally located Roosevelt. Was the telegram delivered to the Tahawus Lodge via telephone and Hall delivered a handwritten note? What was the content of the message or messages? And what was Roosevelt's reaction to the news contained within the envelope, envelopes—or in some versions—a scribbled note on a folded slip of paper in no envelope. Stories of how many men set loose on the mountain in search of Roosevelt and the methods of locating the missing Vice-President are contradictory as well. Was Hall the only herald sent by the Tahawus Club? Did club members join in the hunt, as claimed by some accounts? Or was it, as *The New York Evening World* reported in their front-page story headlined, "Now Searching for Roosevelt: He Is in the Wilds of the Adirondacks on Hunting Trip," that there was an all-out, coordinated assault of club guides launched on Mount Marcy who used "far-reaching megaphone code and the rifle-cracking signals of the mountain-climbing guides" to locate the missing Vice- President?[44]

The *World* article portrayed frantic mountaineers as they scrambled up the slope of Mount Marcy firing rifles, hoping the reports would attract Roosevelt's attention. "Just as the afternoon began to merge with the shades of early evening and as the searchers were nearing the summit of the lofty mountain," the *World* writer described, "the responsive echoes of distant signals were heard and answered, and gradually the scouts and the Roosevelt party came within hailing distance of each other." Was the messenger mounted or on foot? [45] Or, as other tellers of the tale recount, did Roosevelt respond to the rifle shots by firing his rifle and rushing out to meet the messengers? Only a few points in the trail of events are clear. Roosevelt did receive a bedraggled written communiqué of some kind from the gnarly hand of the tall weather-beaten Harrison Hall. He was on foot. Framed by the early afternoon mist still clinging to Lake-Tear-of-the-Clouds, surrounded by a picket of guides and hiking companions, an exhausted Hall located the Vice-President. It probably had just gone past two o'clock in the afternoon and Hall had been grinding through the deadwood and mud at top speed since ten o'clock that morning.

Hall volunteered earlier that morning to deliver a message to Roosevelt that stated that the Vice-President should come to Buffalo with all haste. Hall took the shortest, though most difficult, route possible from the Upper Clubhouse at the rustically elegant Tahawus Lodge. No one knew exactly where Roosevelt was, but if anyone could track him down, it would be the swift and seasoned 51-year-old Adirondack's mountain guide, Harrison Hall. From the Upper Clubhouse to Lake Colton, Hall's path was relatively clear, but beyond that where Roosevelt was believed to be, a formidable "black tangle of primeval forest" stood between Hall and the Roosevelt party. [46]

Neither telegraph service nor rail service extend past North Creek, the town nearest to the Tahawus Club, thirty-five miles away. Plus, the Roosevelt family was staying at the Upper Lodge, ten rugged miles from the main lodge where the telephone line terminated. At least fifteen telegrams were sent to Roosevelt at the Tahawus Club regarding the President's status, but somehow the only message the Vice-President received before Hall emerged from the Adirondack thickets suggested McKinley's condition was "splendid." [47] Roosevelt had left his itinerary with friend Ansley Wilcox, whose guest he had been since he arrived in Buffalo after the shooting, but Roosevelt's secretary, White House cabinet members, or doctors attending McKinley were not informed of Roosevelt's schedule. On Friday the 13th, without informing anyone in Washington, the Vice-President had made a spur-of-the-moment decision that he would stay an extra day at the Tahawus Club and explore the upper reaches of Mount Marcy.

The entire party, except the youngest Roosevelt child, Quentin and his nanny, were enjoying a romp in the Adirondack wilds that day. About mid-day, Roosevelt's wife, Edith, and children were returning to the Upper Lodge from a picnic, while the men scrambled further up the mountain when, suddenly, Hall moved past them at a furious clip, yelling back that he had a message for the Vice-President. The guide, with Mrs. Roosevelt's party, shouted back he was going to Mount Marcy. Hall never broke his stride. He reached the Vice-President's party just as they were settling down for lunch on the banks of the small misty tarn on the southwest slope of Mount Marcy—some 4,500 feet above the sea level—the source of the Hudson River and the highest point in the state of New York. The men heard the crackling of twigs snapping in the underbrush and turned in the direction of the noise to see Hall appear in the clearing "grim visaged and grizzled."[48] The party—to a man—recalled how they instinctively knew the news would be as bleak as the gaunt messenger's expression.

Most accounts state that Roosevelt reacted immediately to the news Hall carried and began a frenetic trek for the Upper Lodge.[49] However, there are other accounts, importantly from Harrison Hall himself, that contradict this aspect of the narrative. Several accounts of the encounter state that before Roosevelt started down the mountain, he leisurely finished his lunch. Many years later, Hall's grandson recalled that his grandfather was infuriated by what happened after Roosevelt received the message:

> What happened next angered my grandfather, Harrison Hall. He had hurried as fast as the wet, slippery, foggy trail would permit any guide to travel. He knew the message he bore was urgent, and he had not even taken the time to tell Mrs. Roosevelt about it when they met on the trail below. The Vice-President took the message, read it, said nothing, but calmly turned and finished his lunch. My grandfather never had much to say about that moment. It left him flabbergasted. [50]

120

Sometime after the men finished their lunch, the group gathered their things, and began the trek back to the Upper Lodge. The three hour long scramble down the mountain evidently gave Roosevelt more than enough time to mull over his options. He was not leaving for Buffalo immediately as he had first announced at lunch on Mount Marcy. "I have thought it all over," he declared, "and unless I hear further news, I shall adhere to my original plans, and go down Saturday morning."[51]

Edith Roosevelt reported later that her husband arrived at the Upper Lodge, around five o'clock in the afternoon, bedraggled and wet. He would not be leaving right away, he told her. Disregarding the ominous nature of the communication he received from Hall, Roosevelt chose to interpret the language in the message—or messages—as an update on McKinley's condition, rather than an urgent plea for him to return to Buffalo. There appeared to be no reason now for him to hurry back, he told his wife. Roosevelt appeared more annoyed than concerned. "I'm not going unless I am really needed," he told his wife. "I have been there once and that shows how I feel. But, I will not go just to stand beside those people who are suffering and anxious. I am going to wait here."[52] Still, the telegrams kept coming. Yet, for some profoundly incomprehensible reason—and despite writing in his autobiography that the moment he saw the panting Hall clutching a message in his hand, that he "felt at once that he had bad news, and . . . that I must come to Buffalo immediately"—Roosevelt made no plans to leave.[53] Instead, around ten o'clock, the Roosevelts went to bed.

The Midnight Ride of Theodore Roosevelt

Edith Roosevelt wrote that a messenger awakened the couple around midnight with yet another urgent communiqué for the Vice-President. President McKinley was dying. This time the message was stated in terms that even Roosevelt could not spin in his direction, and besides, unlike on Mount Marcy, he would have a wider audience. The nation was afire for news of Roosevelt. Newspapermen kept the telegraphs and long distance wires alive in front of Roosevelt's trip, reporting news of the couriers' search to reach him, the special train Secretary William Loeb arranged to be waiting at North Creek, and details of his frantic "race against death" to be at the side of his fallen Chief. In truth, at this time Roosevelt's response to McKinley's plight was not induced by either his devotion to the President or camaraderie he felt toward McKinley. It was showmanship.

Roosevelt had little respect for McKinley as either a leader or as a man. Roosevelt—to whom qualities of manliness included determination and unyieldingness—utterly distrusted McKinley's lack of "firmness." Yet, Roosevelt—who famously described McKinley as possessing "all the backbone of a chocolate *éclair*"— became his Vice-President. What was interpreted as concern for McKinley was more likely a frantic response to Roosevelt's sincere belief that since no Vice-President who assumed the office upon the assassination of the Executive-in-Chief had ever been elected to the post, his presidential ambitions were as dead as the political careers of Andrew Johnson or Chester Arthur. However, it appeared to one and all as he plunged into the "elemental chaos and black darkness" of the perilous Adirondack night that his distress was generated by an urgency to be by the side of his dying friend.[54] Keenly aware that the country was watching, Roosevelt was now totally committed to a breakneck relay race through the treacherous darkness to the specialty-chartered train waiting rail station in North Creek.

Roosevelt ordered three buckboards with fresh horses spaced at intervals along the route to the train station. Regardless of his earlier ambivalence about leaving Tahawus for Buffalo, the way to the North Creek station was indeed perilous. The thirty-five miles of twisting, rain-slicked muddy ruts could hardly be called a road, but Roosevelt urged all speed from the drivers, who in turn pushed their horses to the limit of their natural endurance and abilities. Afterwards, the second driver reported his wagon skidded and nearly plunged 100 feet down a ravine, but Roosevelt told him not to slow down. From first-hand accounts of the mad-dash to North Creek, it was something of a miracle that the nation did not lose two Presidents that night. Displaying the urgency that he had failed to muster, Roosevelt jumped from the first buckboard to the other, and plunged wildly on the trail again. Unbeknownst to Roosevelt, while he and his driver were barreling down the mud-slicked narrow blackness of the trail, William McKinley died at 2:15 in the morning.

Roosevelt's utterly reckless dash through the darkness delivered him at the North Creek station around four-thirty in the morning, where Loeb met him aboard the special train and gave him the news that he was President of the United States.[55]

A Cowboy in the White House

The special train carrying the new President to Buffalo where he would be sworn into office, disgorged its solemn riders just before it reached the station. Waiting to escort Roosevelt were members of the Fourth signal corps, his secretary William Loeb, and his friend Ansley Wilcox. The men withdrew to the Wilcox home where Roosevelt could wash off the Adirondack mud and don finery borrowed from Wilcox and his neighbor, and then he called on McKinley's widow at the Milburn house.[56] After returning to Wilcox's house, Roosevelt decided that his friend's library would be an appropriate venue for his swearing-in ceremony. Members of McKinley's cabinet and two-dozen newspaper reporters gathered in the Wilcox library. The scene was somber as a distressed Secretary of War, Elihu Root, conferred with the overwrought raspy voiced Roosevelt.

Roosevelt displayed "extreme nervousness by picking at the lapel of his long frock coat and nervously tapping his heel on the hardwood floor" as he waited for the ceremony to begin. Root managed to choke out the words, "Mr. Vice-President, I . . . " when his voiced cracked and tears begin to stream down his face. It took him a full two minutes to recover. He then continued with his request on behalf of the Cabinet members for Roosevelt to take the oath of office. Roosevelt obliged the Secretary of War and Judge John Hazel administered the oath. He then proceeded to deliver the shortest oath of office speech on record. Roosevelt turned to the assembly. His voice now fully recovered he declared, "In this hour of deep and terrible bereavement, I wish to state that it shall be my aim to continue absolutely unbroken the policy of President McKinley for the peace and prosperity and honor of our country."[57] Though startlingly brief, Roosevelt's message of his commitment to carry out McKinley's policies brought relief to the cabinet members, the financial markets, and members of Congress. No one in the country was more relieved to hear that the new President would pursue McKinley's policies, than the Nicaragua Canal champion, Senator John Morgan.

No doubt Senator Morgan was optimistic by Roosevelt's oath to stick with McKinley policies. Still, despite the declaration, the Senator needed reassurance. Within two weeks of Roosevelt's inauguration, Morgan would call on Roosevelt at the White House to nail down the new President's position on the Isthmusian question. The reorganized French Panama Canal Company had been sniffing around Washington, becoming evermore anxious to dispose of its expiring concession and depreciating assets. Rumors were it would go cheaply. Although they did not believe it at the time, William McKinley's death in 1901 was the best news the anxious investors in the *Compagnie Nouvelle du Canal de Panama* could possibly receive. It was true that the Panama lobby had spent a great deal of time and money cultivating a relationship with McKinley and suddenly the man was dead, but until the shooting in the Temple of Music, the course toward Nicaragua was fixed.

While Morgan was occupied with his Nicaragua Bill, the country was distracted, riveted, on the project of ridding the country of the anarchists like Leon Czolgosz. By September 24, ten days after McKinley died, Czolgosz was tried and found guilty of murder in the first degree.[58] No witnesses were called for the defense. The trial itself consumed only eight hours and twenty-six minutes. Two days later, Judge Truman C. White sentenced him to die in the electric chair for killing "our beloved president."[59] The vigor and speed of his trial was breathtaking, but ultimately satisfying to the scores of Americans who wanted revenge, not only on Czolgosz for McKinley's murder, but also agreed with the Lincoln, Nebraska *Courier* that all anarchists should be exterminated "like rattlesnakes."[60]

SOME ROOSEVELT MAXIMS (or Gatlings)

OR

Old Saws Repaired and New Ones Made.

By T. R.

Success justifies anything.
Despise money, but take it.
Keep yours, but spend Uncle Sam's.
Turn the rascals out; put yours in.
Do others quick; if caught, blame Loeb.
Never mind the dead — plenty more to kill.
People love extremes and their opposites.
Among the good be bad.
Among the bad be good.
Be a college man in Dakota.
Be a rancher in New York.
Be a statesman among cowboys.
Be a cowboy among statesmen.
This inverse system avoids counterfeit detection.
Make a noise.
Talk heaven and raise hell.
All things come to him who takes.
Thou shalt not kill without a bodyguard.
Thou shalt not lie — abed too late.

Edward Garstin Smith's notion of rules Roosevelt lived by.
The Real Roosevelt, 1910.

"Please Buy Our Nice Canal," an anxious France at the gates of the U.S. extends in one hand a barnacle-encrusted tugboat named *"Panama"* and a map of the isthmus in the other. Wrecked machinery and collapsed banks littered the background with the word *"Ruin"* hovering above.
The Washington Times Star, *08 Jan. 1902.*

CHAPTER FOUR

Please Buy Our Nice Canal, 1901-1904

The Panama Canal scheme is a hoodoo to be shunned and avoided.
—Senator William Andrew Clark, 1902

*Legislation, police surveillance, the administration of justice, the
military and diplomatic service, all are chiefly concerned with
business relations, pecuniary interests, and they have little more than
an incidental bearing on other human interests.*
—Thorsten Veblen, 1904

On October 16th, one month and two days after Roosevelt
ascended to the Presidency, Senator John Tyler Morgan called at the
White House to take the measure of the new Commander-in-Chief's
stance on the Nicaragua Canal legislation. Morgan emerged from the
encounter with Roosevelt crowing to the gaggle of newspapermen
anxiously waiting to hear how the crusty, old Southern Democrat
Senator got on with the brash, young Knickerbocker Republican
President. Morgan radiated confidence as he told the journalists that
the new President assured him that the Nicaragua Canal legislation
met with his hardy personal approval and he would do everything
in his power to see the bill pass. After all, Roosevelt had pledged to
follow the fallen President's policies. In his last public address the
day before the shooting, McKinley told the captivated audience that

"we must build an Isthmusian canal," and Morgan and the whole of America understood Nicaragua to be the spot.[1] Brimming with assurance, the scrappy exponent of the Nicaraguan Canal beamed at the reporters, "Isthmusian canal is a certainty. Nothing can stop it. It is a fixed fact."[2] He summed up his triumph proclaiming unequivocally, "The battle for the Nicaraguan Canal has been fought and won."[3] What the aged Confederate warrior did not know was that while the reporters scribbled down his victorious decree, a cadre of pro-Panama lobbyists was preparing the battlefield for a final assault on the Nicaragua Canal project. Far from being fought and won, in a few short weeks, Morgan would see a titanic conflict between Nicaragua and Panama detonate and rage across Congress, spinning the House into a hotbed of insurgency and the Senate into a brutal combat zone.

Yet, standing in front of the White House on October 16th 1901, Morgan did not detect a whiff of defeat. He could only smell victory. Nevertheless, after satisfying inquiries about the meeting with Roosevelt, the clamoring reporters persisted in asking more question of Morgan, questions he surely felt were irrelevant at this point in a game he believed he has won. How did Morgan feel, they wanted to know, about the conference between Isthmus Canal Commission chairman, Admiral Walker and Marcel Hutin, the president of the floundering the *Compagnie Novell du Panama*—the French Panama Canal Company—scheduled for that very day. Was he concerned at all about the rumors that Hutin would make an offer so low the government could simply not refuse, the reporters probed. The elder Statesman was unruffled. "For several years past," a coolly confident Morgan instructed reporters, "the Panama Canal Company has been talking of making some proposition for the use of its route, but I cannot see how anything they can say can affect the situation."[4]

They next asked Morgan about a curious canal contender who had appeared seemingly out of the blue. A letter received by the Department of State the previous day signed by one H.M. Crill, an "expert miner and lumberman" from Michigan, announced that he had discovered the location of an ancient canal while seeking potential mineral extraction opportunities in Colombian territory.

In his letter, he asserted that a primordial interoceanic thoroughfare was situated in a mountain gap "lying midway between the two routes already surveyed" and the "spot was found in an almost inaccessible country clogged with rank" undergrowth that had concealed it for centuries. This prehistoric canal, claimed the intrepid explorer, at one time connected the two oceans and could be easily and inexpensively refurbished to its elemental glory.[5] Reporters wanted to know if this new discovery gave Morgan pause. "Ten governments have been searching for just such a route for the last two hundred years," scoffed Morgan, "and I do not believe this man has succeeded where they have failed."[6] The Department of State dismissed Crill with the same ease Morgan displayed and never investigated his claims.

Morgan exuded confidence that the Nicaragua Canal legislation would sail through the Senate and left his unpleasant experience with the pesky Panama Lobby aside. President Roosevelt had given Morgan and the nation his word that he would follow McKinley's policies, so why should Morgan worry about Crill's imaginary prehistoric waterways or French Panama Canal fire-sale. Even the once "ubiquitous and ever present" thorn in his side that was Cromwell vanished from Washington that summer.[7] Reliable sources had it that Hutin had fired the attorney in July because of Cromwell's "anxiety to induce the New Panama Canal Company to sell [and] his syndicate operations" rather than attending to the welfare of the company.[8] This "anxiety" on Cromwell's part, no doubt confirmed for Hutin another rumor that their counsel had actually formed his own company, quite separate from the Panama Canal Company of America that Hutin endorsed to Americanize the project in 1898. The goal of Cromwell's new company, so the gossip went, was to surreptitiously gain control of the *Compagnie Nouvelle du Panama del Canal*. Even if the reports were unproven, Hutin had had quite enough of "the methods he had employed, and the large sum of money he had spent," and sacked Cromwell.[9] The great dissatisfaction and frustration that Cromwell created for his French clients must have deeply satisfied Senator Morgan. Morgan detested the Fox of Wall Street. Cromwell's absence must have intensified Morgan's sense of elation after his reassuring visit with Roosevelt.

Victory in the House

By the close of 1901, barriers to Morgan's success with his decades' long fight to get the Nicaragua Canal seemed to melt away. Admiral Walker responded negatively to Hutin's asking price for the French ditch. Hutin, disappointed by the rejection of his latest offer to sell the bedraggled French project for bargain price of $109,000,000, had slunk back to France thoroughly defeated. By mid-November, the Isthmusian Canal Commission had unanimously endorsed the Nicaragua route making the Panama question just a footnote in the Congressional record as far as the Alabama Senator was concerned. Morgan had little to worry about. Taking Roosevelt's encouragement to heart, Morgan planned to introduce another Nicaragua Canal bill—one that once again that mirrored Representative William Hepburn's bill so that House agreement would be assured—in early December.

On December 6th, Representative William Hepburn—who like Morgan experienced years of defeats and delays on his Nicaraguan isthmian legislation—introduced a bill authorizing the appropriation of $180,000,000 for the construction of the Nicaragua Canal. The same week, two other Nicaragua Canal bills were introduced in the Senate, one by Morgan to construct the canal and the other by Senator George Perkins to lease in perpetuity the land upon which the canal would be constructed. It seemed that both Houses of Congress and the stars were aligned and arrayed for a Nicaragua victory. Not only had Roosevelt reassured Morgan in his face-to-face meeting in October, but also in his first Annual Address on December 3rd, the new President outlined the importance of the Isthmusian canal and described the genial negotiations between Great Britain and the United States toward an abrogation of the Clayton-Bulwer treaty that had hamstrung completion of the Nicaragua project for decades.

Even though Roosevelt used the term "Isthmusian" instead of "Nicaragua" in his remarks, his references to Great Britain, canal treaty negotiations, and the economic boon to the Southern Atlantic states, left no doubt in anyone's mind that he was calling for the speedy construction of the Nicaragua Canal. Roosevelt declared:

I am glad to be able to announce to you that our negotiations on this subject with Great Britain, conducted on both sides in a spirit of friendliness and mutual good will and respect, have resulted in my being able to lay before the Senate a treaty which if ratified will enable us to begin preparations for an Isthmian canal at any time... In this treaty, the old Clayton-Bulwer Treaty, so long recognized as inadequate to supply the base for the construction and maintenance of a necessarily American ship canal, is abrogated... No single great material work which remains to be undertaken on this continent is of such consequence to the American people as the building of a canal across the Isthmus connecting North and South America... While its beneficial effects would perhaps be most marked upon the Pacific Coast and the Gulf and South Atlantic States, it would also greatly benefit other sections. It is emphatically a work which it is for the interest of the entire country to begin and complete as soon as possible.[10]

His statement must have made Morgan positively giddy. Roosevelt could have not been referring to Panama or any other proposed or imagined interoceanic waterway. More good news for Morgan and Hepburn followed as the United States Envoy to Nicaragua, Costa Rica, and El Salvador, William Lawrence, entered into protocol discussions with his Nicaraguan counterpart, to define the terms of the forthcoming canal treaáty on the 10th of December.

With only one of the main sticking points—the Clayton-Bulwer Treaty that prevented the United States from fortifying the Nicaragua Canal—removed, "no considerable opposition to the enterprise has been urged," observed the *New York Tribune*.[11] Nonetheless, an old warhorse like Morgan should have known his enemies better. Although every superficial aspect of the complex act of legislation appeared tidy and stable, a politician as experienced as Morgan should have detected a slight rumble just below the surface of what he thought was solid ground. A change of seismic—if not cosmic—

proportions was afoot, but Morgan did not seem to notice. The confluences of Presidential ambition, corporate greed, and more than a little evangelistic fervor, were converging and would soon swallow up the Nicaragua Canal ambitions of the old Rebel warrior.

EARTHQUAKES, VOLCANOES, AND THE "HANNAMA" CANAL

As a politician, Morgan was accustomed to the underhanded and devious practices of lawyers and lobbyists like William Nelson Cromwell, as well as the political machinations of his Republican opponents like Marcus Hanna and Morgan, as always, was ready for a fight. And, although the fall of 1901 began with victories for the Nicaragua Canal project, a succession of progressively destabilizing rumblings began to reverberate in the press. While the Senate Canal Committee did issue a favorable report on Morgan's Bill and it was introduced to the body, the chamber's Republican managers continually deferred action on the bill.[12] Next, Morgan's old nemesis C.P. Huntington, the anti-Nicaragua railroad magnate whose holdings included the Panama Railroad Company, was up to his old tricks as the mastermind behind a plot to block the Hay-Pauceforte Treaty that abrogated Clayton-Bulwer, the passage of which was critical to Morgan's hopes. After a long period of remission, "Secret influences have been brought to bear" upon decision makers and were "being operated under cover in the executive session of the Senate," a news report revealed on December 12th.[13] But, it was no secret to the reporter who was behind the machinations, "it is quite apparent that they have their origins in the well-understood opposition of the transcontinental railroad."[14]

Meanwhile, reports were flying in the papers that the Maritime Canal Company—the company the United States backed to dig the Nicaragua Canal but had its concession revoked in 1899 by the Nicaraguans—was asserting that they still had the rights to the canal, not their replacement, the Cragin-Eyre syndicate. As discussed earlier, by 1900, the Cragin-Eyre group, headed by former two-time New York City mayor, W.R. Grace, had been awarded the concession after Maritime failed not only to achieve certain construction goals, but also neglected to make their contractually required payment of

132

$4,000,000 to the Nicaraguan government.[15] The Maritime Canal Company had protested delays were unavoidable, but without support from the United States government, they were powerless to prevent their speedy replacement with Cragin-Eyre. Yet in 1901, Maritime emerged from relative obscurity to trouble the waters by claiming that they in fact owned "every foot of land between Lake Nicaragua and the Pacific Ocean," the route through which the waterway was to be built.[16] Even though Secretary of State John Hay refused to consider Maritime's claim, the public agitation from both the materialization of the Maritime assertion, and the exposure of Huntington's anti-canal activities unsettled the political process.[17]

On the 21st of December, more disquieting news for the friends of Nicaragua reached the United States. It was reported that a meeting of the shareholders of the *Compagnie Nouvelle* in Paris was so fractious that gendarmes had to be called in to restore order.[18] Fistfights broke out between factions of the shareholders when a coupe d'état orchestrated by Philippe Bunau-Varilla deposed Marcel Hutin and installed Marius Bo in his place. Urged by a frantic cable sent by his American newspaperman ally, Walter Wellman, declaring that the UnitedStates was ready to accept the $40,000,000 offer—a figure Hutin rejected as too low when first suggested by the Isthmusian Commission—Bunau-Varilla began drumming up fear and anxiety among the shareholders convincing many that if they did not agree to sell the works at that price, they would lose everything.[19] He succeeded. Bunau-Varilla not only forced Hutin's ouster at the meeting, he also successfully argued that William Nelson Cromwell should be reinstated as counsel for the company. The relief Morgan must have experienced over the last six months without the specter of Cromwell haunting Senators' offices, undermining his efforts from his command and control center in the grand salon of the swank D.C. Willard Hotel, disappeared in a flash. Now, not only did it appear that his nemesis, Cromwell, would be back to frustrate his efforts, but the little French adventurer Morgan found so objectionable was also on his way to Washington as well.

The news that the French were "ready to sell out" at the astonishing, rock-bottom price of $40,000,000 captured the headlines.[20] On December 27th, the press began to suggest that a resurrection of sorts was underway for the Panama Canal project. "Chance for the Panama—This Route May be Chosen Instead of Nicaragua," screamed one headline.[21] By December 30th, a story on the front page of the Washington, D.C. *Evening Star* ominously presaged a change in the political wind. The headline read, "Isthmian Canal—Extraordinary Activity of the Panama Lobby—Effort to Block Legislation—Agent Coming From Paris With a New Offer."[22] On December 31st, the last day of what had been a disquieting month for the Nicaragua proponents, the *Indianapolis Journal* declared the "Canal Bill in Peril."[23] And, even though in late December Morgan still labored under the impression that Theodore Roosevelt was a friend of the Nicaragua Canal, it could not have made him rest easier that the *Indianapolis Journal* forecast that when Representative William Hepburn offered his bill the first week of January 1902, "some strong man will be selected to offer an amendment practically killing that bill and substituting therfor[e] one that will authorize the President to select a route for a canal."[24]

"Penniless and Bankrupt in Money and in Character"
January 1902

By the 4th of January, Marius Bo, the newly installed president of the *Compagnie Nouvelle*, cabled Isthmusian Canal Commission chairman, Admiral John Walker, with a formal offer to sell. By noon, Walker had conveyed the offer to Secretary of State John Hay who then rushed the proposal to President Roosevelt. The Panama Canal Company, stated Bo, "was ready to transfer to the government of the United States, on payment of $40,000,000, its property and concessions, estimated at that amount by the Isthmusian Canal Commission."[25] The desperation of the French was obvious to the press. On January 8th, the *Washington Times* ran a cartoon on page one that depicted a bedraggled, anxious woman as France offering in one hand a barnacle encrusted tugboat named "Panama" and a map of the isthmus in the other. Wrecked machinery and collapsed banks littered the background. The text of the cartoon read, "Please Buy Our Nice Canal."[26] Representative William Hepburn's Nicaragua Bill—essentially the same bill that he had offered almost every session

134

since 1899—reached its turn on the calendar in the House the same day the cartoon appeared in the *Washington Times*. There was a slight hint of insurrection in the House of Representatives when the "strong man" that the *Indianapolis Journal* predicted in December appeared, Congressman Robert Morris of Minnesota.

Morris gave notice he would attach an amendment to Hepburn's bill to allow Roosevelt to select the Panama Canal over Nicaragua. The debates that followed, in which the French bargain was considered, continued all through the day and into the next. Hepburn, however, was unstoppable. In his opening remarks to the House, he described the French Panama Canal company managers as "penniless and bankrupt in money and in character," only after American tax-payer dollars.[27] After his speech, he was besieged with questions from his colleagues that he confidently and deftly addressed. If the report of

William Peters Hepburn. John Ely, **William Peters Hepburn,** *1919.*

the cost of the Panama Canal was true, Representative McDermott of New Jersey wanted to know, why he should continue to press for Nicaragua. Practically speaking, the geography had not changed by the Panama Canal price being lowered, argued Hepburn. "Any gentleman who absorbs the commission's report . . . must believe," Hepburn replied to McDermott, "the canal that is 400 miles nearer our territory, that makes New Orleans and San Francisco and New York 374 miles nearer than the other is the better canal for us."[28]

Furthermore, Hepburn called the news that the company offered the works for $40,000,000 a mere rumor, but even if the rumor were true, he told Representative Reeves of Illinois, the United States should deal with Colombia, not the French. There was less than two years remaining on the French's nontransferable, nonrenewable concession and the canal works would then rest firmly and legally in the hands of the Colombian government. For the French Panama Canal Company, Hepburn said, "[T]he jig is up."[29] The following day on January 9, in a stunning victory, the House rejected the company's offer and the Hepburn Bill passed on with an almost unanimous vote of 309 votes in favor of the Nicaragua plan and only just two against. Morris' amendment to grant the President sweeping power to choose the canal route himself, among all but one of the several other proposed modifications to Hepburn's Bill, was decisively rejected. The only alteration to Hepburn's Bill that passed was one offered by Representative Vandiver of Missouri, and that was made in order to correct a minor grammatical mistake in one section.

AN ACCIDENTAL PRESIDENT, ROOSEVELT'S CANAL

Most scholars find Roosevelt's intervening with the Walker Commission's findings, disregarding the House sentiment, and abandoning the American Nicaragua Canal project perplexing. For the most part, they chalk his actions up to his brash, expansionist, imperialist, hyper-masculine exuberance that was endemic to all in the seats of power as nations struggled to maintain or acquire dominance in a changing world order at the beginning of the twentieth century. However, this single, one-dimensional view ignores not only the power and urgency of his political ambitions, but dismisses the potency of his complex family relationships, and discounts unflattering aspects of his personality and character. A closer inspection of the conditions and imperatives of Roosevelt's intricate personal and family life and his role within it reveals a critically important underpinning of his actions.

By Any Means Necessary: Roosevelt's Resolve

Up until January 1902, Roosevelt's tenure as the newly, unelected President of the United States had been pretty lackluster. His first official act came September 20th when he called his cabinet together to reiterate his stay-the-course pledge made at his Wilcox house inauguration that he would "carry out in all its details, the policy mapped out by President McKinley."[30] The newly minted President must have experienced a sinking feeling in the pit of his stomach that he, like the other Vice-Presidents of felled Presidents in American history, was doomed to an ineffective, tedious political career, and then political extinction. Vice-Presidents John Tyler, Millard Fillmore, Andrew Johnson, and Chester Arthur had all finished out the term of his respective dead Commander-in-Chief, but not a single one went on to become President in his own right. One of them–Andrew Johnson–carried the dubious distinction of being the first President to ever be impeached. Roosevelt desperately wanted out of this colorless club of impotence and obscurity, but in the early hours in his Presidency it looked as if he was a shoe-in for a lifetime membership.

At the beginning of October, Roosevelt made the front page of the *New York Tribune*, not by distinguishing himself as an innovative, courageous leader of the American people, but by once again following McKinley's policies and plans. He appointed an attorney general for the state of Kansas that McKinley had chosen, not the one party leaders were promoting. Despite powerful Kansas Senator Burton's vigorous lobbying to the contrary, the newspaper reported that Roosevelt insisted upon upholding McKinley's wish to name John S. Dean Attorney General of Kansas. "Senator Burton," the article read, "is fully convinced that when President Roosevelt said he would carry out the plans and policies of President McKinley, he meant it."[31] With Burton's remarks, Roosevelt must have sensed the corner he had painted himself into as narrow as something with the dimensions of a grave, yet he seemed to be unable to do otherwise. Roosevelt got kudos for being McKinley's stand-in, not for being the Rough Rider that distinguished him as the alpha male in the pack of ordinary politicians. December 4th, 1901, in his first two-and-one-half hour message delivered to Congress, he continued to highlight his approach to his Presidency of replicating McKinley by adhering to the dead President's policies. A grief-stricken country might have been comforted, but Roosevelt despaired. "It was a dreadful thing," he wrote his friend Henry Cabot Lodge, "to come into the Presidency this way."[32] Given the disdain for McKinley he privately expressed, Roosevelt was undoubtedly grieving more for the loss of his presidential campaign ambitions than the loss of the President himself.

Henry Cabot Lodge standing next to Theodore Roosevelt. Library of Congress, 1902.

McKinley's death unsettled Roosevelt and Lodge's long-laid plans for a Roosevelt presidential campaign in 1904. Part of the duo's political calculus in early 1900 was to use any high-profile federal office he could get as a steppingstone to Roosevelt's election to the highest office in the land. At the end of McKinley's second administration, the Republican ticket would be wide open and Roosevelt planned to fill the void.[33] Lodge had tried every possibility, including angling for the then Governor of New York to position himself for a run at the office at the end of McKinley's term. As Governor of New York, Roosevelt was growing as weary of the state's political machine as the machine was with Roosevelt. He was experiencing "a lot of ugly things recently… and [I] feel like throwing up my hands," he confided to his mentor, Lodge.[34] Still, he preferred to remain as Governor, rather than sign on for the purgatory of the Vice-Presidency. Roosevelt believed that the position of Vice-President would hamstring him, render him impotent to project his own particular brand of power and authority. A Vice-President always had to ask for permission and Roosevelt was more about giving the orders than taking them. If he left Albany for Washington, he wanted a robust, manly position: something in the War Department—"a Secretaryship of War if things go right," or best of all, the first civil Governor General of the Philippines, he wrote to Lodge. Besides, he told Lodge, the Vice-Presidency simply did not pay enough. "The money question is a serious one for me," he revealed to Lodge:

> I have a very keen regret that I did not have some money making occupation, for I am never certain when it may be necessary for me to sell Sagamore and completely alter my whole style of life. As Governor I am comparatively well paid … but great pressure would come upon me if I went in as Vice-President. A Vice-Presidency … would cause me continual anxiety about money … I could only live simply."[35]

Moreover, to add insult to his Knickerbocker notion of insolvency, the fact that Roosevelt was not McKinley's first choice, left the Governor's delicate ego more than a bit bruised. The only reason

William McKinley with his first Vice-President and friend Garret Hobart.
Oscar King Davis and John Kimberly Mumford. **The Life of William**
McKinley, *1901.*

McKinley considered Roosevelt as his running mate in the first place was because Garret Hobart, McKinley's immensely popular Vice-President in his first term, had died while in office.

Some of Roosevelt's powerful allies wanted to see him as Vice-President, especially his Western supporters, but some urged him not to take the position that has been described an "impenetrable vacuum."[36] They also feared he would languish, choked off from visibility and the power to showcase his independence and originality, but thought the risk was worth it to position him for his own Presidential campaign in 1904. But, Roosevelt wanted out of his governorship and the New York state Republican leadership made no secret of their desire to rid New York of the obstreperous Governor.[37] McKinley finally and unequivocally indicated there was no office in the War Department open to Roosevelt and let Lodge know in no uncertain terms that the Philippine Governorship was out of the question; Lodge beseeched Roosevelt to take the Vice-Presidency. Lodge told his young protégé, "in the deadliest confidence," that the Vice-Presidency would be "a true stepping stone to the Presidency," and at length Roosevelt yielded to his elder's considerable political savoir-faire.[38] Despite all of the political caché of Lodge and his active publicity machine, the position of Vice-President of the United States of America was the best Roosevelt could do.

Vice-Presidential Nominee

While the Vice-Presidency was the last choice for both Roosevelt and Lodge, the position had been a pathway to the Presidency for a few men. Three former Vice-Presidents—John Adams, Thomas Jefferson, and Martin Van Buren—were in actual fact elected President after years of languishing in the obscurity of the Vice-Presidency. The duo strategized that with careful management the same could happen for Roosevelt. The success of the project, of course, depended upon the increasingly popular Roosevelt's ability to actually campaign for the office, and not to tread into the Presidency over the corpse of McKinley. That would be, as history had dictated, a political death sentence.

Although Lodge finally persuaded Roosevelt to offer his name as a running mate for McKinley, his acceptance by the party was far from assured. McKinley was the only nominee for President, but there was predictable wrangling for power and control of the Vice-Presidential nominating process. There were many moments during the 1900 Republican Convention nomination process that it was not clear that Roosevelt would even get the chance at obscurity or opportunity the Vice-Presidency offered. The powerful Senator from Ohio and President McKinley's great friend and advisor, Marcus Hanna, despised Roosevelt and pleaded with him to select another running mate. "What is the matter with all of you? Here's this convention going headlong for Roosevelt for Vice-President. There's only one life," Hanna warned McKinley, "between that madman and the Presidency."[39]

Hanna, of course, had his favorites, but the seasoned political operative and Senator was out maneuvered by Republican heavyweights, Matthew Quay of Pennsylvania and Thomas Platt of New York whose choice was Theodore Roosevelt. McKinley, for his part, was ambivalent about filling the position. He was still grieving for the loss of his friend and chosen partner, Hobart, to care very much one way or the other who was nominated to be his Vice-President. Absent McKinley's endorsement of any particular man for Vice-President, Roosevelt won the nomination. Within a year McKinley was dead, Roosevelt was in charge, and 1904 would give the "madman" four more years to rule. Nevertheless, in his obscure position as Vice-President before the assassination, with no political machine behind him, the swarm of devoted Roosevelt fans across the country seemed to desert him. "Among the time-serving politicians," as political observer, Albert Shaw, and Roosevelt friend noted, as Vice-President "Roosevelt's stock had declined to a low figure."[40]

Hamstrung by a Ghost

After McKinley's death, Roosevelt's old, fair weather friends returned in obsequious droves, but still he felt the weight of the pronouncement of history profoundly upon him. By the middle of January 1902, Roosevelt could see he needed a way to escape the oblivion to which McKinley's death seemed to sentence him. Hope for his Party's nomination was beginning to dim. Hanna publicly supported the new, young President, but privately and fervently worked against him. The New York Republican political establishment hoped the former governor of New York, Benjamin Odell, or possibly ex-Speaker Thomas Reed, might lock up the support of the New York delegation and carry off the Presidential honors in 1904. At first, it seemed like displacing Roosevelt was an accomplishable goal.

Keenly aware of his precarious position, Roosevelt and Lodge began laying a foundation that would allow him to break free from the dead President's curse when Panama was offered to him on a plate. Not only was the conversation about an interoceanic canal a focus of discussion across America, it had the attention of the world. A radical surprise deviation from Nicaragua as the site of the canal would differentiate him from McKinley, exploit his reputation as a political maverick, and appeal to a base of followers who increasingly viewed Roosevelt's kind of "independence" as the hallmark of American masculinity. With the 1904 election always in the forefront of his mind, Roosevelt would use the Panama formula with his approach to National Securities Company later in the month, cementing his reputation, by no means earned at this or any later date, as the trust-busting friend of the "little man." It was all politically risky, but if history had the attention of fate, Roosevelt really did not have much to loose. Fortunately for Roosevelt, both forcing the Isthmusian Canal Commission to repudiate its findings and his lawsuit against National Securities paid off.

Yet, as powerful as his desire for election in 1904, a cynical political stratagem was not the only force at work upon Roosevelt's decision to discard Nicaragua and hurry into buying the near valueless assets of a bankrupt company. There were no competitors, no other potential buyers, and Colombia was anxious to have the United States take over the franchise from the disappointing French company as soon as their concession expired in 1904. What, indeed, was the rush to secure the Panama Canal? There were other forces at play that went beyond the field of political gamesmanship. There was family to consider.

Douglas Robinson: A Family Affair

When Roosevelt decided to move against decades of studies and the longstanding popular and political preference for Nicaragua, he was not only using the Panama issue as a device to sharpen his image of rugged cowboy individualism, he was insuring that his sister Corrine and her husband Douglas Robinson, amassed even more wealth. Robinson, a big, quick-witted Scotsman and heir to a real estate fortune, was a ubiquitous character in the political, social, and domestic life of Theodore Roosevelt. In Roosevelt's rise to power, Robinson was vital to his decision-making process as both a source of reassuring familial connection and constant reliable business counsel. The New York real estate mogul was a constant

Douglas Robinson with Theodore Roosevelt. Library of Congress, 1910.

companion and faithful political advisor to Roosevelt throughout his governorship and throughout his Presidency. Roosevelt trusted him. Time and time and again, he deferred to Robinson in matters both great and small, both political and personal. Robinson was family after all, one of them.

The successor to a great real estate fortune and Astor Trust Company manager—a J.P. Morgan holding—Robinson handled Roosevelt's financial investments even before he wed Roosevelt's baby sister Corinne in 1882. A month before he and Corrine exchanged vows, Robinson became Roosevelt's business partner in his Elkhorn Stock Company, Roosevelt's Dakota cattle ranching venture. Roosevelt was enthusiastic about the opportunity to make a financial killing in the cattle business, while at the same time rehabilitate his reputation from a "Jane-Dandy" into a manly, chaps wearing, gun-toting, Western cowboy. At first, in the halcyon days of the cattle boom, Roosevelt ran the fourth largest ranch in the Dakota

Territories, but still, he was not much of a businessman, and he looked toward solving some of his capital loss issues by incorporating his business with older and wiser Douglas Robinson as his partner. Even with Robinson's business acumen, the ranch fell victim to the bitter winter of 1886-87. Half of the future President and part-time rancher's herd froze to death that winter. The greatest portion of Roosevelt's inheritance was lost. Douglas Robinson remained Roosevelt's financial advisor. Roosevelt spent the rest of his adult life focused on his financial stability and with Robinson's help, at his death Roosevelt's estate—not including his Sagamore property—was valued around $800,000—$10,000,000 in 2014 dollars.

Among the hard-driving businessman's assets, Robinson secured a substantial interest in a speculative enterprise with *Compagnie Nouvelle Du Canal de Panama* and Panama Railroad director, attorney William Nelson Cromwell, financier J.P. Morgan, friend of Marcus Hanna and president of the Panama Railroad Company, banker J. Edward Simmons, and other tycoons to "purchase shares of the *Compagnie Nouvelle Du Canal de Panama*... and place them in the hands" of the syndicate, the American Panama Canal Company.[41] Once the syndicate amassed enough shares, their energies and resources would be directed on getting the United States government to buy the *Compagnie Nouvelle* with the proceeds of such a sale to go to the American syndicate as the major shareholders, not to the French. Robinson's involvement in Cromwell's syndicate began in May of 1900, long before Roosevelt entered national politics, when Roosevelt was still Governor of New York. There would be no reason, given the nature of the intimate relationship between the brothers-in-law, that Roosevelt would not have known and discussed Robinson's position in the American Panama Canal Company.

Robinson was the go-to man when a problem, financial or familial, was too complicated or too uncomfortable for Roosevelt. He was both buffer and conduit for Roosevelt. Potential blowback for Roosevelt was absorbed or mitigated when Robinson hosted meetings that his brother-in-law might be criticized for taking at his offices. Robinsons' presence offered the cover of informality. For instance, when former Governor of Kentucky William Taylor— indicted for complicity in the murder of the sitting Kentucky governor William Goebel—wanted to discuss his situation with then Governor Roosevelt, they met in Robinson's Madison Avenue private residence, not in the Governor's Mansion. Robinson was also entrusted with managing family embarrassments and mitigating the personal losses experienced by the Roosevelt family. When the premier Keeley Institute for the Treatment of Liquor and Drug Addictions failed to produce a positive outcome for the Roosevelt's tragically alcohol addicted younger brother Elliot in 1892, Robinson put the young inebriate to work developing one of his Virginia mining properties. The hope was that meaningful employment would lessen Elliot's desire for strong drink. Unhappily, Robinson's efforts to refocus his younger Roosevelt brother-in-law failed and Elliot returned to New York finding neither meaning nor sobriety in Robinson's employ.

Elliott's drunken escapades filtered in and out of the headlines. Roosevelt—who had tried unsuccessfully to get Elliott declared insane and the court to name him as trustee of his brother's finances—finally declared that his brother "can't be helped" no matter what interventions were attempted and admitted that he had "a hard heart about Elliott."[42] The following year, Elliott committed suicide in New York. Katy Mann, a former maid at the Elliott Roosevelt home in New York, came forward to claim that Elliott had fathered her son. She demanded $10,000 for child support and to maintain her silence. It was to Douglas Robinson that Mann presented her claim and presumably, since the matter never reached the scandal sheets, Robinson handled the distribution of the funds Mann demanded.[43] Although he failed to have any meaningful outcome with Elkhorn or Elliott, the Roosevelt clan—Theodore, in particular—continued to exhibit an extraordinary level of confidence in him. Even if Corinne did not seem to have much affection for her husband, Robinson nonetheless was a highly regarded and indispensible feature of the family's operating system.

Hundreds of letters, diary entries, and newspaper accounts demonstrate Roosevelt's increasing reliance on Robinson to get things done. His presence was woven into almost every important interaction or decision Roosevelt made. The two were constantly in each other's drawing rooms and pocket books. Robinson handled

146

Elliott Roosevelt with his daughter Eleanor. National Archives, 1889.

all of Roosevelt's income as President, his various investments, and managed his trust left to him by his wealthy father and uncles.[44] He advised Roosevelt on personal matters, like helping the President understand the balance sheets for his trust accounts, to running errands for his brother-in-law, like purchasing three "high-stepping horses" for the new President's carriage.[45]

Robinson made numerous political recommendations to Roosevelt regarding the relative fitness of individuals for Presidential appointments and took meetings with Roosevelt, Supreme Court Justices, military commanders, and the United States Attorney General.[46] He lobbied, almost always successfully, for Roosevelt to grant audiences to his friends and business associates. Robinson had business relationships with investment bankers who were very interested in having the President pave the way for their financial adventures and he was not timid about connecting political power with private capital. Writing Roosevelt in February of 1902 to encourage him to meet with wealthy financier, William Salomon—forerunner of the prestigious, then scandalous Salomon Brothers investment firm of Wall Street—to arrange a loan with a mysteriously unnamed "South American Republic" was not an unusual sort of request for Robinson.[47]

By the time Roosevelt was to make a decision on the Isthmusian Canal in 1902, his brother-in-law's consortium with Cromwell owned almost all the shares in the French Panama Canal Company, giving Roosevelt a huge personal stake in the project as well as a political reason to choose Panama over Nicaragua. With the quality and quantity of interaction between Roosevelt and his brother-in-law, it would be naïve to believe that Douglas Robinson never mentioned his involvement in a syndicate that would prosper or fail according to legislation that the President could endorse or veto. Given the structure of their relationship—the interlocked framework of both personal, kinship, and business bonds underlying the special role Robinson played as Roosevelt's confident and advisor—it is more likely than not that he was completely aware of his brother-in-law's deep connection to Cromwell and the Panama Canal syndicate, the true owners of the French Panama Canal. And in the first month of the new year of 1902, Roosevelt had it within his power to change his future, the future of his friends and family, and the future of the country. With one well orchestrated move, Roosevelt would assure the financial interests of his family for generations to come and emerge from McKinley's shadow to radiate the robust, no nonsense cowboy image he was certain would get him elected in 1904.

January 10, 1902: Dragooning of the Commission

The day after Hepburn's brilliant victory in the House, The *St. Louis Republic* reported that, "with redoubled vigor the struggle between the advocates of the Nicaragua and Panama routes for an isthmian canal went on to-day … the scene of the conflict having been transferred from the House to the Senate."[48] The same day the clash over the canals began in the Senate, Roosevelt ordered Admiral Walker to telephone the members of the Isthmusian Commission and lay the matter of the new offer from the French before them on Monday, the 13th. Senator Morgan immediately went on the defensive. He swiftly moved to neutralize the French Panama Canal and its momentum by issuing subpoenas for Edouard Lampre, secretary of the French Panama Canal Company and Jules Boeufve of the French Embassy to appear before his Interoceanic Canal Committee at 11 o'clock the next day. The men were to answer charges that the French Panama Canal Company, owner of Panama Railroad, conspired with the Southern Pacific Railroad—by this time controlled by longtime Nicaragua opponent C.P. Huntington—to fix freight rates.

This "most wicked monopoly ever attempted upon the people of the United States . . . already cost the Pacific Coast millions upon millions of dollars," stormed a bellicose Morgan on the floor of the Senate.[49] Morgan's chief purpose of course, was to draw public attention to the fact that the Panama Canal Company, now seeking to do business with the United States government, was engaged in unsavory, unscrupulous, and illegal business practices. This accusation, predicted The *St. Louis Republic*, "will not add to the friendliness felt for the Panama project. Senator Hanna, who is in favor of considering the Panama offer ... will attend the meeting tomorrow to take a hand in the melee."[50] The Saturday morning fracas did not last long, but it encompassed a lot of territory. The testimony of Lampre and Boeufve covered 175 typewritten pages. Although no indictment resulted from the investigation, the witnesses affirmed Morgan's allegation that the Panama Canal Company was merely engaged in the charade of building the canal with the aim of keeping the project alive. When Morgan asked Lampre whether the Panama Canal Company ever intended to complete the canal, the witness answered candidly, "No," validating Morgan's claim that the French company was foisting its valueless chattels on a gullible buyer, the United States. The purpose of the sham activity in Panama that the company touted as proof of its vitality, just as Morgan suspected, was to hoodwink a naive America.

As he faced a renewed assault from the Panama Canal Lobby, Morgan still felt the Nicaragua Canal would go ahead, because for one thing President Roosevelt had given him his personal assurance that he supported the project. But on January 14, during another extended meeting of the Senate Canal Committee in which the discussion became "very animated," Marcus Hanna felt obliged to take Morgan aside and privately disabuse his colleague of that notion. "The President," revealed Hanna, "intended to ask Admiral Walker to call a meeting of the [Isthmian] Canal Commission" to review the French Panama Canal Company's offer with a view toward accepting proposal."[51] A flabbergasted Morgan refused to believe that Roosevelt was leaning away from his October pledge to him on Nicaragua and toward Panama. This, the old Rebel general insisted, he had to hear for himself. Morgan and a contingency from his committee stormed out of the meeting, determine to see the President and clarify Hanna's obviously erroneous understanding. After Morgan's exit, Hanna placed an anxious call to Roosevelt, warning him that he could expect a rather exercised Morgan to call upon him shortly.[52]

Precisely what was said in his conference with Senator Morgan cannot be known. No minutes of the meeting were taken. It can, however, best be understood by the truncated comments of newspapermen in their reports of Morgan's brusque demeanor after his meeting with Roosevelt. The normally expressive and communicative Morgan was taciturn and abrupt, "declining emphatically to discuss the interview between himself and the President."[53] Roosevelt must have revealed to Morgan that at 3:15 that day, just as Hanna had revealed to Morgan, he had ordered Admiral Walker to call the Isthmusian Canal Committee to discuss the Panama Canal Company's offer and to provide him a "supplemental report" no later than Saturday, the 18th.[54]

The sense of urgency Roosevelt conveyed to Walker is curious when considering that the United States was the only buyer the Panama Canal Company had ever managed to wrangle into negotiations. "I think this is a very important matter," the President emphasized to Walker, "and there should be no delay." [55] The "now or never" tenor from the White House stretches credibility. Several other options were opened to Roosevelt. Debate in the Senate had not yet begun, and had Roosevelt wanted a reassessment of the Panama route as a viable option because the price had been suddenly and dramatically lowered, he could have, without the Isthmusian Canal

Commission, the Interoceanic Canal Committee, or Hepburn's or Morgan's approval, used the "bully pulpit" to ignite such a discussion. The worst case scenario would be that he veto any bill that called for a Nicaragua Canal. Roosevelt needed to act urgently because he knew that the Panama Canal project, more fully examined, would not withstand scrutiny. If carefully read, even the Commission's endorsement of the Panama route would cause a truly deliberative body to ignore its findings and call for a Nicaragua Canal. The report read in part:

> We for many reasons—commercial, military, hygienic, seismic, and otherwise—believe the Nicaragua route to be the better route for an isthmian canal, and we so report and recommend. But inasmuch as the construction of the canal over the Panama route, which commercially, military, hygienic, seismic, and otherwise we believe to be inferior to the Nicaragua route, can be constructed for $5,630,704 less than the other, therefore, we in our final supplemental report, recommend that route.[56]

Some leaders, like Senator John Hipple Mitchell, were aghast that for the savings of an estimated $5,630,704, the Senate would "permit this comparatively paltry difference in the cost of construction, this mere bagatelle compared to the magnitude of the enterprise and its cost to control its action to the extent of setting aside the better route."[57]

Mitchell's demand that "The Isthmian Canal Commission must furnish me with a better reason than this before they can expect me to reject and set aside their report of November 16, 1901," was ultimately ignored.[58] Roosevelt decided that Panama was more useful to him, politically and personally. All the Panama Canal proponents obscured the details and highlighted the final determination of the report. The supplemental report clearly states that Nicaragua was the best choice for strategic and commercial reasons, but Roosevelt counted on a national quirk of the American collective character's response. The nationwide narrative, with the help of Roosevelt's

The Isthmian Canal Commission, American Monthly Reviews of Reviews, May 1902.

publicity machine and Cromwell's "literary bureau" that was said to have as many as 225 newspapers on their payroll, was turned from the "most practicable route and feasible that is known as the Nicaragua route," to a story about the great deal Americans got from France.

It must have been the old soldier's fury and sense of betrayal that left him speechless when reporters plied him for information about the meeting. Either he did not want to tip his hand about his next moves to neutralize the Panama threat, or Morgan needed some time to regroup. Either way, his uncharacteristic reticence with reporters was a silent signal of how desperate the situation was for the Nicaragua Canal. That evening the Washington, D.C. newspaper, the *Evening Star*, perhaps smelling blood in the water, reported in a front-page article that rumors were flying that the Commission would recommend Panama.[59] At the January 18 meeting, Commission member and friend to both Cromwell and Roosevelt, George S. Morison, moved that the changed conditions brought about by the offer of the French company gave sufficient reason to retract the previous findings of the Commission and to deem the Panama route preferable over Nicaragua. There was a definite difference of opinion among the commissioners: not every member went down easily.

Commission members Lewis Haupt, Samuel Pasco, and Alfred Nobel were manifestly disinclined to abandon Nicaragua, but the President had made it painfully clear to Admiral Walker that he expected an undivided decision by the Commission and Walker pressured the men. Roosevelt intended to accept the Panama Canal Company's offer and he warned Walker that anything less than unanimous agreement by Commission members would be unacceptable. Noble and Pasco finally caved in to the coercion, but Haupt could not be moved to repudiate the Commission's months of work and deliberation in one afternoon. Haupt, a member of the first Walker Commission, the Nicaragua Canal Commission, was no stranger to controversy. He was a man of strong convictions and spoke his mind, often too plainly to be political. When in 1899 McKinley instituted the second Walker Commission at the urging of William Nelson Cromwell, Haupt publicly declared the move was nothing more than a delaying tactic, initiated by self-serving "friends" of the new French Panama Canal Company. The interview almost got him fired. Now in 1902, he was the last man standing in the resistance to a Commission coup d'état being carried out by the new President.

Contrary to most accounts of the meeting that state Walker called Haupt out of the meeting to privately counsel him on the reasons he should reverse his stance, Haupt later told reporter Earle Harding that it was Roosevelt himself who called him out of the committee room and demanded that he sign the report.[60] Apparently, Roosevelt finally moved Haupt to giving what he wanted in a shrewd appeal to Haupt's patriotism. As recorded in the minutes of the meeting, Haupt understood that the issue had moved well beyond the scope of which route offered superior engineering advantages into the realm of the political. Roosevelt convinced him that a divided report would be used by canal enemies, like the powerful transcontinental railroad interests to defeat any canal legislation and so the issue had become, "a question, therefore, of Panama or nothing."[61] As Haupt categorically believed an isthmian canal was essential to the general good of the United States, "he concluded that his duty to his country would best be fulfilled by waiving his objections and signing the report."[62] When Haupt finally consented to put his name to it, he insisted that his reasons be formally entered into the minutes of the Commission.

The following Monday, Roosevelt sent the supplemental report to Congress and Bunau-Varilla, newly arrived from Paris, checked into the Willard Hotel, the "swellest" hotel at the national capital.[63] The little Panama Canal zealot could not leave the outcome to chance. He would be present to midwife the rebirth of the Panama route. Two days later, Roosevelt's sister Corinne, Douglas Robinson's wife, wrote to her brother imploring him to meet a fascinating expert on Panama, Philippe Bunau-Varilla. Morgan's war for the Nicaragua Canal was lost in the parlor of Corrine and Douglas Robinson and the grand salon of the Willard Hotel. Morgan's complete miscalculation of the artfulness of his Commander-in-Chief and his underestimation of the potency of the Panama Lobby unsteadied him. Yet, he might have recovered his equilibrium and forced his way forward on the Nicaragua Canal legislation, except for the one ingredient in this political brew he never fully measured: Philippe Bunau-Varilla.

154

Darling Theodore—

This letter refers to M. Bunau-Varilla who is most anxious to have a little talk with you. He is now at the New Willard in Washington. Theodore knew from [Sun Brummid] you who he is. I know how busy you are, but thought you might care to see him on the Panama question —
Corinne [Robinson]

January 22nd 1902

Letter from Corrine Roosevelt Robinson to Theodore Roosevelt. Corrine Roosevelt Robinson suggests that President Roosevelt meet with Philippe Bunau-Varilla, who is "most anxious to have a little talk" with him about "the Panama question." January 22, 1902. Theodore Roosevelt Papers, Manuscripts division. Library of Congress.

NICARAGUAN CANAL IN DANGER.

Cartoon depicts Marcus Hanna as a Mt. Hanna volcano with "daily erup-
tions" indorsing the Panama route and spouting statistics as Senator John
Tyler Morgan looks on stunned by the blast. **Minneapolis Journal,**
07 June 1902.

CHAPTER FIVE

PANAMANIACS AND VOLCANOES, 1902-1903

Any one doubt[s] the superiority of the ... Nicaragua route over ...
Panama makes himself liable to denunciation as ... an emissary of
the Panama lobby, the Pacific Railway lobby, or some other
power of darkness.—ROBERT C.V. MEYERS, 1902

———————————

When Senator John Tyler Morgan met Phillipe Bunau-Varilla in 1901, the two almost resorted to fisticuffs. Morgan found the little Frenchman obnoxious and transparently venal; Bunau-Varilla thought the old Senator's brains were addled by age and obsession. Now, with Bunau-Varilla steering the course of the *Nouvelle Compagnie,* it seemed he was having his revenge for Morgan receiving him in a most indecorous manner. As for Morgan, he immediately sprang into action, hoping to reverse the course of events. His Committee on Interoceanic Canals took testimony for two months after the startling reversal of the recommendation of the Isthmian Canal Committee. Throughout the hearings, during which reams of testimony were taken, Committee member and Morgan's Republican rival Senator Marcus Hanna, couched his questions to the witnesses and the members of the Canal Commission in such a way as to highlight any comments about the Panama route that were in the least way positive. Hanna's incessant solicitation of remarks from witnesses that could be framed as sanguine about the Panama Canal was rehearsed by hours of coaching by the Cromwell. The object of the exercise was to have an authorative record to which

Hanna could refer to when delivering the Committee minority report in favor of Panama before the full Senate—a report that would be entirely authored by Cromwell.[1]

Everyone on the Committee understood that the issue would not be settled in the hearings, but that the real fight would take place on the floor of the Senate. Hanna, as well as Senators Kittredge and Spooner, were using their considerable personal influence to convert Committee colleagues to Panama. Finally, in the first part of March, the Committee decided by a vote of 7 to 4, to reject a bill offered by Senator Spooner—a man with personal and professional ties to both William Nelson Cromwell and Theodore Roosevelt—in favor of the Hepburn Bill with no amendments. Sponer's bill would haved authorized the United States President to build an Isthmian Canal in Panama if the necessary rights could be obtained, or Nicaruagua if they could not. The minority, however, submitted a report of its own in which Senator Hanna pitched a robust case before the Senate in favor of the Panama route.

The final struggle in the Senate lasted from June 4 to June 19, 1902. As the fight heated up, Cromwell and his subordinates were back in Washington coaching, preparing, writing responses, and giving talking points to their allies. Nicaragua was still the favorite of most lawmakers, until in the middle of May when the resourceful little French engineer Bunau-Varilla reached into his bag of tricks and came up with a simple and brilliant slight-of-hand that would lead to a decisive victory for the Panama Lobby. His plan was rooted in his first American trip in 1901 to save the "great French enterprise" with his series of lectures to bring "Truth and Justice" to the discussion of interoceanic routes.[2] When the theatrical Frenchman lectured in 1901 to his rapt audiences in Cincinnati, Chicago, Cleveland, Boston, Philadelphia, Princeton, New York, and Washington, D.C., he always raised the specter of Lake Nicaragua as a bubbling caldron of volcanic activity. Bunau-Varilla's vivid and dramatic language evoked the fears in the minds of his audiences of a maniacally patient geologic horror that lurked in the heart of Nicaragua, just waiting to incinerate and entomb its unsuspecting victims, Mount Momotombo. "In the center of Lake Nicaragua is a volcano in constant eruption," Bunau-Varilla cautioned his audience.[3]

At the time of his lectures, his American supporters, like George Morrison who was now sitting on the Isthmusian Canal Commission—thanks to Cromwell's influence—counseled him to cease his dramatization of the dangers of volcanoes. The references to volcanic activities made Bunau-Varilla seem a bit of a hysteric, Morrison warned. Even though he followed Morrison's advice and toned down the fervor of his delivery, the Panama zealot was keenly aware of the effect the topic of volcanic eruptions had on audience members. Of all the questions raised by Bunau-Varilla during his lecture tour, he said the volcanic dangers he presented were the only point "which was accessible to the general public, the only one which would be correctly appreciated by a body of hearers."[4] It was of little concern to the preacher of Panama that there had not been a volcanic disturbance of note in the country since 1835.

At last, on May 8th 1902, fortune smiled again on Bunau-Varilla as it turned a blind eye to thousands of islanders on Martinique. Mount Pelee, without warning erupted with a force that, according to Bunau-Varilla, had "no parallel since the destruction of Pompeii."[5] He fervently believed that once the terrifying headlines and the gruesome images of the destruction in Martinique, once related to Nicaragua as he had in his speeches, would loosen the grip the idea of a Nicaraguan Canal had on Americans. And he was right. Bunau-Varilla seized the "unexpected turn of the wheel of fortune . . . to turn against Nicaragua the terror of which the disaster of Mount Pelee had produced," and changed the course of history.[6]

The destruction was indeed appalling. St. Pierre on Martinique was called the Paris of the Caribbean before the pyroclastic flow from Pelee engulfed the city. Over 30,000 of its inhabitants suffocated or burned to death with a mixture of gas, steam, glowing dust, ash, and pumice in one day. Only two people were reported to have survived the blast: a prisoner tucked away in the bowels of a jail cell and an individual whose home was on the outskirts of the city. Sensational, lurid descriptions of the volcano's effect began appearing in the American press just as debate on accepting the recent recommendation of the Isthmusian Canal Commission of the Panama route heated up. One witness to the aftermath described in the *San Francisco Call* streets of St. Pierre littered with "thousands of dead bodies, scorched black and shiny as if they had been plunged into boiling pitch."[7] Dozens of "volcano experts" stepped up to lend their expertise to a hungry press, thus, paving the way for Bunau-Varilla's ingenious gambit.

On May 15th, volcano expert and *Popular Mechanics Magazine* editor, Henry H. Windsor was quoted saying that Mount Cosigüina on the northwestern corner of Nicaragua would be the next serious volcanic eruption. "A canal through Nicaragua," warned Windsor, "will eventually be destroyed."[8] The volcano, totally dormant since 1859, was sited as an example of the molten terror that lurked beneath the surface. Bunau-Varilla bided his time, letting the volcano paranoia spread, until he decided the time was right to contact the President of the United States with his concerns. Roosevelt, who knew Bunau-Varilla through his sister Corinne Robinson, received the letter from the Frenchman that included his monograph regarding Nicaraguan geological instability and a cutting from a newspaper that supported his claim.

Cromwell, of course, had understood the publicity value of the horrific disaster for his cause and sought to leverage American fears, even if he had to invent a few details to insure insecurity. Suddenly, stories extolling Panama's relative geological stability over that of Nicaragua appeared. "These terrestrial disturbances will have a distinct and powerful bearing on the construction of the Isthmian canal" wrote the *Indianapolis Journal*, "While there have been a considerable number of earthquakes in various parts of Panama, they have been comparatively light, and there are no volcanoes, active or extinct, in that vicinity."[9] Naturally, in a piece that was inspired by Cromwell, the story referred to Bunau-Varilla and his expertise on the subject, stating that:

> M. Varilla, former engineer-in-chief of the Panama Canal, has declared that there are even no volcanic rocks within 180 miles of the proposed Panama route, as the isthmus was formed in a geological era that precluded earthquakes and volcanoes. On the other hand, Nicaragua has suffered severely from earthquakes, and has a number of active volcanoes of its own.[10]

160

Cromwell also used his swarm of paid newsmen to plant fictitious stories about the seismic activities of Mount Momotombo and prepped Senator Hanna to demand the Panama location because of the volcanoes in Nicaragua. Senator John Tyler Morgan fought back against the hysteria roused by the false claims, quoting the Nicaraguan officials denying that any such activity had taken place, thus refuting the claims on the Senate floor.[11] Still, the pull of the sensational lurid and macabre deaths trumped Morgan's speech by a press capitalizing on the public's panic. Newspapers continued to report dangers of Nicaraguan volcanic activity that did not actually exist as though they were facts.

The Hanama Canal

On June 7th, 1902, the Senator from Ohio, Marcus Hanna, began a scathing denunciation of the Nicaragua route in the Senate that included colorful maps, volumes of testimony gathered from seafaring captains, rivers pilots, and reams of warnings of seismic instability along the route by so-called volcano experts. When Morgan asked if the information he was quoting as fact was derived from the Interoceanic Canal Committee on which he served, Hanna said his information, "came to him in the course of his own investigation, [and that] he obtained the information from thoroughly accurate business sources."[12] Cromwell would later admit to being the accurate business source that Hanna cited, an honor also claimed Bunau-Varilla.[13] Cromwell had carefully prepared the material for Hanna's speech and had a team of two subordinates by his side to prompt the Senator during his speech.

As Hanna spoke to the Senate, he had in front of him two sheets of paper. The only notes on the pages were references to the page numbers of the various publications, maps, and reports Cromwell had supplied the Senator. Cromwell's junior associates sat behind Hanna, poised to locate within the over fifteen books and pamphlets, the quotations Hanna intended to use, and passed them up to Hanna. "Backed up by this material, he talked to the whole Senate just as he had already talked to many Senators in person—explaining in a conversational way the reasons which made the Panama route more desirable. He spoke on the first day for over two hours, until his knees gave out, and on the day following he concluded with a somewhat shorter additional argument."[14] As well received as Hanna's remarks were—many would later say that this was one of the best speeches ever delivered in the Senate—the Panama Lobby still needed something to boost them into the majority. It was at this point that inspiration struck the fastidious former Panama Canal engineer, Bunau-Varilla. He would counter the otherwise credible claims that volcanic activity in Nicaragua were historic features, not relevant to contemporary circumstances, and help defeat Morgan's Nicaragua Canal legislation with a humble postage stamp.

Bunau-Varilla recalled that the postage stamps of the Republic of Nicaragua depicted an active, smoldering volcano. This was the very "official document" he was looking for to substantiate the claims that Nicaragua was a literal hotbed of volcanic activity. He later wrote that he began the search among Washington stamp collectors from whom he purchased ninety stamps, "one for every Senator, showing a beautiful volcano belching forth in magnificent eruption. It was the up-to-date proof of the existence of these volcanoes in activity,"

The little Nicaragua stamp that made the big impact. Philippe Bunau-Varilla. **Panama; The Creation, Destruction, and Resurrection.** *London: Constable & company, ltd, 1913.*

he glowed, "which the officials of the Nicaraguan Government denied."[15] Bunau-Varilla, fearing the opposition would calm the volcano fears, "shot this final arrow," sending each Senator a stamp and a plea for Panama.[16] Directly after receiving the stamp, Republican Senator Gallinger posed the question to the Senate, of whether it could be considered rational to make such a massive investment "in a country that had taken as its emblem on its postage stamps a volcano in eruption."[17] Seeing the desired effect of his postage stamp carpet-bomb, Bunau-Varilla wrote that he knew then that "the battle was won. Truth at last triumphed. But how narrow was the margin between success and defeat!"[18] On the evening before the vote, the *Washington Times* front page story led with "Volcano on Postage Stamp and Seismic Disturbances—Remarks by Mr. Morgan Apparently Foreshadows Selection of Panama Waterway."[19]

The Senate response to Panama was miraculous. Hanna had delivered the best speech of his long career, the demonstration of active volcanoes in Nicaragua by the postage stamp, and the profound impact produced by the disaster in Martinique—all had contributed to Panama's victory. "These active and powerful forces had washed away, one by one, the members constituting the majority for Nicaragua," beamed Bunau-Varilla.[20] In the end, on June 19, 1902, the Senate substituted the Spooner Bill for the Hepburn Bill and sent it to conference. The Panama side won by only eight votes and the question for the friends of Panama were what kind of compromise would the House demand. However, despite a near unanimous endorsement of Nicaragua just five months previous to the passage of the Spooner Bill, news reporters were speculating that the House would give way to Spooner. "Representatives will accept the isthmian canal bill, as it passed the Senate yesterday, declared the *San Francisco Call*, "and the President will sign it."[21] Representatives, it was reported, would cheerfully agree to the Panama route, if not doing so meant no canal at all. The sentiment in the House was overwhelmingly in favor of an isthmian canal—any Isthmusian canal—whether it was Nicaragua or Panama seemed of little matter to the House members at this point. It was an attitude, the newspaper suggested, of "fearing to go before the country with no Nicaragua canal legislation passed . . . [Representatives] are now bending their efforts toward getting

163

IN WHICH DITCH WILL HE SINK THE WALLET?— From the *Herald* (Boston).

Uncle Sam stands between the two canal routes seemingly unable to decide. The caption reads "In which ditch will he sink the wallet?" Reprint, American Monthly Review of Reviews, Vol. 25., 1902.

acceptance of the Spooner substitute."[22] Spooner's Bill insured that one canal or the other would be built.

A meeting of the House Committee on Interstate and Foreign Commerce was called and Hepburn was instructed to get his bill into conference immediately. Hepburn asked unanimous consent to take the bill from the Speaker's table and proceed to the Senate for conference. Because the Spooner Bill contained a provision that called for the President to negotiate immediately with Nicaragua if there was any delay with the Panama transfer, Morgan publicly endorsed the bill because he believed the issues between Colombia and the Panama Canal Company were so great, no agreement would be reached, and the law would force a Nicaragua Canal. The Speaker of the House, David Henderson, named two Republicans,

Hepburn and Loren Fletcher of Minnesota, and Democrat Robert Davey of Louisiana as conferees. Because Fletcher was one of only two members of the House who voted against the Nicaragua canal bill in January, Henderson's choice of Fletcher was interesting to say the least.

Davey—whose constituency included the Southern port city of New Orleans that would unquestionably benefit from a canal route through Nicaragua—held an unenviable, minority position along with Hepburn. Not one to easily admit defeat, Hepburn declared that he would hold out as long as possible for the Nicaragua bill to be passed by the House. However, since even Senator John Tyler Morgan who had "worked every day for thirty years" on the Nicaragua canal and in the end voted for the Spooner Bill, Hepburn's prospects did not seem good. Seemingly above the fray, the cagey and politic Morgan told reporters that his primary goal was to get an Isthmusian canal and the Spooner legislation would give America "her waterway." Hepburn was pressured to declare whether he was "first, last, and all the time a Nicaragua man," or whether, if he like Morgan, would yield to the Spooner Amendment if it was apparent an agreement could not be reached through the conference process. Hepburn patriotically replied that America's best interest came first for him too, and declared that first and foremost he was "for a canal."[23] Although at the time both men seemed resigned, the language in the Spooner Bill left the door open for Nicaragua and it was through this door Morgan was preparing to charge.

Morgan's Counterassault

On the 28th of June, Senator Morgan came out swinging. He offered a resolution providing for the Interoceanic Canal Committee to ascertain whether any "unlawful or corrupt methods" had been used by the "swarm" of Panama Canal Company lobbyists to obtain any part of the $40,000,000 for the purchase of the waterway.[24] It was not his intent, claimed Morgan to impugn the character of the Senate or House, but because "large stipends and bribes" were commonly paid to those who "conduct great negotiations" this investigation would "clear the atmosphere of all floating charges."[25] Spooner called

Morgan's resolution "mischievous" and Hanna—who was already annoyed that Morgan had thrown a "cloud" upon the question of the title to the property claimed by the Panama Canal Company—said that if such a lobby existed, it was news to him.[26] This resolution started Morgan upon a relentless course of investigation of Cromwell and his Panama Canal syndicate that would not end until Morgan's death in 1907.

The dog days of the summer of 1902 were filled with news other than the Panama Canal purchase. According to reports, on July, Senator Bailey of Texas "first threatened to kill his colleague from Indiana and then choked him fiercely until dragged away by Senator Spooner of Wisconsin and the Sergeant-at-Arms."[27] Britain, Germany, and Italy were still engaged in a joint naval expedition to blockade the Venezuelan ports to force payment of debts by the South American country, causing Monroe Doctrine jitters in all quarters. Workers were striking in the coalmines and rail stations of America, grabbing headlines that warned of anarchists' plots. Stories about the end of nasty blood letting of the American-Philippine War filled the papers, and Panama still kept bubbling up in the news.

In June, Roosevelt summoned Cromwell to the White House. The meeting led to Cromwell, through his press agent Roger Farnham, leaked to the press that the President was determined to have the Panama route, and that should the treaty be rejected, Panama would secede from Colombia, and the President would promptly recognize the new Republic. Toward the end of July, not revealing that the United States had already chosen sides in the rebellion, the United States gunboat *Ranger* broke up a skirmish between Colombian and Panamanian insurgent gunboats in Panama Bay.[28] And in August, more news about unrest in Colombia regarding Panama began to circulate. It was reported that some Colombian officials objected to Secretary John Hay's call for a perpetual lease of the Panama Canal strip of land and the establishment of United States tribunals and police force with a provision in the zone, both of which violated the Colombian constitution.[29]

Suddenly, in September certain "defects" in Panama Canal Company's concession were unearthed in Paris, calling to question the Company's right to sell the property.[30] A month later, U.S. Attorney

166

General Philander Knox issued an opinion that the Company had the right to sell the canal. The publicity machines of Cromwell and Roosevelt sprang into action, transforming the public conversation from one of stating Colombia's right to maintain its sovereignty over Panama, to one in which their position was characterized as "Colombia's haggling attitude."[31] The double standard of this attitude was overlooked by most, buried beneath emotional patriotic rhetoric. If the U.S. Congress believed that a treaty negotiated with a foreign power was to the detriment of the nation's interest and not only violated the sovereignty of the U.S., but also violated its Constitution, no criticism would be levied if they refused to ratify such an instrument. However, the refusal of the Colombian Congress to sign the treaty

Uncle Sam swinging a big Monroe Doctrine stick and enforcing order for the Panama Railroad, **American Monthly Review of Reviews,** *Vol. 25, 1902.*

was characterized as "banditry" by the White House and almost every newspaper in the country took the jingoistic bait Roosevelt was scattering about to a ravenous press.

Reflecting the bullying attitude that Roosevelt functioned under while dealing with a less powerful nation, the Department of State announced that "the United States Government will not wait to conclude a treaty with [Colombia], but will begin digging the canal and discuss terms afterwards."[32] With a publicity onslaught, the discussion centered around how to fulfill what Roosevelt and Cromwell described as Colombia's "moral obligation" to ratify the treaty, something that the Colombian Congress—just as the U.S. Congress would be in similar circumstances—was under no obligation to do. Still, the connection eluded most journalists. By the end of November 1902, the *San Francisco Call* reported that, "threats have been made by persons interested [in selling the Panama Canal] as to the dreadful things that would happen to Colombia if she did not speedily negotiate a treaty," helping to prime the country for a confrontation.[33]

Nicaragua proponents clamored to invoke the Spooner Bill provision to build in that country if the process hit a snag with the Panama Canal purchase, but the Department of State declared that no talks with Nicaragua would occur "until present negotiations with Colombia are declared off."[34] The day after Christmas, Iowa Congressman Hepburn, who had so successfully marshaled the Nicaragua Canal bill through the House, had enough. Something foul was amiss, he feared and the delays meant one thing to him—political corruption—and he set about to prove it. The Panama Canal Commission, relayed newspaper accounts of the Congressman's charge, "has made places for the sons of army and navy officers and of senators and representatives and others prominent in political and social life, and has given them pay far beyond their availability for any practical purpose."[35] Hepburn introduced a resolution, calling on the Secretary of State for a list of the officials and employees of the Commission who "played fast and loose with government money."[36]

Throughout all the resistance and charges presented by the Democrats and other friends of Nicaragua, Cromwell never wavered from his course. He forged ahead with his plan to set the diplomatic framework to separate Colombia from any part of the millions he and his syndicate were getting from the sale of the Panama Canal works to the United States. Working alongside Roosevelt and Secretary of State John Hay, Cromwell constructed the perfect instrument in the language of the treaty between Colombia and the United States. If the Colombians ratified the treaty, they would receive a pittance of the $40,000,000 and lose all control over their Panama territory, or if they balked at the terms and refuse to sign, Roosevelt would have the perfect pretext for assisting Panama to secede from Colombia. In the end, it was actually Cromwell who drafted the treaty with Secretary John Hay's Colombian counterpart, career diplomat Dr. Thomas Herran, but he first had to deal with Colombia's ambassador Jose Vicente Concha's resistance. After months of negotiations, Concha—

Secretary of State John Hay. Lorenzo Sears, **John Hay, Author and Historian,** *1914.*

169

who by all accounts, was "erratically brilliant, though boorishly bitter in his antipathy toward North Americans"—could no longer abide the disunity of his own politicians or his distrust of the Americans and assigned Herran the role of negotiator.[37]

Much to Cromwell's relief, Herran—who had also worked in harness with Cromwell and Bunau-Varilla to defeat the Nicaragua route legislation—was drawn into the negotiations when Colombian minister to the United States, Jose Vicente Concha, called him in late December of 1902 to take his place. Herran was as suspicious as Concha, but he became convinced that the Americans would abandon Panama for Nicaragua if an agreement could not be reached.[38] The part he played in helping the construction of a document that Cromwell knew the Colombians would reject would eventually earn the scorn of his countrymen, but he carried on and Cromwell achieved what he wanted: the advancement of the Panama Canal Company's interests and the Colombian disenfranchised. The Hay-Herran Treaty was signed January 22, 1903.

Although the Cromwell crafted Hay-Herran Treaty stated that, "[I]t is understood that Colombia reserves for herself all her rights to the special shares in the capital of the New Panama Canal," one week after the signing Paris managers of the syndicate declared Colombia's 50,000 shares "non-negotiable." Cromwell would later boast that he crafted both the document and negotiated it with Hay and Herran, and he was the lone witness to the midnight signing of the treaty. With these mechanisms in place it was assured that the $40 million went to Cromwell's American Panama Canal syndicate and the $10 million originally offered to Colombia in the Hay-Herran Treaty went eventually to Panama—which ended up flowing through the hands of none other than William Nelson Cromwell. Anticipating a Panama revolt, Cromwell envisioned a provision in the constitution of the fledgling country would provide for a fund to "secure for posterity" of the Panamanian people. In due course, $6,000,000 would be set aside for such a fund that William Nelson Cromwell, appointed Fiscal Agent by the President of Panama in 1908, would manage. The investment of the endowment included funneling millions from the funds through the real estate firm of Douglas Robinson, Roosevelt's brother-in-law.

170

The Sheep and the Wolf: Forcing Colombia Out, 1903

Since Cromwell had written the treaty for the Panama Canal Company in its own interest, contravened Colombia's sovereignty, and thereby violated its constitution, Colombian lawmakers were understandably opposed to its ratification. Colombia was not actually asking for major concessions in the agreement. They asked that the accord respect its sovereignty and that their rights to compensation be not less than those of any other stockholder in the Panama Canal Company. Yet, despite their reasonableness of their requests, Colombia was portrayed as a bad actor, a petulant and greedy child, standing in the way of progress. When the Colombians protested their harsh portrayal, a campaign of distorted information about the agreement and vilification of the Colombian government was unleashed through the White House and Cromwell's private army of newspaper lobbyists. The Colombian government had no luck in breaching the wall of disinformation.

Colombian authorities repeatedly attempted to get the citizens and the government of the United States to understand the difficult position in which Cromwell's treaty placed them. "[Our] government has been presented this dilemma," one official wrote, "Either it lets our sovereignty suffer detriment, or renounces certain pecuniary advantages, to which, according to the opinion of many, we have a right."[39] Senator Morgan, at least, agreed. From the Senate floor, Morgan accused Cromwell's employers of "riding down the Colombian constitution," trampling it underfoot.[40] Yet, attuned with the *zeitgeist* of turn of the century American exceptionalism, Roosevelt and the majority of the American public would not accept Colombia's position as one of principle. Roosevelt claimed to be dumbfounded by the refusal of the "jack rabbits'" in Bogota to abandon their constitution and their autonomy for the opportunity to rake in some cash.[41] Not that any self-respecting American would do the same, but the Colombians should be happy to change their constitution, he told John Hay, if the price were right.[42]

The Public Conversation: Walter Wellman

The public conversation in the American press revolved around the question does a "comparatively backward nation have the right to block the world's progress?" The Roosevelt administration thought not. While denying the rumors that the President had "threatened to seize the Isthmus," journalist, Roosevelt apologist, and long-time Bunau-Varilla backer, Walter Wellman, wondered in a widely published editorial whether such an action would not be in the best interest of the entire civilized world. Wellman's gusto about eliminating barriers to the advancement of the world caused by the "half-civilized" Colombians triggered the *National Magazine's* remarks that the journalist should be given a "conspicuous place in" the creation of transoceanic history.[43] Since his encounter with Bunau-Varilla in Paris in 1901, Wellman was a true devotee of the Frenchman's Panama Canal doctrine.

Journalist Walter Wellman. Library of Congress, 1910.

It was Wellman who had first cabled Bunau-Varilla on December 23, 1902 the short but explosive message, "Confidential information from Congress and Isthmian Canal Commission indicates that $40,000,000 offer would be accepted. Imperative no higher. Act quickly."[44] And act quickly, Bunau-Varilla did. "This cablegram, which cost Mr. Wellman $4.20, worded with his characteristic directness," stated the *National Magazine,* "changed the tide of negotiations involving several hundred millions [of dollars]."[45] In Paris while Bunau-Varilla speedily orchestrated the shareholders *junta* in the United States, Wellman busied himself "crystallizing sentiment for the Panama route by publishing facts that fell like bomb shells into the camp of the Nicaragua people."[46] The foundation of the argument Wellman presented supported the idea of snatching the territory of Panama from the Colombians for the sake of progress and civilization. The proposition was an attractive one to many Americans.

In a lengthy article, Wellman insisted "It is not true that our government is intriguing to bring about a secession from Colombia by the state of Panama . . . with a view to the ultimate acquisition of the canal territory by the United States." Rather, explained Wellman, "the administration has taken a firm stand in favor of the general proposition that Colombia shall not be permitted to block the world's progress."[47] Wellman drew the comparison between Colombia and the "primitives" subdued by larger, complex, and civilized nations for the sake of modernization and prosperity—like Vasco Núñez de Balboa's pacification of the Panamanian natives in 1513, for example. "For instance savage tribes are not permitted to prevent the opening of continents to civilization and commerce," he argued, "and backward nations which are advanced far beyond savagery must also conform to the world's necessities."[48]

His argument articulated a principle that would guard against barbaric people from impeding the world's progress, the principle he called "civilization's right of eminent domain."[49] Wellman called upon a hypothetical case most expansion minded Americans would be inclined to support:

> For instance, if nature had placed in the Atlantic Ocean
> a long strip of rock, standing in the path of commerce

between the old world and the new, inhabited by a million or two people who maintained a sort of government, and it was desired to cut a channel for ships, if that government stood in the way, either declaring it should not be done or attempting to exact exorbitant terms, how long would it take the governments of America and Europe to dispose of this obstacle? Civilization's right of eminent domain would be exercised and a channel would be cut for the world's commerce. Nature did not plant such a strip of rock in the Atlantic Ocean, but she planted one in the American isthmus separating the great seas. And it is with that obstacle to progress the United States is now dealing. [50]

This line of reasoning struck a cord with the values of a newly imperialistic America that defined Manifest Destiny, not as confined to the geographical borders of its Western boundary, but as a spirit of progress ordained by providence, propelling the Nation forward regardless of the location.

The *Literary Digest* reported at least half-a-dozen important newspapers supporting the same line of thinking. "The Indian, the Hindu, and the Filipino have given way before the march of civilization and commerce, now it is the turn of the South American," argued the Boston *Advisor*. "If you can not come to terms with the Colombian brother," it suggested, "why not exercise the right of eminent domain again, a process which has proved so easy with the Indian and the Hindu?" The Indianapolis *Sentinel* proclaimed, "The simplest plan of coercing Colombia would be inciting a revolution in Panama and Costa Rica and supporting the insurrectionary government. That is what European nations have been doing to accomplish their ends. It is hypocritical, but it preserves appearances, and in this case it would be almost justifiable."[51]

At the time, as Roosevelt entertained the idea of a military occupation of Panama, America was distracted in both the minutia and the monumental of every aspect of the governance of the new territories recently liberated from Spain's oppression, only to exert a cruel domination of its own. The Philippines was officially pacified in 1902, but the Irreconcilables—remnants of resistance groups—still troubled the United States authorities for four more years, with savagery and bloodshed displayed on all sides. The Cubans seemed to feel that it might be time for the Yankees to go home. Hawaii was restless and resentful. "Horrible atrocities" committed against the Christian Bulgarians by the Turks added to the impression for the average American that Western, white and progressive civilizations like America were under attack.[52] People of color who were in lesser stages of development—as Wellman suggested of Colombians—inhabited all these United States' protectorates and it was an accepted principle that the burden of guiding the underdeveloped, "little brown brothers" out of the way of progress, was a responsibility of a civilized white America—even if it meant using force.

In the interim, while the public debate about Colombia's gluttony and pettiness were circulating through the press, Panama's rivals in the United States Senate clung to the thread of hope written in the Spooner Bill that upon the failure of Colombia to ratify the treaty "within a reasonable time," the President would immediately proceed to negotiate for the Nicaraguan right-of-way.[53] All the while, the Colombian government, who wanted a canal in its state of Panama, rejected the characterization that they were highjacking the process. They appealed to calm and reason, but received only bellicose insults in return. The Colombians agreed to the negotiation, they argued, which is a process that does not obligate acceptance. "The fact of Colombia having initiated the negotiations does not demand the approval of the same by that Government," responded Hay's counterpart, Luis Carlos Rico, "for the approval of Congress is necessary to the ratification of them, to which is given the constitutional power of approving or disapproving the treaties which the Government makes . . . If such were the case, the preparing of the pact would be the occasion of a serious danger instead of an element of peace and progress."[54]

This all, of course, pleased the friends of Nicaragua. If Colombia did refuse to ratify the Hay-Herran Treaty, the Spooner stipulation would be evoked, the anti-Panama Canal Company group believed, and they could return to the business of building a Nicaraguan canal.

While Morgan and his Nicaragua friends breathed in a sigh of relief created by the likelihood that Roosevelt would in the end be forced to abandon the Panama project, the President and his administration along with William Nelson Cromwell and Philippe Bunau-Varilla were ratcheting up the game to a whole new level.

A Cromwellian End: Instigating the Revolution

The Colombian senate unanimously rejected the treaty on August 12, 1903. "Naturally," wrote peace advocate and Roosevelt critic Annie Riley Hale, about Cromwell, "such a versatile genius was not to be turned from his purpose of having the United States build a canal across Panama, by a trifle like the failure of the Colombian government to ratify the treaty."[55] Actually, the Colombian failure to ratify the treaty was just what the dexterous New York lawyer had planned for when he guided the Paris managers of the Panama Canal Company—of which he was one—to the corporate excommunication of Colombia. Cromwell, hedging his bets, had structured the treaty in such a way that even if the French had agreed to pay Bogota the fee it demanded, the South American lawmakers could not in good conscious sign the agreement. It required them to forfeit their sovereignty over territory and even if the Colombian lawmakers were so inclined, it would take a constitutional amendment to undertake the exercise. Thomas Herran was vilified as a traitor for having participated in such a sham treaty. Outraged, Dr. Juan B. Perez y Sota, senator from the State of Panama, fired off an angry missile which appeared in *El Correo National* stating:

> The Herran Treaty will be rejected, and rejected by a unanimous vote in both chambers. That is what I hope, since there will not be a single representative of the nation who will believe the voice of the people who have sold themselves; who have had the brazenness to recommend the shameful compact. The insult, however, which Herran has cast upon the Colombian name will never be wiped out. The gallows would be a small punishment for a criminal of this class.[56]

The complication of Colombia's refusal to be silent during the legal mugging enacted by the Panama Canal Company counsel was no inconvenience for master political stage-manager Cromwell. He set in motion a series of diplomatic exchanges using John Hay and the United States State Department to insure that his clients—who were by this time one as the same as the syndicate he controlled— would not have to pay out one cent to Colombia. After meeting with Hay and Roosevelt, Cromwell recommended that Hay issue a severe warning to Colombia, threatening grave consequences if they did not comply with the treaty as written.

On June 9th, Hay sent a cable to American minister in Colombia, Arthur Matthias Beaupre, to warn his hosts, "If Colombia should now reject the treaty or unduly delay its ratification, the friendly understanding between the two countries would be so seriously compromised that action might be taken by the Congress next winter which every friend of Colombia would regret."[57] To the world Colombia would look as if they reneged on their obligation and the Roosevelt administration would appear strong by refusing to submit to the blackmail of the people of the United States by "rapacity of a band of men who abused their authority."[58] Presenting terms to the South American nation that they could never accept and then depicting them as petulant and greedy thugs standing in the way of progress, accomplished the first tactic of the Cromwellian strategy to concentrate the proceeds of the sale in his hands. What prevented the ratification of the treaty was not Colombian bandits "holding up" the United States, but William Nelson Cromwell.

All of the many amendments to the treaty introduced by the Colombians relating to compensation for the concession for the right of way were rejected by the United States. It was instead Roosevelt's position that the treaty prepared by the attorney for the Panama Canal Company was inviolate and "covered the whole matter, and any change would be in violation of the Spooner Law and not permissible."[59] This assertion by the President of the United States, that the Colombian Senate could not modify a treaty submitted for its deliberation, toughened by Secretary Hay's ultimatum, led the Colombian Senate to reject the treaty. Because of the "imperative nature of the notes" from Hay "regarded as offensive and highly humiliating," even the Colombian senators who were in favor of the treaty and friendly toward the United States, joined in rejecting the treaty.[60] It then directed the Colombian government to carry on with negotiations with the United States with an agreeable settlement as their goal.[61] Yet, Hay and Cromwell's goal was "to initiate a Panama *uprising*," Riley later wrote, "which with the timely and efficient backing of United States gunboats, might grow into a Panama *revolution* which would serve every Cromwellian end."[62]

Military Intervention

The administration moved with militant alacrity to ensure the success of the Panamanian separatists' project. While Hay was busy issuing confrontational ultimatums to Bogota, Roosevelt was conferring with international law expert, John Bassett Moore, about a legal framework for invading Panama and simply taking what he wanted. The clause in the 1846 treaty signed with Colombia giving the United States the right to maintain free and open communication of the Panama Railroad would be enough for Roosevelt to send in troops. On October 19th, Roosevelt ordered the Navy Department to hold warships within striking distance of the Isthmus of Panama on both the Atlantic and Pacific sides. Orders were issued that day to "send the *Boston* with all possible dispatch to San Juan del Sur, Nicaragua. She must arrive by November 1, with coal sufficient for returning to Acapulco. Secret and confidential. Her ostensible destination Acapulco only."[63]

The message was sent to the Navy Yard in Brooklyn that the *Dixie* must be ready to set sail on the 23rd. Orders were given to place a contingent of 400 Marines on board the *Dixie,* and the USS *Atlanta,* was ordered to proceed to Guantanamo. Roosevelt, as Commander-in-Chief also gave instructions to the General Staff to prepare for the eventuality of a military campaign on the Isthmus. Roosevelt was providing more than enough muscle to neutralize Colombia's attempt to suppress an insurrection in Panama. While Roosevelt was preparing to prevent Colombia from asserting its sovereignty by blockading the ports and landing Marines in early autumn,

178

Cromwell and Bunau-Varilla had been preparing to rule since late that summer.

The Panamaniacs in America

During the month of August, 1903 swarms of Panama revolution conspirators—most of whom were employees of the Panama Railroad Company—came to New York seeking the guidance of Panama Railroad shareholder and legal counsel William Nelson Cromwell. The only Panama insurrectionary to appear in his offices that was not connected with the railroad was J. Gabriel Duque, editor of the *Panama Star and Herald* and quite possibly the wealthiest man in Panama. After a long discussion detailing the plans of the revolutionary committee—approximately six men from the City of Panama's Municipal Council and two from the Panama Railroad Company—Cromwell offered the job of President to Duque when Panama attained its independence. The offer was conditional, however, upon whether Duque, a Cuban born citizen of America, would finance the revolution. Duque turned the offer down. Even so, Duque's involvement was critical to the success of Cromwell's plans. He called Secretary of State John Hay and made an appointment for Duque to confer with him. When Duque left Cromwell's New York office, he went straight to Thomas Herran, Colombia's minister to the United States and revealed the content and character of his discussions with Cromwell and his planned meeting with Hay.

During his New York visit, Duque—often called "the king of Panama" by members of the press because of his extraordinary wealth and influence—gave a number of interviews in which he announced that for some time, a plan had been in the making to break away from Colombia and seek American protection. Afterward, he travelled to Washington to meet with Hay and discuss the *coup*, an event that was reported by no less than three major news outlets. *The Times* reported that in his meeting with Hay, Duque was said to have informed the Secretary of State that the insurrection was scheduled to take place on September 23rd, the day after the time for the ratification of the treaty expired. Duque asked for United States aid in carrying out the plan.

Hay's official response was, of course, he could not promise help, but then he made an astonishing remark to the Panama secessionist that his timetable was a bit premature. "It seems to me," Hay continued, "it would look better if you waited six weeks or so... You understand that if there is a revolution, the United States will keep the Isthmus open and allow no fighting near the railroad. If there is to be any fighting it will have to be done before our Marines get there."[64] With a wink and a nod, Hay made sure Duque appreciated exactly what he meant, even if he did not directly say it. "You understand don't you," probed the elder statesman.[65] "We will prevent traffic across the Isthmus from being interfered with and we will also prevent bloodshed anywhere on the Isthmus."[66]

Not being naïve or simpleminded, Duque concluded Hay was telling him that the plotters must delay their seditious act.[67] A guarantee that the United States would not permit any fighting around the railroad obviously meant there would be some force that would be brought to bear to backup that statement. The most unambiguous declaration—that the most unsophisticated person could easily understand—was the phrase "our Marines" would "get there" to prevent the Colombians from interfering with Panama's interoceanic transit route. Duque went back to New York and reported his interview to his colleagues on the same day. The secessionists followed Hay's prompting and the revolution did not come off on September 23rd as previously planned. In concurrence with Cromwell and the Roosevelt administration's wishes, the rebellion was postponed to November 3rd to take advantage of the U.S. news cycle's preoccupation with the November 4th elections. By then, the United States would be ready.[68]

When Duque turned down Cromwell's offer of the Presidency of Panama, the Fox of Wall Street did not miss a beat. It made little difference to him if Duque accepted or not, because he knew that on the same ship that carried Duque from Panama to the United States was another leader of the conspiracy more easily directed than Duque. Dr. Manuel Amador was an employee of Panama Railroad Company—like most all the conspirators—in which Cromwell was not only the legal council, but also a major stockholder. In other words, Cromwell was the boss of most of the Panama plotters.

180

The Panamanian secessionists chose Amador—the railroad's chief medical officer and elder member of the faction—to represent them to the United States' powerbrokers, starting with Cromwell. Among the cabal relying on Amador to secure American assistance with their intrigue were American soldier of fortune H.O. Jeffries—who as a youth worked for the candidacy of New York Assemblyman, Theodore Roosevelt—railroad middle-managers James Shaler, Herbert G. Prescott, J.R. Beers, and for good measure, United States Army officer William Murray Black.[69]

Amador visited Cromwell on the heels of Duque. Cromwell was very assuring to Amador, but about this time Colombian diplomat Thomas Herran—to whom Duque had confided the lawyer's complicity in the uprising strategy—made it known to Cromwell that he would hold him personally responsible if such an event as described by Duque were to take place. To minimize his exposure, Cromwell immediately cabled insurrection advisor and Panama Railroad employee, James Shaler, not to allow any railroad employees to participate in revolutionary activities.[70] Having produced a document that could support a claim of non-involvement, Cromwell publicly distanced himself from Amador. The story usually is told that Amador, who at first was deeply optimistic because of Cromwell's support, was left uncertain and angry at what appeared to be Cromwell's indifference. It is more likely, piecing together the evidence and what is known about the operational style of Cromwell, even if he was in the background, he was pulling the strings of his Panamaniac marionettes. Or using another apt metaphor beyond puppetry, Cromwell was the *deus ex machina* contriving to resolve Amador's problem without seeming to be present. Cromwell summoned his petite knight in shining armor, Philippe Bunau-Varilla to handle Amador.

Before Bunau-Varilla took the helm, Amador travelled with Cromwell aboard the Congressional Limited train to Washington, D.C. On this trip Cromwell drafted the manifesto of independence for the proposed Republic of Panama. Once in Washington, the pair went to the White House near midnight and remained locked in conference with Roosevelt until nearly dawn.[71] They emerged just in time to catch a morning train back to New York. On September

23rd, Philippe Bunau-Varilla arrived in New York and, although he claimed to have come on his own accord to observe the dramatic political drama himself, there is strong reason to believe that Cromwell had the Panama Canal Company send him to New York to provide the Panama insurrectionists the funds necessary to hold a successful revolution.[72] Bunau-Varilla, as he had claimed throughout his career, declared that providence put the two Panama partisans together when a mutual acquaintance, J.J. Lindo, happened to mention to his friend Amador that the Frenchman had just arrived from Paris and was staying at the Waldorf-Astoria Hotel. Amador immediately sought an audience with the man he was sure could help him and his cause. Sometime after their introduction, Amador told fellow conspirator that he and Bunau-Varilla had also traveled to Washington, where he waited in the lobby of the White House while the Frenchman met with Roosevelt.[73] After the meeting with Bunau-Varilla, Amador returned in great revolutionary spirit to Panama.

Follow the Money

Bunau-Varilla promised Amador everything he had been looking for from Cromwell: money and muscle. The Frenchman vowed to Amador that he would deliver to him the cash he needed for the revolution, that the U.S. Secretary of State and the President would support the *coup d'état* with the armed forces of the United States, that Panama would be promptly recognized by the United States, made financially secure, and that American warships and soldiers would safeguard the new republic from reprisal by Colombia. The sum of $100,000 for the enterprise was telegraphed over by the *Credit Lyonnaise* to the account of the New Panama Canal Company, then over to Heidlebach, Ikleheimer and Company, then credited to Bunau-Varilla. The $100,000 that Bunau-Varilla had so generously offered the revolutionist Panamanian group was in the future and the revolutionist committee needed funds immediately, so in addition to the forthcoming funds, a loan of $100,000 from the Bowling Green Trust Company backed by securities—later shown deposited by

William Nelson Cromwell—was earmarked for the immediate use of the revolutionaries.

Revolutions were not cheap and they needed to meet the expenses of the revolution, which in their case meant several thousands of dollars were required to bribe the Colombian soldiers to desert their posts. The commander of the Colombian troops in Panama alone required $35,000 to abandon his post. The money to bribe him and the other soldiers and officers of the Colombian army stationed on the isthmus were advanced by the Panama Railroad Company and the bank of Ehrman—of which the senior partner, Felix Ehrman, was also the vice consul general of the United States in Panama. The financial firms Isaac Brandon and Brothers, as well as employers of Bunau-Varilla's pal J.J. Lindo who arranged to have him meet Amador in New York, Pisa Nephews bank.[74] Interestingly, the transfer of funds may offer an explanation for the acrimony and resentment that developed soon afterward between Cromwell and Bunau-Varilla. It looks as if Bunau-Varilla was not the moneyed, debonair man he appeared, but a man of modest means—much too modest for a person with such grandiose sense of self.

In total, Bunau-Varilla surrendered just half of Cromwell's money to the revolutionary committee coffers and he pocketed the rest. Only $25,000 of the $100,000 went to Amador before the revolution, and another $25,000 was pried away from the crafty Frenchman after the revolution with the greatest of difficulty. When questioned later about delivery of the funds to Amador, banker J.J. Lindo testified that at the behest of Amador, he called on Bunau-Varilla asking him to make good his promise of funding for the fledgling government. At first Bunau-Varilla refused. After much haranguing, the Frenchman finally relented and signed over $25,000 to Lindo.

Publicly, Bunau-Varilla bragged that he, not Cromwell, had bankrolled the insurgents with $100,000 of his own money, and that Cromwell had nothing to do with the finances. Bunau-Varilla claimed that as a man of means, $100,000 was a pittance and anyway, Panama's cause was so worth the cost. In fact, Bunau-Varilla would assert, Cromwell had let the Panamanians down and abandoned the revolution in a most cowardly way. However, despite his protestations

"Christmas on the Isthmus" shows Uncle Sam as Santa Claus handing $10 million dollars to Panama while other Latin American countries get nothing. Udo Kepper, **Puck**, Library of Congress, 1903.

of magnanimity, his 1903 sojourn in New York strongly suggests that Bunau-Varilla's estate was negligible, perhaps nonexistent. He did maintain a room at the Waldorf-Astoria as his diplomatic headquarters, but it was literally a $5-a-day accommodation—a mere $132 in today's dollars—while living with his family at the more modest and moderate-priced New Amsterdam Hotel on Fourth Avenue; hardly the arena of a man to whom $100,000 was an insignificant charitable donation to a commendable cause. Bunau-Varilla appeared in posh and exclusive venues, but at the end of the day, he had to walk down the hall of the hotel to the bathroom.[75]

It is reasonable to conclude that this dispute over money was at the core of the mutual distaste and antipathy Cromwell and Bunau-Varilla displayed toward one another after the Panamanian succession from Colombia.[76] Cromwell—a man who knew where every penny he spent, including to how many light bulbs lawyers in his practice used—would have been furious at the Frenchman's liberties with his money. And for his part, it is logical that Bunau-Varilla—whose sense of entitlement permeated his every gesture—enjoyed unauthorized appropriation of Cromwell's cash as the money he had earned. But, the disintegration of the compact between Cromwell and Bunau-Varilla would come after Amador returned to Panama and to share the good tidings of his successes with his new friends in America. Amador's associates were at first dubious of the intentions of the United States. However, their anxiety turned to relief when the gunboat *Nashville* arrived off Colon November 2nd, one day before their planned uprising.

Shows Philippe Bunau-Varilla clutching a bundle of Panama Canal stock and $40,000,000 under one arm while candling a giant egg by the light of "intrigue." A chick representing the new republic of Panama burst forth from the egg presenting a smiling Theodore Roosevelt with Bunau-Varilla's credentials empowering him to represent the new nation. Title: "The Man Behind the Egg!" Reprinted in Albert Shaw's A Cartoon History of Roosevelt's Career, 1910.

CHAPTER SIX

Rough Riding Diplomacy 1903-1908

We were thus to see the Monroe Doctrine evolved into a new doctrine that is entitled in all justice to be baptized the Roosevelt Doctrine; and that generally, a centralized, a personalized, and a kind of vi et armis *theory of government was to be set up for our worship.*
—JOSEPH S. AUERBACH, 1904

When the rumors that Panama would declare its independence from Colombia on November 3rd reached officials in Bogota, naturally the government was furious. Bogota responded in the manner of any early twentieth century sovereign nation when threatened with territorial losses by sedition and intrigue; they sent warships to subdue the insurgents. On November 2, 1903 the Colombian battleship *Carthenga* sailed into Limon Bay to land troops in Colon on the Atlantic side of the breakaway territory, and the gunship *Bogota* steamed into the Gulf of Panama on the Pacific coast to the city of Panama where it lobbed bombs on the surprised citizens of the city of Panama.[1] However, the commander of the *Bogota* proved nearly as hapless as the residents of the city he was attacking. All the bombardment accomplished was to kill one luckless Chinese merchant and his unfortunate mule, destroy a few uninhabited buildings, and invite the displeasure of the United States government who publicly demanded the Colombians cease the shelling because the Panamanians were not given proper notice of the impending attack, therefore, the attack violated international law.[2]

Yet, perhaps more inauspiciously for Colombia than its artillery inaccuracies or becoming the recipient of open criticism from its most important ally, President Roosevelt also had prior knowledge of the date of the revolt and was sending a sizable armada to interfere with Colombia's exercise of its authority over the recalcitrant province. In September Roosevelt, Secretary of State John Hay, Secretary of War Elihu Root, William Nelson Cromwell, and Acting Secretary of the Navy John Loomis had decided that the Colombians would fail at any attempt they made to discipline its rebellious territory. The decision was made and the military campaign designed soon after the Panamanian insurrectionist millionaire J. Gabriel Duque's Washington visit to Secretary of State John Hay in the autumn of 1903, long before the Colombians responded to the rumors of the planned rebellion.

Roosevelt's plan to shepherd Panama into the nations of the world sprang to life in August of 1903 when the Colombian senate rejected the proposed Panama Canal treaty offered by the United States. Roosevelt's plans were put in motion by October. Roosevelt knew with certainty that a civil disturbance would erupt in Panama because he had personally discussed plans with mastermind William Nelson Cromwell, canal crusader Philippe Bunau-Varilla, and separatist leader Manuel Amador. He also knew when the mutineers would declare independence because Hay had done his job of communicating the administration's preference to the revolutionary committee through the "wink and nod" conversation with Duque. In fact, the knowledge of the Roosevelt administration's sponsorship of the rebellion in the territory of an ally and the chorographic nature of its support were commonplace.[3] The newspapers reported,

> In a roundabout way, it was later learned that the President would like to have the revolt delayed until after the election, but no longer. Always striving to please, the revolutionary committee of the Isthmus gave the final order that the new government should be proclaimed immediately after the close of the polls on November 3rd. It was [thus] proclaimed at Panama.[4]

On October 7, William Nelson Cromwell briefed the President on the Panama situation "pretty thoroughly," as reports of the meeting were conveyed by the press.[5] Knowing that a revolt in Panama would produce potentially awkward questions, Cromwell had suggested the November 3rd *coup d'état* so any news coverage would then have to compete with headlines screaming about the election results. The administration agreed. Hay had made quite certain that the leadership of the Panama insurgency understood that any declaration of independence should coincide with the November 3rd state elections. All that was left was for the United States Navy to pull the trigger, so to speak, by coordinating so-called training exercises that would put them on Panama's doorstep in time to back the rebels. With eleven states, including influential state heavyweights like Ohio and New York, electing state legislatures—which in turn appointed United States Senators—plus myriad ballot initiatives, governorships, and mayoral seats on the line, the distraction was another stroke of genius by the Panamaniacs. The public demonization of the Colombians was another.

At first Roosevelt had refused to officially comment on the Colombian refusal to ratify the Panama Canal Treaty, but in the Rooseveltian off-the record fashion, he established when he invited his favorite reporters to attend him at his morning shave, the country understood that Roosevelt regarded the matter differently. While he feigned indignation to reporters, he knew all along that the series of diplomatic events orchestrated by William Nelson Cromwell could come to no other conclusion. The administration wanted to create the impression that Colombia had reneged on an agreement—broken a vow to America—when in actuality the Colombians had never agreed with the United States proposal in the first place. Publicly, he called the Colombians bandits. Roosevelt denounced the government in Bogota and some pundits prognosticated trouble for the frail South American republic.

Others took it in stride. The President, according to the Roosevelt-friendly and Republican leaning *San Francisco Call,* had "no authority to use what appears to be coercive or threatening or dilatory measures to complete the negotiations for the Panama route."[6] Indeed, the intention of the Spooner Act was not to allow "this Government to express to Colombia any desire that the Colombian Senate's action be reconsidered," but that Roosevelt should "wait the necessary time for the Colombian Congress to adjourn finally without ratifying the treaty before actually beginning negotiations with Nicaragua and Costa Rica."[7] Some saw the rejection of the United States proposal not as banditry, but as confirmation of the superiority of the Nicaragua canal location:

> If President Roosevelt is as free from the influence of the transcontinental railroads as his admirers would have us believe, he will . . . at once [enter] into negotiations with Nicaragua and Costa Rica to secure a right of way for an interoceanic canal across their territory. It is now plain that Senator Morgan of Alabama was right in his insistence upon the Nicaraguan route and that the obstructive tactics he pursued in order to defeat the Panama bill were actuated by the highest patriotic motives.[8]

Yet, more balanced voices frequently spoke about the legitimate rationale of Colombia for rejecting the treaty terms. All the while, a sustained public discussion echoed about the Nicaraguan option that ran through the press. The Colombian legislature was, of course, in no way required to ratify a treaty that its lawmakers believed to be harmful to their country any more than the United States Senate was obligated to ratify a pact because the treating party wished them to do so. Roosevelt was now obligated under the Spooner Bill to "turn to Nicaragua and apply the appropriation carried in the bill to that route" and not send troops to Panama to impose his personal and political agendas.[9] Instead, Roosevelt readied his battleships. By October 15th, orders were issued to begin the positioning of warships within range of Panama by the November 3rd target date. "It is positively stated that these [Naval] movements on the part of our Navy are in no way connected with a canal project," reported a November 3rd story buried on page six in the *Washington Evening*

190

Star.[10] The official rationale for sending all the firepower of the Pacific and Caribbean Squadrons to Panama was to uphold the provision of the 1846 Treaty with Colombia calling for the United States' military help to ensure the open transit across the isthmus on the Panama Railway in case of civil disturbance.[11]

By the end of October, the press was taking notice of the Navy's preparation for training exercises within range of Panama. Headlines reported rumors that Panama "Is Ready for a Revolt" and "President Roosevelt was moving energetically to meet it."[12] The account of how this was accomplished by Roosevelt's ordering of Acting Secretary of the Navy Charles Darling to dispatch warships to "maintain an open transit," was vividly covered by an enthusiastic American press corps.[13] But of course, that was subterfuge.

Since the news of the uprising had to compete with headlines of the important United States elections, just as master publicity manipulator William Nelson Cromwell had planned, the big questions regarding the role the United States played in defeating the political goals of an ally were delayed, truncated, ignored. "Panama Revolution: Revolt Started in Isthmian Canal Interests" was tombstoned on the Walla Walla *Evening Statesman* with "Tammany's Clean Sweep: McClellan's Big Victory." The *St. Paul Globe* ran "Panama Declares its Independence" headline half the point size of the "Democrats Win in New York" splayed across the entire width of the front page. "Panama Declares its Independence" was below the fold of the *Bismarck Daily Tribune* where "Election Results" dominated above. "Tammany Wins Great Victory" separated "Revolution on Isthmus Spreads" from "Democratic Successor to McComas Assured in Maryland" on the front page of the *Washington Times*.

The reports on Panama, as expected given the vigor of the Cromwell publicity machine and Roosevelt's "untiring press-bureau," capitalized on United States military prowess and its moral obligation to protect American interests from the insufferable vagaries of unruly South American politics.[14] It took days before the public and Congressional attention could focus on the remarkable events in Panama. During the action against Colombia, over 1,000 of its soldiers, more than enough to contain the rebellion, were prevented from landing in the mutinous province of Panama by American gunboats on both coasts, or at least that was the plan. Ironically, as it happened, Roosevelt's pride and the quintessence of American political power and martial prowess, the United States Navy, very nearly missed the revolution.

Pinching Panama

By the close of the three month long Spanish-American War in August of 1898, the United States claimed the fifth most powerful navy in the world. By the time Roosevelt sent warships to Colombia's small province of Panama in 1903, it was ranked third. The growth of American sea power was thanks in large part to the jingoism of Theodore Roosevelt, Senator Henry Cabot Lodge, Secretary of State John Hay, maritime mastermind Captain Alfred Thayer Mahan, and—perhaps more potent than all these powerbrokers combined— the collective hypermasculine impulse of American imperialism powered by the romanticism of American exceptionalism. Roosevelt, and his likeminded professional politicians and opinion leaders, grew and enhanced the martial and technical capabilities of the Navy so that by 1903 Roosevelt had full faith that the naval operation at Panama would conjure what has become to be known as shock and awe. Yet ironically—even though his strategy was successful in the end—the operation was more than a bit haphazard.

Roosevelt's ardor for enhancing the Navy was well known and even better played in the press by the President. Five days after Colombia rejected the Panama Treaty with the United States, Roosevelt grabbed headlines by reviewing a "magnificent and impressive naval spectacle" on Long Island Sound. "For the first time in the history of the country," reported the *Daily Pioneer*, "the President of the United Sates, reviewed and inspected, in peace time, a great fleet of United States warships."[15] Toward the end of the display, the *Barry*, running at twenty knots in formation with four other destroyers, swung wide on a turn and rammed the starboard side of the *Decatur* at the very moment Roosevelt was receiving congratulations for the success of the maneuvers. The collision was tremendous; the *Decatur* listed sharply to port and appeared to be sinking before the startled eyes of Roosevelt, Admiral Dewey, and the other social, political, and maritime dignitaries. Within moments, the *Decatur* righted itself and the ceremony continued yet the awkward, uncoordinated performance of the *Barry* was a harbinger of the execution of the Panama operation. Roosevelt had at his disposal one of the three the most modern, efficient, technologically upgraded, killing fleets ever afloat. He took it for granted that when he ordered more than nine warships from his great American fleet to pounce upon an easy prey like the backward and weak Colombia, the operation would go like clockwork. Yet only one gunboat, the *USS Nashville*, made it to Panama on time and even then, the effect of its arrival miscarried. Naval communications, also among the best systems in the modern nautical world, stuttered and failed. If the Americans had been sent to engage the Germans or any other first rate navy and not the Colombians, they undoubtedly would have been routed.

The naval command had been under orders to proceed to Panama since October 15th. The Pacific Squadron under Rear Admiral Henry Glass commanding the cruisers *New York, Boston, Marblehead* and the gunboats *Ranger* and *Concord* received orders to conduct naval exercises beginning the 22nd near Acapulco, Mexico with a view to being within hours of Panama by November 3. Four days later on the 19th of October, Glass was ordered to send the *Boston* toward San Juan del Sur, Nicaragua, with a goal of arriving no later than November 1, and keep the remainder of the fleet "ready to proceed to the Isthmus."[16] In the Atlantic, orders came on October 24 for the cruiser *Dixie* to embark a battalion of Marines at Philadelphia and set sail for Guantanamo, Cuba. In the next few days, the cruiser *Atlanta* also received orders to sail to Cuba and the gunboat *Nashville* received orders to proceed to Kingston, Jamaica, where it would be only thirty hours from Colon, Panama. The *USS Nashville, Dixie, Prairie, Marblehead, Concord, Baltimore,* and *Boston* were positioning themselves for an intervention with the Colombians at Panama where they would face United States ally Colombia's two small and dilapidated ships the *Bogota* and *Cartagena*.

As the United States ships set sail for Colon and the city of Panama, orders not to allow Colombian troops to land were issued, but the *Boston* and the *Dixie* were hamstrung by mechanical and

193

fueling difficulties preventing them from reaching Colon. Rear Admiral Glass' entire fleet suffered crippling delays for the same reason—dodgy equipment and a lack of coal. The *Nashville* did not receive the orders until the day after they reached Panama. Before the commander of the *Nashville*, John Hubbard, received the communiqué, 400 Colombian troops from *Cartagena* had already landed at Colon. Hubbard, who arrived the evening before on November 2 and saw the troops disembark, having an understanding the provision of the treaty, saw no reason to interfere with the Colombians at that time.

Blue Jackets on the Isthmus

The following day, Tuesday, November 3rd, Hubbard received his belated orders and he raced his Marines to shore. He and his forty-two Marine "blue-jackets" set about minimizing the effect of the Colombian troop presence by making sure the Panama Railroad would not transport them across the isthmus. After conferring with the Panama Railroad superintendent, Hubbard cabled his commanding officer:

> Receipt of your telegram of November 2 is acknowledged. Prior to receipt this morning, about 400 men were landed here by the Government of Colombia from *Cartagena*. No revolution has been declared on the Isthmus and no disturbances. Railway company have declined to transport these troops except by request of the Governor of Panama. Request has not been made. It is possible that movement may be made to-night at Panama to declare independence, in which event I will * * * (message mutilated here) here. Situation is most critical if revolutionary leaders act.[17]

How the cable was mutilated is still as mysterious as the missing words in Hubbard's message. At the same time, Hubbard was assuring his command that the situation was calm, Assistant Secretary of State Loomis was ratcheting up martial enthusiasm, sending a cable to the

United States Consuls-General at Panama and Colon, "Uprising on Isthmus reported. Keep Department promptly and fully informed."[18]

On Wednesday November 4th, Hubbard informed his superiors at the Navy Department that he had "landed force to protect the lives and property of American citizens here against threats [by] Colombian soldiery."[19] Concerns from press reports that were much more lurid than the actual events warranted caused Hubbard to reassure the Navy that Americans in the port city of Panama were safe.[20] The "reported bombardment" of Panama, cabled Hubbard, "is much exaggerated." Fears that United States citizens and their property were at risk from the Colombians were unwarranted, assured Hubbard, as the British man-of-war *Amphion* was capably protecting American interests at Panama while the *Nashville* was at Colon. By then, the battalion of blue jackets commanded by Captain John A. Lejune aboard the tardy *Dixie* reinforced Hubbard's small, but determined detachment of Marines. On the following morning, Hubbard reported that he withdrew his Marines declaring, "No bloodshed. I do not apprehend difficulty of any serious nature."[21]

By Friday, November 6th, pacification of Panama was ensured prompting the Navy Department cable to Washington, "All quiet. Independents declare Government established as Republic of Panama . . . Independent party in possession of Colon, Panama, and railroad line. *Nashville* withdrew force."[22] The Colombian soldiers stationed at Colon and Panama had been bribed by money supplied to the separatists by William Cromwell and Philippe Bunau-Varilla. The *Boston* and *Dixie* eventually arrived and intimidated the *Cartagena* and its soldiers to head back to Bogota, and a small group of Panama Railroad employees and members of the Panama municipal council declared the isthmus independent.

Legitimizing a Revolution

Twenty-six hours and fifty-five minutes later, Roosevelt recognized Panama as a new nation. On November 18th the Hay-Bunau-Varilla Canal Treaty was signed. Colombia's $10,000,000 went to the Panamaniacs, and the $40,000,000 paid by the United States for the New Panama Canal Company's property was delivered through J.P. Morgan and Company to Cromwell, Bunau-Varilla, and holders of the French Company's stock—among whom were Roosevelt's brother-in-law, Douglas Robinson, and William Taft's brother. All this came to pass before Panama had anything that bordered on a constitution, before it held an election or preformed any of the customary undertakings of a sovereign nation. Secretary of State Hay signed the final treaty with Bunau-Varilla who was, as a payment for his assistance to the revolutionists, appointed the First Minister Plenipotentiary and Envoy Extraordinary "with full power to conduct diplomatic and financial negotiations" for the infant nation.

Bunau-Varilla, who had not visited Panama for seventeen years before the episode nor indeed after his appointment as envoy, never again set foot on the Isthmus. Through his purchase of the diplomatic post, the little French engineer was instantly elevated to a position in society that his birthright could never provide. Ever in search of the limelight, Bunau-Varilla took credit for Roosevelt sending the United States Navy to keep the Colombians at bay, thus, securing Panama's independence. He later wrote that, "The revolution was made because the connection between the request of a boat to me and the arrival of the boat materialised [sic] in the eyes of the confederates the reality of the influence which Amador had asserted to them I possessed over the American Government."[23] Nothing and no one stood in the way of the new interoceanic canal treaty with the new country of Panama, brokered by its new ambassador, Philippe Bunau-Varilla, a citizen of France.

Pax Rooseveltiana

Once attention was no longer diverted by the elections, Americans began to react to the extraordinary news about Panama and the United States' role in its insurrection. Reaction was mixed to say the least. The narrative that Roosevelt had no choice, but to act "in the interest of collective civilization" played well in some quarters, but in others, people were offended that America acted as Civilization's thug, snatching a weaker nation's property. The *Milwaukee Daily News* did not buy Roosevelt's December 4th justification, writing:

VOL. LIV. No. 1395.   PUCK BUILDING, New York, November 25, 1903.   PRICE TEN CENTS.
Copyright, 1903, by Keppler & Schwarzmann.

"What Fools these Mortals be!"

Puck

Entered at N.Y.P.O. as Second-class Mail Matter.

A REVELATION IN REVOLUTIONS.

UNCLE SAM—"Well! Well! You boys have at last had a revolution which will help the whole world."

Uncle Sam, holding a huge roll of "Canal Plans" under his arms bends down and congratulates a tiny smiling, puffed-up Panama. Uncle Sam pats Panama on the back saying, "Well! Well! You boys have finally had a revolution which will benefit the whole world." A U.S. gunboat in anchored in the background. Puck, 25 November 1903.

197

The President's justification in its last analysis is that the ends justified the means. True, he undertakes to establish that the means employed were proper and that there has been no infringement of Colombia's rights by the United States, but in this he is not convincing. He resorts to the "manifest destiny" plea—that the revolution and its resulting advantage to the United States was the work of Divine Providence rather than the fruit of chicanery, intrigue and greed. In this, he has followed well-established precedent. No modern world Power ever grabs territory or preys upon the weak and defenseless. When it becomes necessary for it to despoil the weak, it does so in the interests of civilization and humanity as an instrument of a Higher Power.[24]

It was obvious to many—Senator John Tyler Morgan among them—that without the United States' muscle, Colombia would have maintained control of its wayward province. "I am compelled to say," said Morgan wryly, "that to-morrow if the United States Government should withdraw its fleet and marines from the Isthmus or confine their operations to the protection of their railroad and to the passage across the isthmus, Colombia would march in and capture the eight men who organized the Panama government."[25] Panama, according to many other observers, such as the intellectual former governor of South Carolina, Daniel Henry Chamberlain, "was the northern province or State of the Republic of Colombia, and an integral part thereof, standing in substantially the same political relations to the republic as do the several States of our Union to our republic. [It] was as much a part of the territory of the Republic of Colombia as the territory of Massachusetts or South Carolina is of our republic."[26] To interfere with Colombia exercising its authority over a rebellious state would be tantamount to declaring that Lincoln had no right to stop the Confederate States from seceding, claimed Roosevelt critics.

While there were undoubtedly many Americans who would have made that claim, a majority saw Lincoln's action of preserving the

Union as both reasonable and righteous. The message of disregarding the treaty's obligations to preserve Colombian sovereignty, Roosevelt and his Panamaniac advisors proclaimed that American interests not only trumped the provisions of the accord, but violated the very essence of "fair play" that many Americans held up as a defining value of their national character. Secretary John Hay declared that the protests were nonsense, that the United States was "simply pursuing its time honored course in executing its obligations under the treaty of 1846," as well as preventing bloodshed.[27] It was for those reasons and those reasons alone that the United States had dispatched "an adequate naval force" to ward off the Colombians from their sovereign territory.[28]

When Roosevelt and Hay claimed they acted on the behalf of the progress of civilized nations, the press and many individuals challenged the notion that "progress" demanded violating international norms or that "collective civilization" had anything to do with the events in Panama. "The President has invented his obligation [to civilization]," cried *The Nation*, "and gives the world to understand that his hasty and unwarranted action in affronting a friendly nation, and entangling us with a band of conspirators, is only his way of establishing a *Pax Rooseveltiana*."[29] The *Philadelphia Public Ledger* wrote that the phrase, "in the interest of civilization" was the common justification of "land-grabbing" governments from time immemorial.

Later, in an open letter to John Hay published in the *New York Times*, an outraged Chamberlain confronted the assertion that progress was being held hostage by Colombian brigands or that there existed such a character as "collective civilization" on whose behalf Roosevelt claimed to have acted. "I wish I could get from you a definition or description of 'collective civilization.' Who is he?" Chamberlain demanded of the Secretary of State: "Where may he be seen or known? Where and when has he spoken in this Panama affair? Has he confided his 'interests' or views to you? Do you hold a brief for him, or are you his designated mouthpiece? These queries puzzle me."[30] Chamberlain continued to pursue the rhetorical justification made by Roosevelt and his supporters to its logical conclusion:

Do the files or archives of your department hold any document which is the expression of the wish or will of the nations collectively? You are in fact trying to beguile the people by an empty form of sounding words, nothing more. The world at large has never shown any but a very vague and languid interest in an Isthmian Canal . . . 'Collective civilization' you may think a fine phrase in which to disguise a despicable job; but, if it serves even that office it will on the principle strictly of *ignotum pro magnifico*. I can hardly pardon myself for dwelling even so long on an idea so tenuous.[31]

Despite the fact that numerous Americans were aghast at Roosevelt's "indecent haste" in recognizing Panama, scores of others supported the President's view that "civilization" demanded action.

Some are pouring out the vial of wrath on the President for what they call his indecent haste in recognizing the new State of Panama. For my part, I am very glad that we have a man at the head of our nation that can see through and embrace the opportunity. For the life of me, I can't see why the wheels of progress should be blocked by a few grasping politicians at Bogota. The President gave them a dose of their own medicine and by the way they act, it seems hard to take.[32]

At first Congressional Democrats seemed as furious as Chamberlain grew to be, but seemed to be "in the dark" about whether to make Panama an "issue" or endorse the President's moves, according to an article in the *Minneapolis Journal*.[33] "Early last week the democrats were delighted with the prospect," the writer reflected, and was pleased that "the administration had given them ready-made that which they so earnestly seek, an issue on which to go before the people."[34] But, only eight days after the Panama succession they were in doubt. Democrats were nervously discussing the uncertainty of whether it was good party policy to condemn the administration for having "advanced American interests."[35] Since

Democratic opinion in both the House and the Senate had "not as yet shaped up, so that it is possible to foretell what is to be done," the writer predicted:

> The probabilities are that after another day or two of reflection, the leaders will advise the "rank and file" that, after all, it is not a good issue and that nothing is to be made by thundering against the administration concerning it. This does not mean that no democrat will criticize the president.[36]

Nevertheless, all that most Democratic politicians wanted was an interoceanic canal no matter what. Republicans balked, too, at first because they worried about the reaction of the Great Powers, but their concern very quickly gave way to the recognition of its value as Panama, a domestic diversion. The Republican Party was "growing sick of the Philippine business" and it was growing "wearied with its costs, its profitlessness, and the waste of men involved "in the project and would prefer if the public focused on another issue.[37] Roosevelt's victory in Panama offered an instant, clear and decisive, military, and policy success for their Party. Soon enough, both sides came around to supporting the President's lightening fast, unorthodox move. The *de facto* acknowledgment of Panama's legitimacy came on November 6th; November 13th the United States formally recognized Panama; and on November 18th, the convention on the treaty for constructing a canal across the isthmus was concluded. No Panamanian signed the treaty. Before Thanksgiving was celebrated on the 25th, the new Republican majority ousted old Senator Morgan as Chair of the Senate Canal Committee and Marcus Hanna took his place. Miraculously, all committee hearings into improper business dealing between William Nelson Cromwell, the New Panama Canal Company, and the administration abruptly came to a halt.

Colombian and European Reaction

For their part, Colombia was at once appalled, angry, perplexed, and indignant. The little country knew they could not fight the United States with its military and first appealed to Roosevelt "to extend the hand of Justice."[38] Apparently, thought some Colombians, the President was hoodwinked, or misinformed, or simply did not understand the situation. Colombian General Rafael Reyes sailed to Washington with a "peace commission" to have an audience with the President. The General had no doubt that once he told the President that they "simply wanted the United States to keep their hands off," as said Reyes to reporters covering the event, Roosevelt would retract his support for the rebellious territory.[39] "The fight is ours, between patriotic Colombians and unpatriotic Colombians, and if we are permitted to exercise our rights, we will crush the Insurrection, take back our rightful property," said the Colombian envoy of peace.[40] "The Panama canal," stated Reyes, "is as much ours as the harbor of New York is that of the United States."[41] Failing to convince the United States government as he did, General Reyes advanced the idea that the world tribunals at The Hague should settle the issue, a proposition that Roosevelt flatly rejected. [42] Why bother going through the process of arbitration, the Administration responded; the question was settled. The Great Powers had already recognized "Uncle Sam's foundling" and nothing would be gained at The Hague.[43]

When the blockading of Panama to prevent Colombia from guarding its territory from the seditious act of "eight men" first happened, the rest of the world, undistracted by United States' election results, immediately weighed-in on Roosevelt's actions. Of the Big Powers, the German laudatory response of the Roosevelt's bellicosity was noteworthy. The newspaper *Frankfurt Zeitung* unreservedly endorsed Roosevelt's hyper-masculine, Wild West-style muscle-flexing. "A mighty state will not permit itself," declared the paper, "to be thwarted in its civilizing work through the stubbornness of a land three-quarters barbarous."[44] France took a "wait and see" attitude, while some in Great Britain wondered if they should not take a hand in the matter because of Panama's proximity to their territorial interests in the West Indies. However, some foreign diplomats on assignment in Washington were flabbergasted by Roosevelt's interpretation of the treaty provisions and relayed their astonishment to the press.

"I do not want to appear to criticize the United States government for American naval commanders to refuse to allow the Colombian government to put down an insurrection in Colombian territory," one unnamed diplomat remarked. "The refusal of the United States to allow the Colombian troops to attempt to retake Panama . . . would be to aid and abet in a revolution," a move to which European powers must strenuously object. Closer to home, the *Toronto Weekly Sun* seemed resigned that America's actions were lamentably common among great nations:

> Even if the conduct of the American government has been as bad as appears, other governments are not qualified to cast the first stone. Russia wants Finland . . . while a British writer of eminence justifies her action on the principle that force makes law. Great Britain wants the Transvaal that she may paint South Africa red; and she takes it, solemn pledges notwithstanding. We are apparently drifting into a renewal of the age of Machiavelli, when in politics expediency, or what to rapacity seemed expediency, made right."[45]

Panama's acceptance by the republics of the world was a *fait accompli* by Christmas. As Chamberlain described the birthing process of the nation of Panama, "He [Roosevelt] adopted the child before it was born, midwifed its birth, and became sponsor for it during its puling infancy," and Germany, France, and Great Britain were persuaded without much difficulty to recognize the legitimacy of the birth.[46] By January of 1904, Roosevelt expressed his unswerving conviction that the domination of the great English speaking powers over the underdeveloped nations in general and of the United States supremacy over Latin America in particular, portended good fortune for all concerned, especially the subjugated people. Roosevelt saw himself and his actions as blameless in the situation, and just as Wild West cowboys who "if justified in their own minds, would shoot a man instantly, and regret the necessity, but not the shooting, afterwards," expanded the Monroe Doctrine to include America's neighbors.[47] He wrote to his close British friend, Cecil Spring Rice:

It was a good thing for Egypt and the Sudan, and for the world, when England took Egypt and the Sudan. It is a good thing for India that England should control it. And so it is a good thing, a very good thing, for Cuba and for Panama and for the world that the United States has actually done during the last six years. The people of the United States and the people of the Isthmus will be better because we dig the Panama Canal and keep order in the neighborhood.[48]

Roosevelt maintained a constant emphasis before the public on developing the one weapon lethal enough to enforce the Monroe Doctrine by intimidation, the Navy. His likeminded friends and allies also stressed the danger of breeches in the Doctrine at every opportunity. Roosevelt's new Secretary of War, William Taft, generated support for the continued and aggressive armed intervention in Latin America beyond Panama, calling this time not only for a larger Navy, but also for an enhanced Army for good measure. Taft—whose brother Charles' interest in the Cromwellian American Panama Canal Company before the purchase of the Zone would cause an unwelcome public conversation for him later—acted as Roosevelt's special agent to square American interests to those of the interests of the new Panama republic. Upon his return from Panama, Taft's public addresses were peppered with the language calling for an assertive American fighting force to police the neighborhood of the Western Hemisphere.

VI ET ARMIS THEORY OF GOVERNMENT: THE ROOSEVELT COROLLARY, 1904

President Theodore Roosevelt submitted his annual message to the Congress of the United States on December 6, 1904. In this message, Roosevelt wrote at length about a great many national problems, from railroad regulation, to Indian agents, to the National Gallery of Art, to conservation of natural resources. When it came to foreign policy, however, one short paragraph of the three paragraphs

Mayol in *Caras y Caretas*, Buenos Ayres.

THE YANKEE PERIL AS ONE ARGENTINE JOURNAL SEES IT.

Of South America he speaks in a frank, sincere style, expressing himself in this way: " Here no one dares lay a hand but myself."

Raymond Gros, TR in Cartoons, 1910.

205

devoted to foreign policy articulated a principle that became known as the Roosevelt Corollary to the Monroe Doctrine. Roosevelt's declaration solidified a foreign policy that ensured American dominance over Latin America by requiring an enhanced Navy to enforce the policy. Through rhetoric that appealed to the American sense of self as the rugged, take charge, go-it-alone cowboy of the Wild West, Roosevelt began winning the battle for the hearts and minds of most citizens regarding his actions in Panama. Still, a few politicians were unrepentantly opposed to Panama.

On the front pages of newspapers across the country, a Senator from Texas, Charles Culberson, accused the President of open defiance of the Spooner Law and of "Boldly Proclaiming the Kingly Dogma of International Eminent Domain."[49] The headline on the *St. Louis Republic* blared, "Panama Incident Most Disgraceful Episode In All Annals Of America."[50] Culberson declared that the claim that the Marines were landed merely to protect the railroad was utterly false and the intent all along was to steal from "Colombia the sovereignty and property of the territory which we obligated ourselves to defend."[51] Senator John Tyler Morgan was so aggrieved by the trajectory of the acquiring of the Panama property that he introduced a bill that the whole territory be annexed into the United States. Since "the President of the United States approved and protected the secession with the naval forces of the United States and that the President and the Senate recognized the independence of, the new republic by appointing a minister to that republic," it only made sense, confirmed Morgan, that "all the rights and portions of the republic of every description shall vest in [the] United States of America without reserve."[52]

This fractious start of the project could have been—and indeed was by many observers—predictable. There was no magic in the mere possession of the property that cleared the "unholy ground" of mudslides and the miasma that Richard Harding had noticed when he first arrived in Panama in 1898 and even less reason to believe Democrats would docilely accept Roosevelt's hijacking Congressional power. Many vociferously declared that what Roosevelt did by assisting Panama to revolt was an act of war against Colombia and that "the President of the United States has no right to

206

make war upon a foreign power that being solely within the province of Congress."[53] In addition to usurping Congressional power, President Roosevelt, according to his Democratic detractors, could not legally refuse to execute a law now on the statutes, the Spooner Act, to build the Nicaragua Canal.[54] Senator Author P. Gorman of Maryland announced that he was "considering the advisability of the impeachment of President Roosevelt," if he failed to negotiate with Nicaragua as required by the Spooner Bill.[55]

How the successful promotion of the Canal was managed through the outrage and obvious distortions of Constitutional authority was a mystery to some, but clear to others. As Edward Garstin Smith opined in his 1908 reflection of the process:

> The Senate was jollied, the House was coerced, the Department of Justice was blindfolded, the press was muzzled, the critics were frightened, the people were hoodwinked, a big noise was made about the commercial importance of the Panama Canal, hundreds of millions more of money appropriated out of the treasury for building a canal at Panama, great digging was done into the Treasury of the United States and clouds of dust were thrown into the public eye.[56]

The powerful Roosevelt publicity machine in tandem with William Nelson Cromwell's army of newspaper reporters in his employ, shifted public opinion and—without too much reporting of the Democratic gnashing of teeth. The process of co-opting reporters was straightforward and effective as Roosevelt critic, Annie Riley Hale, wrote. With her usual fearlessness, Riley listed names and positions of the compromised journalists:

> President Roosevelt has put into the public service more newspaper men and other writers than can be easily enumerated, but the following partial list will convey a general idea of this phase of Rooseveltian activity: Whitelaw Reid, ambassador to England; Robt. J. Wynne, correspondent . . . and president

of a Dining Club in Washington, composed almost exclusively of newspaper men, was successively advanced to the post of Assistant-Postmaster-General, then to the head of the Department, and finally to be Consul-General to London, the best paying post in the consular service. Of the three D.C. Commissioners who govern Washington under the direction of Congress and the President, two were active newspaper men when appointed by Roosevelt. Maj. John M. Carson, of the *New York Times,* was made chief of the Bureau of Manufactures; Francis E. Leupp . . . was made Indian Commissioner; George Horton, appointed Consul-General at Athens; Albert Halstead, Consul at Birmingham, England; J. Martin Miller is Consul somewhere in Europe; and Jos. Rucklin Bishop was . . . made the Secretary of the Panama Canal Commission, at a salary of $10,000 a year. It has passed into a proverb in Washington: "Write a biography of Roosevelt, and pull out a consulship."[57]

THE HUNTER HUNTED
From the *Herald* (Baltimore)

From behind a tree Senator Gorman fires a shotgun blast of "criticism of the Panama affair" nearly hitting an angry Roosevelt. Reprinted in Albert Shaw's A Cartoon History of Roosevelt's Career, 1910.

Yet, a few journalists had the nerve and the prescience to confront the issue head-on. In an opinion piece titled the "Panama Filibuster," the editors of *The Public* answered a series of provocative questions raised by Roosevelt's seizure of Panama:

> Why did President Roosevelt forbid the landing of Colombian troops for the purpose of suppressing the revolt? Why did President Roosevelt recognize Panama as a new nation before Colombia had had any opportunity to act, when President McKinley had declared with reference to Cuba, in his message of April 11, 1898, that "recognition of independent statehood is not due to a revolted dependency until the danger of its being subjugated by the parent state has entirely passed away." Above all, why did President Roosevelt threaten the Colombian government with some mysterious and dire disaster as early as July?[58]

The writers provide several provocative possibilities: positioning for his 1904 Presidential campaign, and the Americans who owned the French Panama Canal stock.

> Is it because $10,000,000 is to be given to the influential gentlemen on Wall Street who own most of the stock of the French company, provided the canal goes through Panama, and that there is no such "watermelon" to be cut in connection with the Nicaragua route . . . That is hardly probable . . . Is it, then, because the continental railroad ring prefers the Panama route as the best way of killing off the canal project? . . . Perhaps President Roosevelt, eager as a schoolboy in circus time for nomination and election to the office he now holds only by accident . . .

Panama opponents were rolled over by the brute force of the Rooseveltian publicity machine. A young journalist during this time, Earl Harding, later stated, "Many editors came to feel that the Panama Canal had become sacrosanct and that the public could not differentiate between exposure and condemnation of the lawless acquiring of the Canal Zone and attacks on the Canal enterprise itself." Harding added in a saddened tone, "Intelligent discussion and honest criticism of the Panama affair was so unpopular as to be almost entirely suppressed."[59] With this level of access and influence in the press, Roosevelt had no trouble influencing public opinion and, therefore, Congress; the Panama Canal Treaty designed by Cromwell and presented to Hay and Bunau-Varilla was signed and the Americans took possession of the canal works in May of 1904. The building commenced at once.

AMERICAN PANAMA CANAL

The same types of disease, mishaps, and mismanagement as the de Lesseps project experienced plagued the American undertaking. Roosevelt was having very little luck in finding the right Chief Engineer for the herculean project. His first appointment to head the project, John Wallace, resigned in June of 1905 and the work languished. The administration painted Wallace as a quitter who left his post for a higher paying job. However, later the brilliant, but beleaguered Wallace said he had resigned because he no longer wanted to be a "tool" in the hands of William Nelson Cromwell.[60] He said that the President and Secretary of War, Howard Taft, had both been possessed by some "strange confidence" in Cromwell that mystified Wallace and that he could not properly do his job because "Cromwell's word was law in all matters pertaining to the canal."[61] By 1905, finding men willing to work on the deadly ditch was turning into a publicity nightmare for Roosevelt. Yellow-jack was either killing workers in droves or the fear of the gruesome disease was causing the remaining able bodied to abandon the project and flee to healthier climes. The number of laborers willing to sign on to replace the dead and escaping healthy workers dwindled precipitously. Overcrowded ships of workers returning to America were packed with panicky people dodging the fever and disease. They spread stories of death and despair. It was beginning to look like the United States would fall prey to the curse of Panama.

By 1906, three Roosevelt appointed governors of the Zone had come and gone. The pubic was looking for someone or something to blame for the trouble with the project that was to define America's place as first among nations. Senator John Tyler Morgan was ready to give them a villain: William Nelson Cromwell. Ailing and old, Morgan, still a member of the Committee on Interoceanic Canals, refocused his energies on "sinister aspects of Mr. Cromwell's connection" with the Panama business.[62] Morgan's confrontational engagement with the antagonistic Cromwell managed to keep his inquiry into the Panama purchase alive and on the front page.

THE FIRST MOUNTAIN TO BE REMOVED

Harper's Weekly, Vol. 49, 15 July 1905.

Cromwell stonewalled, making the news coverage of the event all the more focused on splashy headlines about Panama. People began to wonder why the Silver Fox was so contrary, perverse, and disrespectful to the venerable Senator from Alabama. When news

*Roosevelt stands in front of three men he has decapitated with a sword. The bodies have name tags identifying them as the two chairmen who resigned from the Isthmusian Canal Commission which governed the American Canal Zone Panama Canal—John Findley Walker and Theodore Shonts—and it chief engineer John Frank Stevens who also resigned, leaving the project "headless" as it were. "The Calebra Cut," **The Philadelphia Record** , reprinted in Raymond Gros' **T.R. in Cartoon**. New York: Saalfield Pub. Co, 1910.*

coverage of his stonewalling began to indict him in the minds of the public, Cromwell left the country for Europe, just as he had when he wanted to dodge being involved in the Panama rebellion and Bunau-Varilla took over in managing Amador and his insurrectionist project.

Roosevelt's actions were reviewed in the hearings, but he was not looked upon as a villain in this drama. Still, more and more, the Commander-in-Chief simply looked impotent against the power that was Panama. However, Roosevelt was determined not to let the "crowning achievement" of his presidency go the way of the French. Roosevelt had always understood the power of the visual— for example, loading the Vitagraph moving-picture crew aboard the dangerously overcrowded troop transport to Cuba in order to capture footage of him at his most heroic in 1898 or the staged photos of him capturing boat thieves in the Dakota badlands in 1886.[63] He knew what he had to do to change the direction of the conversation. Through a highly publicized maneuver, unlike his mugging of Colombia where he attempted surreptitious deployments of the United States Navy to Panama in the guise of training exercises, Roosevelt managed the situation through photo opportunities that would herald his domination over the situation. The master of public relations ploys, Roosevelt astounded Americans by announcing that he would go to Panama to "see how the ditch is getting along" with his own eyes.[64]

Not only would it be the first time a sitting President visited a foreign country, Roosevelt announced that his wife, Edith, would accompany him, telegraphing the message that if the Canal Zone was safe enough for Mrs. Roosevelt, it was safe enough for workers. Hundreds of people saw the First Couple away aboard the *Mayflower*. Trumpets, roses, the "Star Spangled Banner," cheering throngs of well-wishers attended their departure as the *Mayflower's* mascot, Buster the bulldog—who was dressed in his official uniform which was a blanket made of a sailor's jeans with his name embroidered in gold thread—frolicked with Roosevelt to the delight of photographers and reporters.[65] The stunt was astoundingly successful. They sailed to the mouth of the Potomac and rendezvoused with the battleship *Louisiana* that would carry Roosevelt and his entourage to Panama. Hundreds of photos captured images of Roosevelt as he merrily trudged through the mud and mayhem of the big ditch and posed in the cockpit on one of the enormous earth moving diggers. The ploy was an enormous success. Public opinion was once again realigned with Roosevelt's version of the reality on the ground and support swelled for the project. In June of 1907, while still in office, the formidable old Confederate General from Alabama, Senator Morgan, died. Buried with him was his obsession to uncover the corrupt associations that converged in 1903 to derail his beloved Nicaragua Canal project. Without Morgan to keep the fires burning, the interest in the seemingly scandalous method to gain the title of the property cooled.

Roosevelt at the controls of a giant canal digger, Library of Congress, 1906.

The work on the project slowly ontinued. Then, the momentum changed in 1907 when Roosevelt appointed the indisputably competent organizational genius Colonel George Washington Goethals as Governor of the Zone. The implementation of Dr. William Gorgas' far reaching sanitary programs improved health conditions dramatically, and the American public began to see the Panama Canal as a project that conferred glory on the nation. Then, in October of 1908 to the surprise of most everyone in America—and to the fury of Theodore Roosevelt—editors at Joseph Pulitzer's *New York World* broke the story of the backroom dealings of William Nelson Cromwell in the Panama Canal purchase, clearly placing Theodore Roosevelt, his brother-in-law Douglas Robinson, and Presidential nominee William Howard Taft's brother, in the frame. Little by little, the story oozed out daily until on October 4, it burst wide open, flooding the headlines of newspapers across the nation. The *World* shook America by demanding an answer to the simple question that, until now, everyone assumed that they knew. The simple question that would eventually lead to a landmark hearing in the United States Supreme Court and discredit Roosevelt was, "Who got the money?"

THE PANAMA ROSETTA STONE,

"The Panama Rosetta Stone" shows William Nelson Cromwell leading a young Panama down a path followed by Colombia being restrained by the U.S. Army and Navy. Behind them is Philippe Bunau-Varilla with Wall Street investors carrying bags of money. Watching over the action from a god-like celestial position is the face of Theodore Roosevelt. Edward Gastin Smith, The Real Roosevelt, 1909.

CHAPTER SEVEN

The Curiously Ingenious Mind of Theodore Roosevelt: 1908-1912

Roosevelt counts with certainty on the hero instinct of mankind. He knows it is easier to stampede a herd than it is to reason with one buffalo. It is easier to control one hundred million people than it is to govern one million intelligent people. Roosevelt has a contempt for individuality, except his own.—Edward Gastin Smith, 1909

The real offense of The World is that for years it has been an uncompromising leader of the opposition against Mr. Roosevelt's jingoism, militarism, lawlessness, violence, centralization and cowboy government.—The Evening statesman, January 28, 1909

It was through a monumental miscalculation on the part of William Nelson Cromwell—the meticulous and astute *deus ex machina* who successfully contrived to resolve the most unsolvable problems in dozens of corporate dramas—the Panama Canal corruption that the late Senator John Tyler Morgan had worked so doggedly to expose, exploded on the front pages of the American press. On October 1, 1908, Cromwell sent his harried law partner, William Curtis—a man who had already suffered a nervous breakdown, he later blamed on the cruel pace of work demanded by Cromwell—to the office of the New York Attorney General William Travers Jerome, to lodge a complaint that "Certain persons," were attempting to extort money from Cromwell.[1] The blackmailers, alleged the long-

217

suffering Curtis to Attorney General Jerome, claimed they were in possession of sensitive material that would implicate Cromwell in misdeeds and corruption in the Panama Canal sale if the information were to be made public. An unnamed sum would buy their silence, but rather than deal with the extortionists, Cromwell decided to use his considerable political connections to intimidate the blackmailers.

The visit of Curtis to the Attorney General's office on behalf of one of New York's most prominent citizens did not go unnoticed and soon word leaked out to Joseph Pulitzer's *The World* newspaper. Acting on the tip, seasoned reporter, Allen Sangree, set off to gather the facts. Jerome agreed to talk with Sangree, and admitted to the reporter that Curtis had been to see him on Cromwell's behalf, but he declined to give out any details about the complaint. In the light of Jerome's reticence, Sangree made a beeline for Cromwell's office to get the details from the Fox himself. Once there, Cromwell received him with courteousness, but when Sangree began to probe Cromwell on details of Curtis' visit to Jerome's office, Cromwell politely refused to comment. Sangree went away empty-handed. Normally, this is where the story would have ended, but Cromwell panicked. Evidently Cromwell feared that Sangree possessed enough detail to run the story, and Cromwell overreacted and imprudently acted to contain the situation.[2]

Only the month before, newspapers exposed the unflattering connections between Cromwell, the election campaign of William Howard Taft, and his association with big railroads, banks, and oil trusts.[3] Cromwell had made the management of news an art form, and the appearance of the series of unpleasant stories challenged the notion he could manage his image. Now threatened by the possibility of more adverse publicity, the normally composed, imperturbable Fox of Wall Street actually lost control of the story by sending one of his press agents, Jonas Whitley, to control it. The following day Whitley, a former employee of the *World*, abruptly appeared in the offices of the newspaper's managing editor, Caleb Van Hamm, to warn him of the dire consequences to his newspaper if Sangree's story was published.[4]

When Whitley materialized in Van Hamm's office, there was no story. Sangree had hit a dead-end, had crossed the story off of his list,

218

and moved on to developing other news articles. Whitley's arrival and his aggressive demeanor had, however, peaked Van Hamm's curiosity. Van Hamm, who was not aware that Sangree was pursuing a story on Cromwell in the first place, calmly invited Whitley to sit down while he excused himself to look into the matter. He discovered that neither Sangree nor anyone else at the *World* was writing a story about Curtis' visit to the District Attorney on behalf of Cromwell—a fact he did not reveal to Whitley. Returning to Whitley, Van Hamm allowed his former colleague to continue in his role of managing the new story for Cromwell and listened patiently to him to chatter on about the heretofore undisclosed facts surrounding the incident. In due course, Cromwell's loquacious press agent revealed to Van Hamm startling details of the attorney's complaint.

According to Whitley, the facts were as follows: Cromwell, through his partner Curtis, had accused unnamed persons of threatening him with blackmail. These scoundrels claimed to possess proof of a speculative syndicate—headed by Cromwell and aided by Bunau-Varilla—formed to buy up the French canal shares and unload them at incredible profit when the United States bought the Panama Canal. Cromwell forged illicit alliances with political figures who, in return for financial rewards, had given him assurances that the Panama offer would be chosen over Nicaragua, claimed the blackmailers, and they threatened to turn the evidence over to authorities if Cromwell did not pay up. This portion of Whitley's tale was of little interest to Vann Hamm. That Cromwell, "the Jesse James of Wall Street," may have acted in his own best financial interest when he negotiated the sale of the French Panama Canal Company was not exactly news to anyone.[5]

Senator John Tyler Morgan pushed the limits of his investigatory powers trying in vain to expose what was to Morgan obvious graft and corruption in the affair. In spite of his relentless efforts, no charges were ever filed against Cromwell and since Morgan's death in 1907, lamented the *Omaha Daily Bee* in retrospect, "There was no successor to carry out his great work of revealing the truth about Panama corruption."[6] So Whitley's outline of unethical and illegal behavior that some unnamed source was now claiming against Cromwell left Van Hamm a bit bored. But when Whitley divulged that the unidentified blackmailers claimed to possess proof that Charles Taft, brother of William Howard Taft, the Republican candidate for the Presidency and Douglas Robinson, brother-in-law of President Theodore Roosevelt were part of Cromwell's syndicate, Van Hamm snapped to attention. For years, gossip had "trickled into all kinds of circles—business, social, and political—that Charles Taft, along with Cromwell, and financier J.P. Morgan, acted "in collusion with powerful persons in the Federal government" to secure the Panama Canal for their own profit.[7] But now, an agent of Cromwell's was sitting in front of Van Hamm, unreservedly talking in a way that suggested that hard evidence actually existed.

The astonished, but composed Van Hamm again calmly excused himself and stepped into an inner office where he dictated the details, as Whitley had related them, to his stenographer. After the story was typed, he returned to Whitley and handed it to him for possible correction. Whitley, at first crossed out Charles Taft's name and substituted that of the youngest Taft brother, Henry, then changed it back to Charles. After completing his edits, Whitley then telephoned Cromwell and read the copy to him. Cromwell approved it and the story was printed the following morning, October 3, 1908. Late that night Cromwell, unwilling or unable to leave good enough alone, telephoned a supplementary statement to Van Hamm. Van Hamm's stenographer dutifully recorded Cromwell's comments, read his notes back to him, and the approved statement was published by the *World* the following day.

In his statement, Cromwell vigorously denied that any syndicate ever existed. He seemed a bit offended that anyone would even allege such nonsense and that neither he nor anyone connected with him had ever made a penny out of Panama Canal securities. "Neither I, nor any one allied with me, either directly or indirectly, at any time or in any place in America or abroad, ever bought, sold, dealt in or ever made a penny of profit out of any stocks, bonds, or other securities of either the old Panama Canal Company or the new Panama Canal Company, or ever received for the same a single dollar of the forty million paid by the United States. I make this the most sweeping statement that language can convey," he emphatically stated.[8] And for good measure he further asserted, "[N]o member of the Taft family or Mr. Douglas Robinson ever had the remotest connection with Panama Canal matters directly or indirectly, and I never saw one of them on this subject before the United States acquired the canal. I never saw Mr. Douglas Robinson in my life.[9]

Curiously, Cromwell discontinued his pursuit of the alleged blackmailers and no charges of blackmail were ever filed against any individuals on his behalf. There is actually more reason to believe that "blackmailers" never existed, but rather that Cromwell was using the tactic to demonstrate his political muscle to the members of the Democratic National Committee—which had made public in August its plans to use the unsettled questions about the Panama transaction as a campaign issue—that he was not a man to be trifled with. Indeed, Norman Mack, Democratic National Committee chairman has said that they were investigating the transfer of the Panama property and he was aware that an investigator, although not retained by the Committee, would be offering his findings to a panel of Committee members. It was publicly speculated that the Committee had engaged the well-known lawyer, Colonel Alexander Bacon, to go to Paris to investigate the matter. Bacon returned to New York from his second fact-finding trip to Paris less than a week before Curits' visit to the offices of the New York District Attorney.[10] Knowing Cromwell's proclivity for obliquely finessing his adversaries into a corner by using his high-powered connections, it seems highly likely that intimidating Bacon into silence, or at least putting him on the defensive, was the goal of involving Jerome.

The World printed six articles on the incidents growing out of the Cromwell complaint to District Attorney Jerome. These were reproduced in many newspapers across the country. Investigatory inquiry resulted in some rather shocking revelations, such as information that at a 1904 banquet attended by both Taft and Cromwell, Cromwell publicly stated that "he had contributed largely to the revolutionists' treasury and was therefore entitled to [Panamanian] citizenship."[11] A report from Paris led to the *World's* disclosure "that very little of the $40,000,000 went to Frenchmen, but most of it to a syndicate of Americans, including, it is said, Douglas Robinson, brother-in-law of President Roosevelt, and Charles P. Taft, brother of William H. Taft, the candidate for President of the

Republican Party and who was Secretary of War in 1904, at the time of the sale of the canal to the United States."[12] The report went on to claim that "the American syndicate, confident that William Nelson Cromwell, the New York lawyer and friend of President Roosevelt and Mr. Taft, would be successful in selling the Panama Canal to the United States, bought up the securities of the canal company at a ridiculously low price compared with the sum paid by the United States Government" of $40,000,000.[13]

Other big city news outlets began to investigate the Panama transaction. On October 27, *The Salt Lake Herald* wrote a scathing story accusing Roosevelt and then Secretary of War William Taft, of covering up evidence discovered by the first military governor of the Panama Canal Zone, retired General George W. Davis, of financial improprieties by Cromwell.[14] During the examination of the financial records of the Panama Canal Company, Davis had discovered that Cromwell, "his fellow directors and stockholders" of the Panama Railroad Company had paid themselves "a large dividend" that the company had not earned.[15] The payments were made at the time the question of title was being resolved, and Davis believed that Cromwell and his associates had "no moral claim to the money" and reported the "questionable methods of the corporate attorney" to the Commission on which he served.[16] Upon learning of the report, Cromwell "brought Secretary Taft and President Roosevelt to his rescue and General Davis was ordered to eliminate all offensive references to Cromwell."[17]

The Chicago Journal published, "It is well known that somebody bought the stock of the defunct Panama Canal Company for $12,000,000 or less, and sold it to the United States for $40,000,000."[18] Several papers, like the *Seattle Star* printed the question of "Who Got the $40 Million?" on the front page, challenging the administration to give an account of the distribution of funds in the Panama deal. Roosevelt completely ignored the calls all through out the month of October.[19] Then on November 2, one day before the election, an editorial asking the President to address questions about the Panama Canal purchase appeared in the *Indianapolis News* and Roosevelt could no longer restrain his rage.

The editorial, which stated that the American people were entitled to know "who got the money," launched Roosevelt into a vindictive and vitriolic assault on the *Indianapolis News* and its editor, Delavan Smith, for his impertinence. Smith, said Roosevelt, occupied the "same evil eminence" as *New York Sun* editor, William Laffan, for an earlier piece questioning Roosevelt's role in Prairie Oil and Gas expansion in Oklahoma. The viciousness of Roosevelt's public attack was unprecedented for a sitting President—even for a man who thrived on condemning his critics to the "Ananias Club," consigning them into political, professional, and social oblivion. If a politician or reporter publicly disagreed with a policy or position —or if the policy or position did not receive the level of support he believed was deserved—Roosevelt was more likely to view any such disagreement in terms of treachery, not merely a difference of opinion. The examples of Roosevelt ostracizing those who disagreed with him are plentiful, but Senator Joseph Burton's banishment in 1902 is particularly illustrative.

Burton disagreed with Roosevelt's Cuba policy and was rewarded by Roosevelt's public snubbing of his fellow Republican. Burton became "persona non gratia" in the White House and his political career was effectively ended.[20] Sinking even lower in the President's esteem, because Burton had allowed a personal note from Roosevelt to be published in an advertisement for the upcoming Kansas City World's Fair, Roosevelt declared that he would henceforward consider Burton "a Democratic Senator" as far as patronage was concerned. To Roosevelt, Burton's indiscretion was a breach of confidence, which was unforgivable. Burton's decline was precipitous. In 1903 Burton became the first Senator in United States history to be convicted of a crime. He violated an 1864 statute that prohibited Congressmen from representing entities that had a claim against the United States. Burton, an attorney, received $2,500 from the Rialto Grain and Securities Company to represent their claim against the Post Office. There had never been a prosecution under the statute until Roosevelt's administration. It was Roosevelt, Burton declared, who "inspired this unjust and cruel persecution of me."[21]

Burton claimed that he was selectively prosecuted on the orders of Theodore Roosevelt because he had defied him against certain policies. What happened to Burton—using the Federal Government to bring Roosevelt's opponents to brook under an obscure law— would serve as a template for how Roosevelt would use an obscure law to persecute his enemies, Delavan Smith and Joseph Pulitzer. Roosevelt's motivation for launching a malicious vendetta against the *Indianapolis News,* then later *The World,* was layered and complex. However, understanding his intolerance for any act that smacked of disloyalty or disrespect toward him is key to understanding how and why Roosevelt reacted with such intensity.

Who Got The Money?

Roosevelt was publicly humiliated because his party not only lost the governorship in Indiana, but just three Republican Representatives out of thirteen positions were elected and the Indiana legislature sent a Democrat to the Senate. Roosevelt credited the poor result to the *Indianapolis News* editorial. "Morally," wrote one observer later, "the election in Indiana was a Republican defeat."[22] But a more potent reason that no doubt pushed Roosevelt over the edge of the rare restraint that he had displayed so far toward the press was his own Vice-President Charles Fairbanks' personal interest in the *Indianapolis News.* Not only was Fairbanks the majority shareholder in the brazen *Indianapolis News,* but he was also the cousin of its audacious editor, Delavan Smith. Roosevelt, who was widely known to be "as vindictive as a Malay," did not suffer even the slightest offense, let alone one that came from someone he considered to owe him fealty.[23]

A former Senator from Indiana, Fairbanks, was a McKinley insider and the Republican Convention had imposed him upon Roosevelt in the 1904 election. The Republican leadership believed that Fairbanks' connection to the slain President was politically soothing for those voters who might doubt the impetuous Roosevelt's commitment to carry out McKinley's agenda as he had promised. Despite his pledge to strengthen the role of the Vice-Presidency, President Roosevelt seemed to go out of his way to ignore Fairbanks. Whether the Vice-President had foreknowledge of Smith's confrontational editorial is a matter of speculation, but what is known for certain is that Roosevelt supported Taft for the 1908 election over Fairbanks, who clearly had Presidential ambitions of his own.[24] Following the *Indianapolis News* editorial, Roosevelt kept uncharacteristically quiet as he implemented a response that would, in his mind, devastate his opponents. At the end of November, Roosevelt used the remaining months of his Presidential term to disparage, mock, revile, and silence his newspaper critics.

On November 29th, Indiana lawyer, civic reformer, and Roosevelt appointee to the Civil Service Commission, William Dudley Foulke wrote the President and suggested, "If the statements of *The News* are true our people ought to know it; if not true, they ought to have some just means of estimating what credit should be given in other matters to a journal which disseminates falsehoods."[25] Far from

Noticeable taut body language in this photo of President Roosevelt and Vice-President Charles Fairbanks, Library of Congress, 1904.

being simply a prominent citizen concerned about the perception of corruption in the highest office of the land, Foulke was a Roosevelt sycophant who at various times brought information to Roosevelt that he had overheard or otherwise gleaned in conversations with other Republican officials. He had written the President in 1903 that Fairbanks was hatching a scheme to "fix the Indiana organization" against Roosevelt's presidential bid and Foulke declared his desire to resign from his post—which he did three months later—to work on Roosevelt's election campaign.[26] He was, however, the perfect straight-man to setup Roosevelt's first public direct response to questions growing out of the revelation made by *The World* of William Nelson Cromwell's alleged blackmailers.

Roosevelt used his 2,000-word reply to Foulke's letter to frame his denunciation of *The Indianapolis News* and then had Foulke make their correspondence public on December 7th. In it, the President addressed Foulke's concerns one by one while denying any untoward activity by anyone other than Delavan Smith and other equally rapacious newsmen. Among other unflattering characterizations, he labeled Smith as a "conspicuous offender against the laws of honesty and truthfulness."[27] It was, according to Roosevelt, all a pack of lies, fabricated to sell newspapers to a gullible public. He asserted that the United States paid the $40,000,000 directly to the French Government and he had the receipt to prove it. More to the point, no one in his administration had the "slightest knowledge as to the particular individuals among whom the French Government distributed the sum."

Roosevelt continued his defense by insisting, "[T]here certainly was no syndicate in the United States that to my knowledge had any dealings with the Government, directly or indirectly" and that "[E]very important step and every important document have been made public." Furthermore, the President declared categorically that any claim American citizens had profited from the sale was an "abominable falsehood" and "a slander not against the American government, but against the French government." It is likely Roosevelt felt assured that the weight of his considerable authority and the public's idolization would give his rebuttal the gravity needed to put his critics back into the box out of which they so noisily rattled.

226

By responding to the convenient letter that Foulke produced no doubt for this very purpose, Roosevelt surely felt confident he had, by the potency of his wrath, cowed his critics into silence. Many papers obliged the President by running headlines that portrayed Roosevelt as the feisty, unjustly accused cowboy squaring-off against craven bullies. Headlines like "Lying Papers are Flayed by the President," trumpeted by the *San Francisco Call* and "Roosevelt Roars" from the *Spoken Press* appeared in papers throughout the country. Roosevelt sorely misjudged the commitment of the *World's* editors to the words Pulitzer wrote on May 11, 1883. When he bought *The World* from robber-baron Jay Gould, Pulitzer committed to "expose all fraud and sham, fight all public evils and abuses that will serve and battle for the people with earnest sincerity."[28]

Roosevelt denounced the conduct of Smith as "not merely scandalous but infamous." Included with Smith was newspaper miscreant, *New York Sun* editor William Laffan, as a type that "practiced every form of mendacity known to man."[29] *The World*, up to this time, had not commented editorially on this latest Panama dustup, but the attack on Delavan Smith and *New York Sun* editor William Laffan—who had published an article that charged Roosevelt with ousting Secretary Hitchcock in the Prairie Oil scandal—struck a deep chord with *The World* editorial staff.

Laying Down the Gauntlet: Joseph Pulitzer's Crew

Reading the attack on Smith and Laffan, on December 8, 1908, William McMurtrie Speer, Yale educated attorney and seasoned editorial and legislative writer for *The World*, could no longer remain silent. Speer ran an editorial calling Roosevelt's assertions, "deliberate misstatements of fact" and his personal attack upon Delavan Smith nothing short of "scandalous."[30] He continued, "The inquiry was originally *The World's* and *The World* accepts Mr. Roosevelt's challenge." Speer then issued a call to "Let Congress officially answer the question, 'Who got the money?'" Speer listed each of Roosevelt's claims to the "facts" of the matter one by one as Roosevelt had laid out his response to Foulke; the United States did not pay a cent of the $40,000,000 to any American citizen; the

Scene shows a part of the vast army of Joseph Pulitzer's World writers just before deadline. Photo taken during the time of the Roosevelt libel case. Joseph Creeland, "Joseph Pulitzer, Master Journalist," **Pearson's Magazine**, *Vol. 21, 1909.*

United States Government had no knowledge to whom the funds were distributed by the French; there was no syndicate. Speer wrote that not only were these claims untrue, but that "Mr. Roosevelt must have known they were untrue when he made them."[31]

Speer observed, "$40,000,000 on the canal properties, and an additional $10,000,000 for a manufactured Panama republic, every penny of both of which sums was paid by check on the United States Treasury to J.P. Morgan & Co.—not to the French Government, as Mr. Roosevelt says, but to J.P. Morgan & Co." And most convincingly, Speer disassembled Roosevelt's argument that no American syndicate existed in the simplest fashion. He quoted the Congressional Record of William Nelson Cromwell's testimony before the Senate. It seemed that in 1904 Senator Morgan had produced a contract— Speer noting that the public record could be verified by simply checking the Congressional Record of the Panama Canal hearings, which empowered Cromwell to produce "an American syndicate, the Americanization of the Panama Canal Company" by his French employers.[32] An American Panama Canal Company with capitalization of $60,000,000 preferred stock and $45,000,000 common stock should be organized, according to the contract, to take over the Panama Canal concessions and all other property belonging to the New French Panama Canal Company. This company and another interoceanic canal company were incorporated in New Jersey with a board of directors comprised of Sullivan and Cromwell law partners. "As to Mr. Roosevelt's statement that there was no syndicate," wrote the scrupulous Speer, "he could have read the 'syndicate subscription agreement' on page 1150, volume 2, of the testimony before the [Senate] committee on Interoceanic Canals —if he had cared for the truth."

The Language of an Angry Fishwife

In a special message to Congress on December 15, Roosevelt let loose his legendary temper in a volley of vitriol rarely, if ever before, heard from a sitting President. In his statement, Roosevelt assured the Congress that "individuals of bad character" were responsible for the allegations of corruption in the purchase of the Panama Canal and "the stories, as a matter of fact, need no investigation whatever."[33] In point of fact, had Roosevelt paid more attention to what was actually being written instead of counterattacking, he would have realized that no charges had been leveled by any news outlet; only questions were raised. Still, Roosevelt—as was his custom and style —singled out an individual on whom to pour his outrage: this time it was Joseph Pulitzer. Roosevelt wrote, "The real offender" in the Panama scandal "is Mr. Joseph Pulitzer, editor and proprietor of *The World*."[34] Roosevelt, next, without indictment or trial, judged Pulitzer to be guilty of "the criminal offense . . . of libel upon individuals," and of "blackening the good name of the American people."[35] This decree was followed by the rhetorical salvo in the opening legal battle between the United States Government and the publisher Pulitzer, as Roosevelt announced, "It should not be left to a private citizen to sue Mr. Pulitzer for libel. He should be prosecuted for libel by the governmental authorities."

After this statement—in a confusing string of phrases in what must have been an effort to emphasize the full range of his indignation—Roosevelt went slightly syntactically off the rails. "In point of encouragement of iniquity, in point of infamy, of wrongdoing, there is nothing to choose between a public servant who betrays his trust, a public servant who is guilty of blackmail, or theft, or financial dishonesty of any kind, and a man guilty as Mr. Joseph Pulitzer has been guilty in this instance." Recovering from the dizzying and confusing sentence, the message went on to say in much more direct language:

> It is therefore a high national duty to bring to justice this vilifier of the American people, this man who wantonly and wickedly and without one shadow of justification seeks to blacken the character of reputable private citizens and to convict the Government of his own country in the eyes of the civilized world of wrongdoing of the basest and foulest kind, when he has not one shadow of justification of any sort or description for the charge he has made. The Attorney-General has under consideration the form in which the proceedings against Mr. Pulitzer shall be brought."[36]

Now the public battle would be between Roosevelt, Pulitzer, and Smith. Roosevelt, in his role as Commander-in-Chief, had already begun to marshal the forces of a powerful state necessary to punish the two newspaper owners. On December 8, the President

230

wrote to Henry L. Stimson, Federal Attorney for New York City, spewing language that would make his December 15th invective look tame in comparison. "Pulitzer," seethed Roosevelt, "is one of the creatures of the gutter of such unspeakable degradation that to him even the eminence of a dunghill seems enviable."[37] After pillorying Laffan and Smith, he then reached the point of his letter in which he asked Stimson to investigate Pulitzer's "various utterances for the last three or four months" on the subject of the Panama Canal and let him know the results of his research. Yet Roosevelt, who had effectively used righteous indignation and fury to crush his critics many times before, misjudged the steadfastness of Joseph

When Roosevelt initiated the libel suit, in 1909 the blind and elderly Pulitzer (left) lived off the coast of the U.S. on the steam yacht, The Liberty, out of fear of being arrested. Here he is seen being guided by a secretary aboard his yacht. Alleyne Ireland, "A Modern Superman: A character Study of the Late Joseph Pulitzer," The American Magazine, Vol. 73, 1912.

Pulitzer and his journalists to uphold the mission of *The World* to "expose all fraud and sham, fight all public evils and abuses."[38]

Response to Roosevelt's Rant

When the name of his cousin and business partner, Delavan Smith, and of Joseph Pulitzer were read, Vice-President Charles Fairbanks rose from his seat as President of the Senate and walked out of the room. Rumors would soon bubble to the surface that if Roosevelt carried through with his threats against Smith and Pulitzer, the Vice-President himself, as majority owner of the *Indianapolis News*, might also be prosecuted.[39] Pulitzer, himself wrote, "Mr. Roosevelt is mistaken. He cannot muzzle *The World*."[40] Criticism of Roosevelt got ugly. At one point, Democratic Representative William Willett from Roosevelt's home state of New York, denounced the President as "a pygmy descendant of Dutch trades people." Willett showed where in his essays and books that Roosevelt had at various times and on several occasions attacked Presidents Washington, Jefferson, Monroe, Jackson, Tyler, and Pierce as well as other American patriots, calling John Paul Jones a "pirate," and Thomas Paine a "filthy little atheist."[41] Roosevelt, concluded Willett, was "frank enough in abusing other Presidents," and it was unseemly that the villifier of Thomas Paine and other American heroes should prosecute Pulitzer—or any other journalist—for some alleged libel.

The foreign press was more diplomatic than Willett, but certainly as direct. "Roosevelt is so great a man in so many respects… it is therefore with feeling of regret and repulsion that we see the President of the United States descending into the gutters of controversy… Roosevelt had far better recommend the prosecution of himself for the heinous offense of degrading the presidential office by mingling in sordid and disgusting disputes… He might surely have spent the last few months of his occupancy of the White House in an atmosphere of personal dignity. To preserve to the end the manner and language of an angry fishwife is not the way to win respect of his own country or of any other."[42]

Problems with the Government Case

One glaring problem for Roosevelt and his Attorney General, Charles J. Bonaparte—descendant of Napoleon Bonaparte—was the stark reality that there existed no Federal libel law with which to charge the "villifier" of the American people.[43] Nonetheless, Bonaparte called dozens of legal experts to Washington to help him construct a case that would satisfy Roosevelt and be actionable. Another fact dogged the legitimacy of Roosevelt's claim that a crime had been committed and although they were entitled to bring libel charges in each of their states, none of the men mentioned in any articles had appealed to the courts for relief. Bonaparte's proceedings finally took shape in the form of indictments obtained from a District of Colombia Federal Grand Jury inquiry into violation of Section 815 of the Code of Laws of the District of Colombia, which provides that "Whoever publishes a libel shall be punished by a fine not exceeding one thousand dollars, or imprisoned for a term not exceeding five years, or both."[44] The Grand Jury summoned several *World* and *News* Washington reporters along with one young newsboy, William Smith, to each present himself on January 16, 1909 to answer questions relating to the distribution of libelous stories in the District.[45] In February, the Grand Jury returned an indictment against the Press Publishing Company, proprietor and publisher of *The World*, Joseph Pulitzer, the President of the company, Caleb B. Van Hamm, Robert H. Lyman, and two of the editors of *The World*, based on the circulation in the District of Colombia of copies of *The World* containing the news articles of October 3, 7, 14, and 16 and the editorial of December 8.[46]

Meanwhile, Henry Stimson, New York City Federal Attorney General, had not been idle in pursuit of some mechanism for charging Pulitzer with libel. March 4, 1909—the day of President Taft's inauguration—the Federal Grand Jury for the Southern District of New York returned separate indictments against *The World's* parent Company, Press Publishing Company, and *The World's* managing editor, Van Hamm, charging them with having distributed *The World* articles in places within the exclusive jurisdiction of the United States within the "fort and military post and reservation of West Point"

233

and within "the tract of land in the Borough of Manhattan, in the city of New York," the address of "a needful building used by the United States as a Post-Office," both places given by the State of New York to the United States of America.[47] The charges read in part that Pulitzer and Smith had a large number of their papers—twenty-nine copies to be exact—that they knew to contain "false, scandalous, malicious, and defamatory" articles about the government's actions in the Panama Canal purchase and that these articles were delivered to military posts when they knew they would be read by cadets, soldiers, and sailors.[48]

The law on which the government relied for this prosecution was reminiscent of the law under which Senator Joseph Burton was prosecuted in 1902, in that it was obscure, unused, and tenuously connected to the so-called offense. "An Act to Protect the Harbor Defenses and Fortifications Constructed or Used by the United States from Malicious Injury, and for Other Purposes," that was enacted July 7, 1898 founded on Sections I and II of a law enacted March 3, 1825. The law, "An Act More Effectually to Provide for the Punishment of Certain Crimes Against the United States, and for Other Purposes," provided for the punishment of arsons committed within any fort, dock-yard had never been used to prosecute libel.[49]

Because over 2,800 government reservations existed that corresponded to the status of West Point and the PostOffice building, if allowed to be used in these cases, no newspaper owner, editor, reporter—or even a newsboy—would be safe from prosecution under this theory of law. On April 8, as if to demonstrate that anyone with any connection to a newspaper that was publishing articles that could "stir up the people," could be hauled before a Grand Jury, Special Attorney General Stuart McNamara resumed questioning witnesses in New York. The first witness that he called was "negro messenger in the office of Jos. Pulitzer, proprietor of the *World*."[50] The next two witnesses called were personal physicians of Pulitzer. When the jury adjourned that day, it was announced that William Nelson Cromwell, Charles Taft, and Roosevelt's brother-in-law Douglas Robinson would not be called until "all other witnesses summoned have been exhausted."

Meanwhile, Taft who had been elected in November, but was not to be sworn in until March, made no effort to halt proceedings initiated by a former President. Yet, already rumors were in the press that his relationship with Roosevelt had deteriorated in a significant way. Taft did not want to start his administration with more controversy, but Joseph B. Kealing, a United States District Attorney in Indianapolis, had no such qualms. Two days before the New York indictments became public Kealing resigned, rather than become a party to the suit. By March 5th, headlines began to appear in newspapers across the county announcing that Kealing "Resigns Rather than Act in Panama Cases."[51]

Most papers published his reflective letter of resignation that he sent to his boss, Attorney General Bonaparte, in its entirety. In the letter Kealing wrote that the guilt or innocence of Smith or Pulitzer did not motivate his decision. He had always, asserted the attorney, "prosecuted all alike, without fear or favor" and if the publishers charged were guilty, they should be put on trial, but only "in the right place, via; at their homes."[52] Kealing further clarified his position by stating, "I am not in accord with the government in its attempt to put a strained construction of the law to drag the defendants from their homes to the seat of the government to be tried and punished, while there is a good and sufficient law in this jurisdiction, in the state court."[53] The principle involved in this undertaking was dangerous. He elaborated, stating he believed, if applied, the theory struck at:

> The very foundation of our form of government …
> I cannot, therefore, honestly and conscientiously insist to the court that such is the law, or that such construction should be put on it. Not being able to do this, I do not feel that I can, in justice to my office, continue to hold it and decline to assist."[54]

Some voices in the press severely attacked Kealing's character for his decision. The *Seattle Republican* called him a "moral coward" and that his refusal to prosecute the publishers showed that he "did not have a single ounce of manhood in him."[55] Others reiterated Kealing's

235

long and distinguished service in the Department of Justice, noting that he amply displayed his moral fiber in his prosecution of the Elkhart Bank case in which one of his close personal friends was convicted.[56]

Judge Anderson's Indianapolis Ruling

On June 1, Delavan Smith and *Indianapolis News* co-owner Nathaniel Williams, successfully resisted the attempt of the Special Attorney General McNamara to extradite them from Indiana to the District of Colombia. The defendants' lawyer, Ferdinand Winter, succeeded in convincing presiding Judge Albert Barnes Anderson that defendants had committed no offense for which they could be handed over to another district for trial.[57] Winter's claim that the defendants were "not guilty of the malice necessary to complete criminal libel, that they had not committed an offence [sic] for which they could be removed from one district to another for trial, and that the indictment charging them with criminal libel was baseless" convinced Anderson.[58] Anderson's ruling made a sharp distinction between malice in civil action and malice in a criminal case, and the prosecution did not meet that measure. While implied malice in a newspaper publication might be sufficient to justify a judgment for damages against the publisher, Anderson stated, in a criminal action "a different degree of malice was required—it must be express malice."[59]

Anderson—ironically nominated for his position by Theodore Roosevelt in 1902—was also profoundly concerned about the principle of freedom of the press and the obligation the press has to its readership. In his summary, he stated:

> It is the duty of a public newspaper, such as owned and conducted by these defendants, to tell the people, its subscribers, its readers, the facts that it may find out about public questions or matters of public interest… So we have this situation here. Here was a matter of great public interest, of public concern. *I* was interested in it; *you* were interested in it; we all

were interested in it. Here was a newspaper printing the news, or trying to. Here was this matter up for discussion, and I cannot say now, I am not willing to say that the inferences are too strongly drawn.[60]

Anderson's ruling effectively ended the government's efforts to remove Pulitzer and *The World's* news editors to the District of Colombia.

Cartoon shows Pulitzer as Barbara Frietchie resisting Stonewall Jackson's advance on Fredericksburg immortalized by Whitter's 1864 poem. Here Pulitzer is waving a flag of Freedom of the Press while Theodore Roosevelt leads armed troops. Alleyne Ireland, "A Modern Superman: A character Study of the Late Joseph Pulitzer," The American Magazine, Vol. 73, 1912.

Although Anderson's ruling offered immediate legal relief to *The World*, Joseph Pulitzer believed if the government's contention went untested—that it was a Federal crime to criticize or question the government in ways it deemed offensive—future journalists could be muzzled by whoever any Commander-in-Chief at the time who was insulted by its content. The newspaper mogul wanted a judgment based on the right to report news of public interest, confident in the veracity of their reporting. Pulitzer went to enormous expense, financing not only his journalists' travel and salary expenses to explore sources in France, Colombia, and Panama, but he also paid for the government's team of investigators to accompany *The World's* staff and collect any information that they found useful. Both sides secured certified copies of records, depositions, and other documentary evidence. When the case came up for trial in the United States Circuit Court in New York City on January 25, 1910, *The World* was prepared to sustain the defense of their justification to print the material because it was based on proof gathered in the fact finding mission. But in the end, the counsel for *The World*, De Lancey Nicoll, thought that the jurisdiction argument was the best route for a quick and certain decision in Pulitzer's favor. Nicoll convinced Pulitzer not to present facts uncovered that would support the truth of the claims made by *The World* stories, therefore, making libel charges moot, but to proceed with the argument the Federal Government did not have jurisdiction to prosecute a libel case that could be remediated by the States. Judge Hough agreed with Nicoll, reaffirming Judge Anderson's decision in the *Indianapolis News* case.

Hough squashed the complaint on January 26, 1910.[61] De Lancey Nicoll, despite his recommendation to Pulitzer to fight the case on grounds of jurisdiction, interpreted the decision as a sign triumph for the freedom of the press and a resounding defeat of Roosevelt. He told the press:

> The curiously ingenious mind… that brought to life for the first time in 86 years the law under which this prosecution was begun, has retired to private life, but has left this legacy behind it. This is not a prosecution

brought by aggrieved or injured private individuals; it was begun by the President of the United States in an attempt to show that a libel had been committed upon the American people. The statute under which this suit was brought was drafted to punish offenses not covered by laws in the section in which they were committed... We had better have the sedition law or even the star chamber again than such a monstrous practise [sic] as the government advocated in this proceeding.[62]

During his summation, Hough had recommended, "This very interesting question can be lawfully presented to the Supreme Court of the United States."[63] While the Government made no move to take Hough up on his suggestion, *The World* was not satisfied with any decision short of the highest tribunal in the land and through a series of articles, it demanded that the Government appeal Hough's decision to the Supreme Court.[64] The Government "took its time" filing its appeal with the Supreme Court on the last day permissible, finally responding to the prodding by *The World*.[65] On January 3, 1911, the Supreme Court Justice Edward Douglass White read the decision to uphold Judges Anderson and Hough's rulings that quashed the indictment on the ground that the Federal Government had no jurisdiction. The Court did not address the question that stimulated the "curiously ingenious mind" of Theodore Roosevelt to retaliate in 1908.

"The Panama Libel Case is dead," declared *Watson's Magazine*, "The only regret the public can entertain at the collapse of the suits, is that they are still in Judge Anderson's state of unappeased curiosity as to "who got the money"... [and] is probably just as well for Theodore Roosevelt, William Howard and Charles Taft, Douglas Robinson, and Wm. Nelson Cromwell." [66] On January 4, *The World* announced that while the "the freedom of the press is established beyond the power of Federal usurpation" by the Supreme Court upholding Hough's ruling, "in due season, *The World* will "present the evidence in its possession to the Congress of the United States and renew its demand for a searching investigation."[67]

In addition to the depositions and evidence uncovered by Pulitzer's investigators in France, Panama, New York, and Washington, D.C., a damning document came into the possession of *World* editors in 1908. According to *World* editorial writer Earl Harding, in 1908 John Hammond, journalist and publicist for railroad interests, told him and *World* business manager Don C. Seitz, that in pursuit of another financial scandal story, he had been promised copies of records of the American Panama Canal syndicate if he ceased his current inquiry. Hammond had the documents in a bank vault and would hand them over to *The World* after the notoriously vindictive Theodore Roosevelt was out of office in March of 1909. Eventually, Hammond delivered a "Memorandum of Agreement," outlining the May 1900 accord between William Nelson Crowell, J.P. Morgan, William Howard Taft's brother Henry W. Taft, and Roosevelt's brother-in-law Douglas Robinson, and others to buy up shares of the *Compagnie Nouvelle Du Canal de Panama*. Senator Chauncey Depew was the man everyone assumed was the target of Hammond's original investigation. Depew gave Hammond the documents. The syndicate was formed while Roosevelt was governor of New York. With no conflict of interest at the time the syndicate was formed and given the level of intimacy between Roosevelt and his brother-in-law, it is unbelievable that Robinson's partnership in the Panama syndicate was kept secret from Roosevelt. In addition, Hammond delivered a sixteen page red leather-bound ledger containing the names of the original signatures of the memorandum, six new names, and the money each contributed to the venture.

THE RAINEY HEARINGS AND THE ROMANCE OF PROGRESS

The writers and editors of *The World* were confident that Congressional hearings would take place on the heels of their Supreme Court victory and they looked forward to the day when all the evidence they had collected would become a part of the public record.[68] In April, Representative Henry T. Rainey of Illinois introduced a resolution demanding a full investigation of the purchase of the Panama Canal. "Of the $40,000,000 paid, nearly all went to a few select persons," Rainey stated. Determined to get to the bottom of the affair, he said that he was willing to "subpoena Roosevelt and William Nelson Cromwell of New York, and we'll show up the whole transaction."[69] However, Rainey's resolution took the form of investigating Roosevelt's 1911 public braggadocios remark "I took the Isthmus," rather than looking into "who got the money."[70] It would not be until January 1912 that the hearings would begin. House Resolution 32 of the Sixty-second Congress, first session read in part that whereas "without consulting Congress," Roosevelt had publicly declared that he "took" Panama from the Republic of Colombia, and that Colombia had petitioned the United States to submit to The Hague Tribunal about the fairness of his action from the beginning of the affair, and that the United States refused arbitration:

> Therefore, be it Resolved, that the Committee on Foreign Affairs of the House of Representatives be, and the same hereby is, directed to inquire into the same; send for books, papers and documents; summon witnesses; take testimony; and report the same, with its opinion and conclusions thereon, to this House with all convenient speed.[71]

Sadly, the Rainey Hearings—despite compiling over 600 pages that included dozens of witnesses, testimony from both investigations by Senator John Tyler Morgan and reams of affidavits and depositions collected by *The World*—had no meaningful impact.

Less than one month into the hearings, on February 20, 1912, the committee called for a recess and through procedural maneuvering, the powerful friends of Panama, particularly Senatort Henry Cabot Lodge, made sure the committee never met again. There was no public outcry for the resumption of the hearings; the nation was more interested in the romance and opportunities the Canal offered than how the canal was acquired in the first place. Thanks to Dr. William Gorgas' brilliant application of mosquito suppression techniques, yellow fever had almost completely disappeared from the Isthmus, and the current Governor of the Zone, George Washington Goethals, had reigned in the unruly project and had made extraordinary progress. By February 8, 1912—in the midst of

WANDAMERE

THE GREAT

Where the Crowds Stop *Where the Crowds Stop*

MORE BEAUTIFUL GARDENS   **MORE SCENIC ATTRACTIONS**

More Amusement Features

SEE THE WONDERFUL **PANAMA CANAL**

A New Lake surrounded by a Scenic Railway and Entered by Locks

GREAT AMPHITHEATRE

Where on June 1 and 3, "As You Like It" will be presented. Other Open-Air Performances all Summer.

Motordrome Races

With the World's Best Riders will be part of the Season's Big Features

Take Wandamere Cars.   Better and Faster Service than Ever Before

Advertisement for a Utah pleasure resort featuring a miniature Panama Canal experience for merrymakers. **Goodwin's Weekly: A Thinking Paper for Thinking People.** *(Salt Lake City, Utah), 01 June 1912.*

the Rainey investigation —the Canal was an astonishing 70 percent completed.[72] Goethals, the organizational and engineering genius who as Governor inherited a pile of mismatched, incompatible, unworkable construction approaches, was producing what the press would label "the greatest engineering accomplishments of modern times."[73] America became enamored with the Canal, conflating patriotism, pride, and prosperity with the project.

Poet Lillian Bailey reflected the population's enthrallment with the project in an ode to the splendor and magnificence of the Panama Canal. Her poem, "The Gates at Panama," appeared in the *San Francisco Call,* next to a full-page allegorical drawing of a regal personification of the spirit of America, Columbia, sitting on her throne, hovering in the clouds over the Isthmus.[74] "My brothers have cut the world in two," penned Bailey, "to set the oceans free."[75] Ads projecting a new affluence the finished project would bring began to appear. Not knowing that the able Goethals would bring the project in a full year earlier than projections, in the summer of 1912, an Aberdeen Washington real estate firm placed a full page advertisement leading with "What are your preparations for 1915?" when a boom in property prices was projected because of the "great era of prosperity" the completion of the Canal would bring Pacific coast residents.[76] America had become Canal crazy. The only digging they were interested in was in the completion of the project, not the dredging up of old scandal rumors. Besides, the papers were filled with a more tantalizing and current political fracas; the political duel between Roosevelt and Taft.

The 1912 Presidential election was heating up, attracting attention. President Taft and Roosevelt—once the greatest of friends—were ferociously vying with one another for the Republican nomination. People were fascinated. Over a two-day period in May, for example, Taft and Roosevelt's competition commanded front-page coverage. Taft declared that the "country no longer needed T.R." and warned the people against a man whose character could allow him to defy the tradition of George Washington and run for a third term.[77] For those reasons and for Roosevelt's "unsound constitutional views," Taft was challenging his former boss for the Presidential nomination.[78] At the same time, "Colonel" Roosevelt was attracting unprecedented

Illustration shows Theodore Roosevelt charging through air at a high rate of speed at an extremely large President Taft who is seated on top of the White House. Title "Stop, Look, Listen!!! . . . witness what really happens when an Irresistible Force meets an Immovable Body." Udo Keppler, **Puck**,
7 March 1912.

crowds of supporters, and continued to uphold his actions in Panama as evidence of his decisive leadership abilities.[79] "Colombia was trying to blackmail the French company," claimed Roosevelt at a May political rally, "which might have landed the French army in Panama. I could have sent a learned report to Congress and there would have been a debate, but I did not. I took the Isthmus and started the canal."[80] Meanwhile, the Democratic challenger for President, Woodrow Wilson, was getting page four coverage, with his unexciting and bookish approach to the topic of tariffs.[81] Eventually, the fiery Roosevelt would split the Republican Party vote with his independent Bull Moose Party presidential bid, handing the Presidency to the staid academician Woodrow Wilson, and George Goethals would astound the world by opening the Panama Canal August 15, 1914, a full year earlier of his original projection.[82]

Uncle Sam, as a giant magnet labeled "United States Protectorates", pulls little figures labeled "Cuba, Nicaragua, Costa Rica, Honduras, Guatemala, Salvador, Colombia" toward himself. A figure labeled "Panama" is already in his back pocket. Udo Keppler. "The Monroe Magnet." Puck 13 Aug. 1913, Library of Congress.

CHAPTER EIGHT

ROOSEVELT AND THE OPENING OF THE PANAMA CANAL: AUGUST 15, 1914

He's loved of the distracted multitude,
Who like not in their judgment but their eyes.
—Hamlet, William Shakespeare

———————————

The day the Panama Canal opened for business, former President Theodore Roosevelt was embarking on a four-and-a-half hour long, bone-rattling automobile trip from Oyster Bay to Hartford, Connecticut to keynote the Progressive state convention. At fifty-six, the bronco busting hero of San Juan, the slayer of black bears and bull elephants, and the subjugator of Bowery criminals and Wall Street tycoons, heaved his stiff and clumsy body into his motorcar like an old man of ninety. For his entire life, Theodore Roosevelt had applied the greatest force of his quite considerable energy to proving his worth—first to his father, then to his country, and now in the early hours of the dew-clad morning of August 15, 1914—to himself.

After warm-up speeches by the handsome and elegant exponent of the eight-hour workday, industrialist Charles Sumner Bird, and the office boy who became J.P. Morgan's "right-hand man," George Perkins, Roosevelt would bring down the house.[1] He always did. His only concern was his voice.[2] In a weakened condition, his voice was the one presentation of self he could not easily stage-manage. His high-pitched voice once made him a laughing stock in his early career as a New York legislator. It was a quality, his mockers claimed, of an effeminate male. The young legislator was often described quite simply, as "pathetic."[3] Any challenge to his masculinity would be agonizing to him personally and jeopardize his ability to inspire his followers. The harassing anxiety of his very public physical decline and the disintegration of his political prowess must have been painful for the man who staked his whole political and public life on vigorous manliness.[4] Betrayed by his party and supplanted by Woodrow Wilson, a man he regarded with contemptuous disrespect, former President Roosevelt had become relegated to page three in the newspapers.[5] His relevance was slipping and he knew it.

Things had changed for Roosevelt since he left office, and not for the better. There was no denying that the glitter of Roosevelt's glorious image had dimmed during his Presidential tenure. Toward the end, some of the members of the press started to respond to his antics, not as the acts of impetuous youth and roguish manhood, but as "the crude and brutal manners of the bully."[6] His pettiness and pique consistently bubbled up to the surface with his handling of the collections of controversies that dogged his last administration. The Spelling Reform debate of 1906 devolved into a farce that made him the butt of a hundred public jokes at home and abroad; the Brownsville Affair; the whispers about Prairie Oil; the Secret Service investigations of Congress; the public 1912 airing of his and Taft's dirty laundry; and finally, the Panama Canal scandal.

Roosevelt was publicly ridiculed when he called for simplified and standardized spelling rules. He ordered changes that Congress refused to implement.[7] "One of the few things that Mr. Roosevelt never was able to get away with was his spelling reform pronunciamento," wrote Irving Norwood in his reflection of the end of the Roosevelt Presidential reign, "which had been largely repudiated by authorities. But . . . 'tis a safe bet that when he returns from his trip [to Africa] and begins to write, 'twill be found that he went "thru" the jungle, "kilt" a lion, "drest" its skin and "shipt" it home."[8]

In the race-related Brownsville Affair, Roosevelt dishonorably discharged an entire regiment of 167 African-American soldiers, one who won the Medal of Honor in the Cuba theatre of the Spanish American War, because white citizens accused the soldiers of starting a riot and murder. Roosevelt did not expel the white officers, who testified that the soldiers had been in their barracks at the time of

248

the disturbance in town. Although no military trial was ever held and a Texas court cleared the soldiers, Roosevelt nevertheless sided with the white citizens who swore the soldiers were guilty.[9] A front-page fracas broke out when, Roosevelt aligned himself with William Randolph Hearst's charges that Oklahoma Democratic governor and Roosevelt critic, Charles Haskell was bribed to open land to the Prairie Oil Company, a subsidiary of Standard Oil that was previously withheld from exploration. Denials and counter-charges about politizing the controversy occupied newspapers for months. [10] In his last annual address to Congress in 1908, Roosevelt stated that the only reason legislation to expand the role of the Secret Service was not passed was "that the Congressmen did not themselves wish to be investigated by Secret Service men." Congress was apoplectic, calling for the President to produce the evidence to support his charge.[11]

He went on a safari to Africa in 1909, not merely to rehabilitate his image, but also to deflect a growing suspicion in the public that his career had played out in "the tinsel of stage-setting," and he himself was nothing more than a seriocomic tragedian "who has interested part of his audience, amazed another, and disgusted the remainder."[12] Roosevelt's professed reason for the year-long safari was for his love of nature and—as he saw himself as a true Renaissance Man—that the 11,400 animals he killed on his African adventure and sent to the Smithsonian to catalog added significantly to the scientific body of knowledge of the Dark Continent. Before he departed from the United States, Irwing Norwood wrote, Roosevelt left "the scene of his years of volcanic official and personal activities, and goes to another land to sound his dominant note. Shots will sound and blood will flow and his knife will find its living hilt. The scalps and skins of the kings of the jungle will dry upon his tent pegs. He will work and sweat and kill and be happy." Norwood correctly predicted that Roosevelt would return "satisfied with the slaughter, fingering his crowded note books, posing amid his trophies. It will be quiet here, but he will not let it remain so."[13]

Roosevelt the historian, literary critic, politician, and cowboy now included in his self-description, "American hunter-naturalist," and turned his eye toward the scientific; never mind that museums had catalogued most—if not all—of the examples he sent back years before he ventured into Africa. A few critics dared to say that they were not convinced that his excessive killing was out of a scientific curiosity, but rather it was a high-minded justification for Roosevelt's blood lust. "Every time Roosevelt gets to the heart of a wild thing," one observer noted, "he invariably puts a bullet through it."[14] And, of course, there was the book that Charles Scribner & Sons had contracted with the ex-President to write. The rumor was that he was offered one dollar per word.

The intense news coverage of his African expedition heightened his visibility and widened the potential readership. "Theodore Roosevelt secured his popularity through publicity; has retained, strengthened, and extended it through publicity . . . The unbroken chain of personal triumphs scored by Roosevelt the President, can be traced directly to the press-bureau of which he is the sole manager."[15] The followership he created and sustained through his delft handling of his public image was impressive. "Newspapers made Roosevelt," wrote Irving C. Norwood in 1909.[16] Roosevelt's antics of "his tree chopping, horseback riding, cross-country walking, tennis playing, and other stunts have made not only good reading, but live news. So far as his athletic performances go, it is not that he does them well, but enthusiastically.[17]

A Mighty Hunter and the Wounded God

Roosevelt's return from Africa was triumphal. At 8:30 on the morning of June 19, 1910, the former President left the steamship *Kaiseran Auguste Victoria* and boarded a review cutter *Androscoggins*, sailing into New York harbor to the roar of a twenty-one-gun salute from the battleship *South Carolina*, a flotilla of eighty warships, 150 merchant vessels, private yachts, excursion boats and "a pandemonium of steam whistles from craft and factories along the waterfront" that hailed Roosevelt's return.[18] Roosevelt disembarked at the Battery where thousands of revelers welcomed him as a conquering hero. As the mighty hunter set foot on American soil for the first time in fifteen months, he was greeted by the continuous ovation of the frenzied throngs. Roosevelt would attempt to repeat

Nelson Harding in the Brooklyn *Eagle*.

Roosevelt wearing a pith helmet bursting through the newspapers.
Title: "Back in the Old Place." Reprint in Raymond Gros'
***T.R. in Cartoon**, 1910.*

the glory of his African triumph with another scientific expedition to
South America to discover the source of the mysterious Amazonian
waterway, the River of Doubt, in 1913. The homecoming from
his South American quest, however, would be a far cry from the
victorious return of *Bwana Tumbo*, the name Roosevelt's African
porters called their "big chief." From his Amazon trek, Roosevelt
returned a fragile and broken man. In 1914, he would limp ashore,
not strut.

   Roosevelt sailed into New York harbor back from his expedition
to find the elusive source of the River of Doubt in South America

Typical headline celebrating Roosevelt's return from Africa,
Seattle Star, *18 June 1910.*

on May 19, 1914. This time unlike the triumphal return of Caesar from his African safari and more like the mythological Ares being carried off the Trojan battlefield—a wounded god, more dead than alive. And like Ares' nemesis, the goddess Athena who hurled a boulder striking Ares senseless on the plains of Troy, the fabled River of Doubt had leveled Roosevelt. The five-month mission to map the mysterious river was meant to enshrine Roosevelt alongside the greatest scientific explorers of his time and restore his public prestige after his 1912 presidential loss, but instead the mysterious Brazilian waterway had spit him up on its shores, leaving him a maimed man.

The River of Doubt

Roosevelt supporter, Catholic priest and scientist, John Zahm had encouraged Roosevelt to join the famous Brazilian explorer Colonel Da Silva Candido Rondon's daring journey to uncover the source of the River of Doubt, called the *Rio da Dúvida* by the South Americans. The exploit was meant to act as salve for Roosevelt's bruising defeat as the third party Bull Moose presidential candidate in the bitter and divisive 1912 election. Roosevelt had become *persona non gratis* with Republicans who blamed him for breaking with the party and dividing the vote, thereby installing Democrat Woodrow Wilson in the White House. Even his old mentor and closest ally, Senator Henry Cabot Lodge, had told him to stay out of politics. Roosevelt later freely admitted to novelist Henry Rider Haggard that his actions in 1912 caused, "The great bulk of my wealthy and educated friends [to] regard me as a dangerous crank."[19] And true to form, when the going got tough—as in his foray to North Dakota after the death of his first wife—Roosevelt sought a wilderness experience to restore his good fortune and reputation. In terms of danger and difficulty, Roosevelt felt it would parallel the relative ease of his African safari and he would be credited with starting a South American "zoo-geographic renaissance."[20] Sadly, that was not the case. Poor planning, inadequate provisioning and the harsh, profoundly alien and unforgiving nature of the Amazon coiled about the Roosevelt-Rondon expedition in an unbreakable embrace like an anaconda squeezing the life from its prey.

In many ways, the journey was the most disappointing of Roosevelt's trekking career. Not only did the River of Doubt fail to grant his lifelong wish to die a romantic hero's death, but on his return, the adventure had cast very public clouds over his integrity.[21] Many

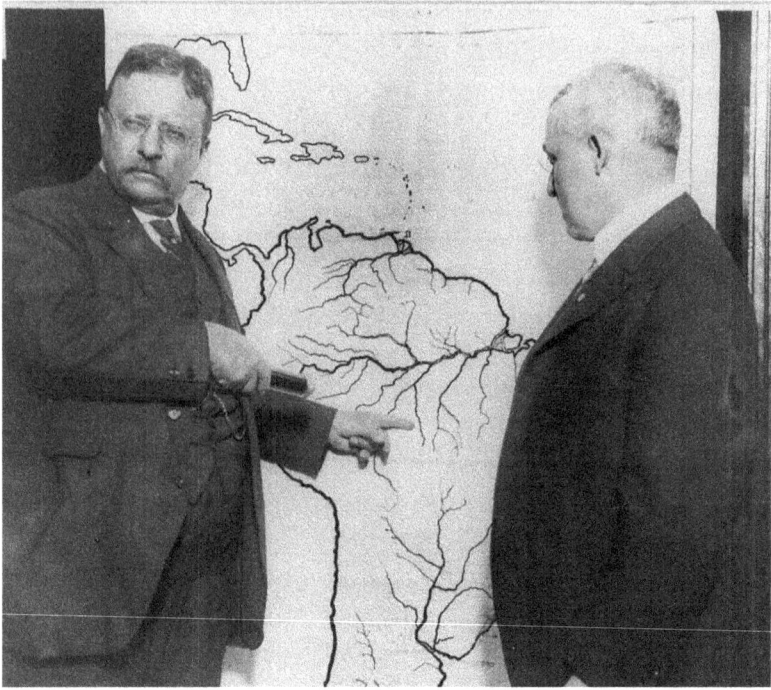

Roosevelt pointing to a map of the area of exploration of Roosevelt-Rondon Scientific Expedition, Library of Congress, c. 1913.

naturalists and scientists disbelieved his claim that he actually discovered the river's source; some questioned whether the river existed at all. "That river," as he called it, washed brutal, penetrating, and lasting misery over the body of the former President. The physical damage caused on the expedition roamed throughout his body until his death in 1919. Yet, he was not alone in his affliction. Everyone in the nineteen-man Roosevelt-Rondon scientific exposition suffered miserably. Three porters died—one drowning, one shooting, and the murderer left to perish in the jungle. Malaria and starvation plagued all the members of the expedition, but Roosevelt seemed closer than any of his compatriots to crossing the threshold of death.[22] Roosevelt's mental anguish during the grueling quest to locate the fount of the great South American tributary was as intense as his physical anguish.

Covered in putrefying insect bites, hobbled by a festering leg wound, and riddled with guilt for holding back the others, Roosevelt thought it might be better to take the morphine "and end it."[23] His torment was so great that he contemplated suicide—a proposition for which Roosevelt had long been prepared. "I have always made it a practice on such trips," he later revealed to journalist O.K. Davis, "to take a bottle of morphine with me. Because one can never know what will happen and I didn't mean to be caught by some accident where I should have to die a lingering death."[24] He begged his companions to leave him to die in the jungle, but one of his fellow explorers, his son Kermit, convinced him that Roosevelt would be leaving the jungle dead or alive. Kermit would carry his father or his father's corpse out of the jungle if he had to. Either way, the elder Roosevelt was going home.[25]

And home he was. Even though his left leg was still as stiff and lifeless as the buffalo heads mounted in his Oyster Bay trophy room, the former President was raring to begin his strenuous five-day political crusade across New England. Roosevelt needed to recover more than his health: the former Executive needed to recover his popularity. In his last sortie into the presidential fray of 1912, the "Big Bull Moose" had split the Republican ticket and lost the last election and until May of 1914, he vigorously denied he would seek reelection.[26] On August 15, 1914, he began his campaign to set the Progressive faithful on fire.[27] As he and his entourage piled into the automobile on August 15, 1914, the old Rough Rider was buoyant. He was—for all intents and purposes—back in the saddle again.

A Masochist's Flare for Mishaps

Physically, Roosevelt was a wreck long before his five-month nightmare exploration of the "strange animals, strange savages, trackless forests, and dangerous streams."[28] With him—along with his Springfield rifle; two Winchester Model 1895 lever action rifles, a 405 and 30-40; a Fox 12-gauge shotgun; a 16-gauge shotgun; and Colt and Smith & Wesson revolvers—Roosevelt carried within his body an impressive collection of broken and shattered bones from his ranching days, a strenuous, intentionally punishing period bordering on the masochistic, as well as permanent damage he had collected while in the White House.[29] Many other men of his

**"I have always been most unhappy that I did
not lose a leg or an arm in Cuba."**

*Drawing shows a smiling, disfigured Roosevelt. Quote from interview.
Irving Norwood, "Exit— Roosevelt, The Dominant,"*
Outing Magazine, *Vol. 53, 1909.*

era pursued the strenuous life as explorers, hunters, and ranchmen
that Roosevelt advocated, but few seemed to court physical injury
the way Roosevelt did.

Almost from the moment he assumed the assassinated William
McKinley's place as Commander-in-Chief, Roosevelt's time as

President had been laced with accidents, violence, and pain. In Pittsfield, Massachusetts at 9:30 on the morning of September 3, 1902, Motor Car # 29—hurtling down the tracks at thirty miles per hour—crashed into Roosevelt's horse drawn carriage. All five passengers in the Presidential carriage were hurled into the air by the explosive collision. Roosevelt's bodyguard, William "Big Bill" Craig, former athletic instructor and USA broadsword champion turned Secret Service agent, was thrown under the trolley, splitting his skull, the eight wheels badly mangling his upper torso. He died instantly. The force of the collision was so great that it pitched one of the four gray horses onto the track as the other three horses bolted wildly, dragging the injured horse and the remnants of the landau another thirty feet across the pavement. The horse was so badly injured that a Secret Service agent jumped from a second carriage, drew his pistol and shot the suffering animal in the midst of the mayhem and carnage of the collision.

Passengers Governor Winthrop Carne of Massachusetts and former McKinley secretary and organizational genius, George Cortelyou, crawled out of the debris with serious, but not life threatening injuries. Presidential coachman, David J. Pratt, who was seated next to Craig survived, no doubt because the body of the downed horse broke his fall. The impact catapulted Roosevelt forty feet into the air, returning him to the pavement in a shower of splintered wreckage. Roosevelt emerged from the pile of rubble with facial contusions and a wound to his left leg.[30] Considering the tremendous violence of the crash, his escape without serious injury was nothing short of miraculous. Or so it seemed at first. At the scene Roosevelt, as usual, underplayed his injuries and brushed away attempts to treat his wounds. "We have no time for such trifles," he roared, "I am in no need of attention. It might have been worse."[31] In actual fact, it did get much worse for the President.

Ten days later in Indianapolis—a major stop on his resumed Western political campaign tour—Roosevelt suddenly required emergency medical attention for the leg he injured in the trolley catastrophe. Characteristically—although he was undoubtedly in excruciating pain from his swollen leg and against the remonstration of his medical advisers—Roosevelt refused to leave for the hospital before addressing the throngs of supporters gathering in Monument Square. He stood on the balcony of the Colombia Club facing thousands of people who had gathered in the Square to hear the Rough Rider President. He spoke for forty minutes. He never flinched. Afterwards, Roosevelt was taken to St Vincent's Hospital where two ounces of putrid fluid were removed from the dangerously infected leg. Later, "in strictest confidence" Roosevelt would admit to Henry Cabot Lodge that his leg was attended to "just in time."[32] A pernicious bacterial infection of the bone, osteomyelitis, had developed in his wounded limb. Despite the successful operation to treat the malicious abscess, pain and instability in his leg continued to plague him for the rest of his life. Many years later the frailty in his leg, reinjured and badly infected, hounded him as he stumbled through the fetid Amazon jungle.

The day before his inauguration in 1904, Roosevelt had a ten-round gladiatorial exercise with the bare-knuckle, middleweight bare-knuckle boxing professional, "Professor" Michael Joseph Donovan.[33] Donovan had been Roosevelt's regular sparring partner since his first days as governor of New York. That same year, this time sparring with a much younger man—an artillery captain—Roosevelt was struck so violently that the retina of his left eye detached leaving the legendary myopic cowboy-president completely blind in one eye. He tried to hide his injury from his wife Edith, but when she noticed him struggling to read, she called in the renowned ophthalmologist, Doctor William Holland Wilmer. Neither Wilmer nor Roosevelt were surprised that the damage was irreversible. Since his Harvard days, Roosevelt was a lover of the gentlemanly art of whacking and being whacked around a boxing ring and it was there his left eye had first been brutally traumatized. His sessions with Donovan added to the damage, leaving the eye vulnerable to permanent injury and after the young army officer landed the final blow, the light in Roosevelt's eye was out forever. For his part, Roosevelt claimed he was grateful that it was his left, not his right eye that was blinded. "Had it been my right eye," wrote in his autobiography, "I should have been entirely unable to shoot."[34]

Roosevelt left office in 1908 while fulfilling a campaign promise not to seek another term. Yet risking the charges of going back on his word, feeling betrayed by his hand picked successor William Taft and feeling jilted by his beloved Republican Party, Roosevelt ran for the chief executive spot in 1912 on the Bull Moose ticket. In October of that year, Roosevelt's campaign was seriously curtailed by John Schrank, a disturbed New York saloonkeeper who shot Roosevelt in his chest with a .38 caliber handgun. Schrank's reason for shooting the former Commander-in-Chief alternated between claims he felt outrage at Roosevelt for running for a third term and acting as an avenging angel for the ghost of William McKinley who appeared to Schrank in a dream and told him that Roosevelt was responsible for his murder. Either way, Schrank needed to "Free the country from the menace of Roosevelt's ambitions."[35] Again, as in Pittsfield, Roosevelt was lucky.

Deflected by a metal glasses case and a thick manuscript in his breast coat pocket, the bullet traveled into Roosevelt's body superiorly and medially for about three inches after breaking the skin, and lodged in the chest wall. With Schrank's .38 slug lodged in his chest, blood oozing over his suit jacket, Roosevelt demanded—as

Roosevelt's stenographer, Elbert Martin, holding Roosevelt's bullet pierced speech. Library of Congress, October 1912.

259

he had done in 1902—that he should be driven to the auditorium where he was schedule to speak, not to the hospital. He would deliver his speech or die trying. "I will deliver this speech or die," glowered Roosevelt defiantly, "one or the other."[36] Always a showman at his most vulnerable moments, Roosevelt held up the bullet-pierced, blood stained manuscript declaring, "The hole is in it that the bullet went through, and it probably saved it from going into my heart. The bullet is in me now, so I cannot make a very long speech. But, I will try my best."[37] Roosevelt spoke for an hour and a half. Only then did he allow himself to be taken to the hospital for treatment. At the hospital, he bantered with the doctors and staff. "He didn't get me and I gave my speech," grinned Roosevelt.[38] The doctors determined that an operation to remove the projectile was more dangerous than to leave it in his chest. Roosevelt carried the metal near his heart for the rest of his life. His blind eye and his rheumatism were secrets carefully guarded from the public, but he wore the embedded bullet like a badge of honor, never admitting to any pain or discomfort. Although he carried on with his campaign, he could never regain his lost momentum.

Roosevelt arriving at Oyster Bay after the Schrank shooting, Library of Congress, 22 October 1912.

In grim contrast to his carefully cultivated image as the quintessential vigorous American male, in reality the renowned Rough Rider was far from robust well before he left for Brazil. Despite appearing to accept the reality of his blinded eye with relative ease, Roosevelt's accelerated physical deterioration required more and more effort to disguise. He once confided to a friend that the crippling pain of his rheumatism made it impossible for him to climb on or off a horse "at any speed," but the general public would not know the extent of his physical deterioration until after his death in 1919.[39] Until then, half blind, half deaf, and crippled, Roosevelt did everything in his power not to allow the public to see his frailty.

After his return from the Amazon basin, Roosevelt had a lot more to hide. And in spite of an energetic publicity campaign to convince the public that he never felt better, his disabilities were on public display. To add to the misery of his festering leg wound, the penetrating dampness of the jungle aggravated his chronic rheumatism, Roosevelt had to use a cane when he disembarked the SS *Aiden*. After he regained over 20 of the nearly 60 pounds he lost in his malarial haze in the Amazonian jungle and he no longer required a cane to walk, people still saw that the physical effects of the jungle ordeal clung heavily to him. "Once the most robust of men . . . he looks ten years older than he did two years ago. His system is filled with malaria," reported the *Montgomery Advisor* on June 29. "The terrible siege of illness he experienced in the tropics lowered his vitality." And worse for Roosevelt, as the peerless media manipulator to whom image was everything would instinctively recognize, "the Colonel sick," astutely noted the *Advisor* writer, "would be much less interesting than if well and robust."[40]

Roosevelt knew all too well the *Advisor* was right and the impression that he had returned from the River of Doubt an ill and impotent man had to be extricated from the public's consciousness for him to regain the Presidency in 1916. Almost certainly, his desire to maintain the public image of manly vigor and famous cowboy resilience motivated him to have the cameramen, returning with him from South America aboard the *Aidan*, film him in a short, brisk stroll with the captain on the deck of the ship.[41] The burning pain in his damaged left leg and his malaria-ridden system would have made the nine-second walk almost unbearable, unbearable for anyone other than Theodore Roosevelt, that is. Roosevelt's imperviousness to pain was legendary from his youth. Once, while fox hunting on Long Island—before his construction of his cowboy identity in the Dakota Badlands—Roosevelt's mount struck the top rail of a fence, fell on Roosevelt and rolled him over a mound of rocks. Roosevelt, his face covered with blood from cuts and bruises, his left hand dangling from his fractured wrist, remounted and continued for another five miles, "taking twenty more fences and catching up with the survivors of the slaughter."[42]

If there was one issue that Roosevelt could use to resuscitate his headline status besides his views on the warlike Europeans and Wilson's pacific Presidential demeanor, it was the Panama Canal. It was risky to stir up the dust around a controversy that had for most Americans been long forgotten, but Roosevelt always bet on the public's positive response to his aggressive, combative style. For years, Colombia sought redress for the role the United States played in the Panamanian insurrection that cost the Colombians millions of dollars and an incalculable loss of prestige. The Wilson Administration, eager to soothe the injuries caused after Roosevelt admitted he "took" Panama in 1903, sought to end the twelve-year estrangement between the two countries with a $25,000,000 indemnity to Colombia. It was, Wilson supporters held, "a matter of justice."[43] Since June, Roosevelt ferociously defended his actions against critics who alleged that he facilitated the Panama uprising against Colombia. With the same ferocity, he mercilessly attacked the Wilson administration for paying "blackmail" to Colombia.

Wilson's action had caused, according to Roosevelt, the United States to be held in "contemptuous derision" by every other country in the world.[44] Roosevelt calculated the fray would return him "into popular esteem on screaming headlines and editorial leaders."[45] The two factions lobbed allegations at each other across newspaper headlines for months, an activity that kept Roosevelt in the public eye throughout much of the summer of 1914—no doubt feeding Roosevelt's ravenous presidential appetites. He would later claim, when it was clear that the country's appetite for Roosevelt's bombastic affectations had diminished, "It would be a mistake to nominate me [for President] unless the country has in its mood something of the heroic." While left unarticulated, when Roosevelt spoke of "something heroic," it seemed an invocation of his "man of action," aggressive—and unconstitutional—dealing with Colombia over the Isthmus of Panama. In his responses to Wilson's diplomacy with Colombia, Roosevelt was clearly and decidedly differentiating himself and his foreign policies from those of the incumbent. Roosevelt's hammer-and-tong attack upon the Wilson Administration over the Colombian indemnity captivated the attention of the editors and kept him in the limelight of the press. Still, however much the amplified press coverage of the Colombian debate over reparations for Panama improved his chances for the 1916 Republican—or Progressive Party for that matter—Presidential nomination, for Roosevelt the topic of Panama was a double-edged sword.

Although Roosevelt did find some measure of support from the press, he also encountered a growing amount of mockery and derision. Roosevelt was frequently met with cynicism, which came from a new generation of journalists, neither infatuated with the Colonel's ability to sell newspapers or books, nor indebted to him for exclusive stories from the White House. Lately, he was treated as a caricature, rather than the hero of San Juan Hill of the past. The Press Club lampooned him at their annual dinner in New York in a blistering satire about a court of inquiry into the facts of this claim to have located the source of the River of Doubt.[46] In the sketch, his character appeared with a dagger clinched between his teeth and two small cannons strapped to his waist. The article describing the raucous event showed little deference to his former position as President of the American people.[47]

With all the attention on Wilson's conciliatory position toward Colombia, newspapers were dredging up credible evidence that the Colonel did, as the Colombians accused, play an unseemly part in fomenting Panama's revolt.[48] Editorials dismissed Roosevelt and his response to the proposed treaty as an unimportant rants, and always before him was the resurrection of Pulitzer's *World's* 1908 exposé of a tangle of unethical and corrupt connections between Roosevelt's strong-arm tactics with the Senate Committee on Interoceanic Canals to purchase the bankrupt *Compagnie Universelle Du Canal Interoceanique De Panama*. [49]Slowly and steadily, stories began to reappear after years of relative quiet about the fastidious French speculator Philippe Bunau-Varilla, the high-powered New York attorney, William Nelson Cromwell and his "gang of rich Americans" —which included Roosevelt's family among other millionaires —exercised an unseemly influence over Roosevelt's sudden and astounding decision to abandon the strongly supported Nicaragua canal plan in favor of Panama.

The Opening of the Canal

The two events—Roosevelt's trip to Hartford opening hia Progressive Party tour happened the same day as the official opening of the Canal—concided. As Roosevelt prepared to rattle off to Hartford, it was not the method of acquiring the Canal that was making headlines, but the news that the 8th Wonder of the World was officially—though somewhat confounding, not formally— opened for business. Secretary of War Lindley Garrison and Acting Secretary of the Navy, Franklin D. Roosevelt, had been tight-lipped about details of the official opening. It was not until June 29 that an announcement was made that the SS *Ancon* would officially open the waterway to the world on August 15, 1914—the day Roosevelt began his whirlwind New England tour. Roosevelt had declared that without his actions in the Isthmnus—which many, including his own Secretary of War at the time, Elihu Root, had called "the rape of Panama"—the debate over the Panama Canal might still be going on, rather than *l'exploit a accompli*. Yet, he had no more involvement with the opening ceremonies than ordinary citizens who first read Garrison's announcement in late June.[50]

The festivities of the opening in Panama suggested little of the international significance of the event. "There will be no ceremonies incident to the occasion," announced Garrison.[51] A formal affair of international proportions to celebrate the opening—an event that actually never occurred—was set for the following spring in conjunction with the 1915 Panama-Pacific Exposition in San Francisco. Plans for the formal opening were extravagant. An armada of ships—twenty-seven foreign battleships and seventeen American vessels carrying heads of state, including the unlikely trio of President Wilson and former Presidents Taft and Roosevelt, aboard the battleship *Oregon*–were slated to gather on the Atlantic side of the canal, penetrate the Isthmus and cruise up the coast to San Francisco to the Expo. Nothing remotely akin to this carnival of global military prowess and cooperation would ever happen. It was not until July 12, 1920, more than a year after Roosevelt's death, that Woodrow Wilson, in a brief written statement to Congress, declared the "formal opening of the Panama Canal for use and operation in conformity with the laws of the United States."[52] But on August 15, 1914 he was silent on Panama. The eruption of the European war diverted his attention. Headlines like "Germans March to Meet United Foe," "Japan on Verge of War," and "Battle lines 250 Miles in Length: Millions of Men on either side," shrieked across newspapers in four inch type.[53] All relevant United States officials were readying for the American response to the conditions of a war unprecedented in scope and sale. Except for the cadre of minor American functionaries and their families who had long been in the Canal Zone, the United States was not formally represented.

The SS Ancon and Roosevelt's Road Trip

The *SS Ancon*, an aging cargo ship owned by the Navy and leased to the Panama Railroad Company, was to have the distinction of being the first official ship to cross the gigantic 51-mile trench. Its sister ship, the *SS Cristobal*, along with the seagoing tugboat *Gatun*, successfully negotiated trial runs earlier, thereby removing any real anxiety—but not the excitement—from the first official transit. The decks were crowded with canal administrators, Panamanian officials—including the mustachioed, President Belisario Porras of Panama—and their wives and families but no United States representative of any prominence was aboard that day. The guests of George Goethals—chief engineer and undisputed overlord of the

Guests of George Goethals aboard the S.S. Ancon celebrating the official opening of the Panama Canal. John Barrett, "The Opening of the Panama Canal," Bulletin of the Pan American Union, Vol. 39, 1914.

Canal Zone—packed the promenade. The seventy-four officers and men aboard the *Ancon* wore dazzling white uniforms and the ship itself glistened with new paint.[54]

The men in white linen suits and broad-brim white hats significantly outnumbered the women in light colored summer dresses and decorative plumed hats. The few children aboard were as sparkling in their Sunday best as the *Ancon's* newly polished fittings. As the ship headed into a waterway lined on both sides by tropical vegetation, except for the tops of dying trees in the lake and the fresh earth and broken rock of the Culebra Cut that could be seen in the distance, the "impression that it had existed from the time of Balboa" was communicated by the scene to the passengers.[55] As promised by Colonel Goethals, the flag of the American Peace Society floated in the light breeze from the *Ancon's* masthead. Ironically, at the same time beneath the fluttering flag of peace and undoubtedly unknown to the Society members—deep within the *Ancon's* cargo bay—two gigantic pieces of artillery destined to enhance the Canal's gun emplacements were stowed.[56] The fully loaded *Ancon*, polished to a high gloss for the local dignitaries and cameramen, left dock number nine at the port of Cristobal at 7:10 am, about the time Roosevelt would have been getting underway for his trip to Hartford. His speech at the Parsons theater was later that evening, but first on Roosevelt's agenda was lunch with his sister, nicknamed "Bye" at her home in Farmington, just west of Hartford.

Roosevelt had been a guest at Oldgate, his sister, Anna "Bye" Cowles' home in Farmington, many times. Bye was one of his closest confidants and strongest supporters. Her Washington residence was called "the other White House" because of the frequency of Roosevelt's visits to confer with her. Only a few political or personal decisions Roosevelt made were taken without first getting the input of Bye.[57] To arrive for lunch with his sister at her Main Street house in Farmington as he had planned, he and his entourage would have had to been on the road around the time the *Ancon* was plowing through the seven miles from the Limon Bay on the Atlantic to the Gatun Locks. Roosevelt was probably just settling down for one of his legendary eight-course luncheons after the *Ancon,* enclosed in the watery embrace of the triple flight of locks, seemed to levitate the 85 feet from the level of the Atlantic Ocean to the level of Gatun Lake. About the time Roosevelt would have tucked-in to his dessert, the *Ancon* steamed away from the Gatun Locks out onto the vast open span of Gatun Lake and into the 24-mile channel leading to the mouth of the snaking Chagres River. Approaching the eight-and-a-half mile gash across Panama's continental divide, the Culebra Cut, the *Ancon* headed toward the menacing Cucaracha Slide.

The French began excavation of the Cut in the 1880s, but the mountains overwhelmed them: they were no match for frequent floods, unexpected landslides of the mountains that the workers referred to as Hell's Gorge. A little further, the *Ancon* passed "that terror of the canal, the destructive Cucaracha Slide. Other slides, some of them quite large . . . seemed pigmies" when compared to the colossal Cucaracha.[58] It took the technology of the new decade to design the machinery and the methods to remove the 262 million cubic yards of soil necessary to carve this section of the canal that the *Ancon* was now gliding through. Roosevelt probably had not left Farmington for Hartford and the Parsons Theatre where he was to address the Progressive party faithful when the *Ancon*—steaming at full speed 24 miles through the lake to Bas Obispo—entered the Culebra Cut.

The 10,000 ton vessel seemed to those aboard to be tiny, dwarfed by the gargantuan Culebra, as one guest aboard the *Ancon* recalled. It bore straight through the Cut to reach Pedro Miguel, where it entered a single lock and descended 30 feet. A crowd of spectators, among them 100 female schoolteachers from England, gathered at the lock to greet the *Ancon*. The school teachers—as unique as a assemblage of 100 women in the Zone was—did not capture the attention of the passengers aboard the *Ancon* as did the sight of Goethals himself as he "stood at the entrance of the lock in shirt sleeves, wearing a characteristic small straw hat and carrying in his hand his ever present umbrella."[59] A mighty cheer erupted from the passengers when they saw Goethals, who ignored the adulation "with characteristic modesty" and continued inspecting the operation of the lock.[60] In thirty minutes, the *Ancon* descended into the water of Miraflores Lake and onward to slide down the two flights of the Miraflores Locks.

Now, the *Ancon* was only eight miles away from the deep water of the Pacific Ocean and "the gateway to its mighty commerce of uncounted millions of dollars and population."[61] Presently, the *Ancon* passed Balboa with its repair shops, dry docks, and the old Panama Railroad wharves. The shriek from whistles of the several ships gathering, waiting their turn to cross from the Pacific to the Atlantic the following day, and from shops and launches, pierced the air until to the passengers of the *Ancon* it "seemed as if bedlam was veritably let loose." Increasing its speed, the *Ancon* headed past the breakwater, beyond the fortified islands of Naos, Perico, and Flamenco, past the last buoys marking the entrance to the canal and "majestically stuck her nose into the deep water of the Pacific Ocean."[62] It then swung around and headed back to Balboa. About 2,000 miles away, Roosevelt would have also reached his destination, the Parsons Theater, around the same time that the *Ancon* merrymakers were returning to Cristobal aboard specially chartered Panama Railroad cars.

On his way to the theatre to deliver his speech, Roosevelt's automobile passed through streets that were deserted except for the usual Saturday night shoppers and people gathered to read the bulletins about the European war. Few people recognized him as he rode through the hushed streets of Hartford until he reached the stage door, where he was quickly ushered inside. The expectant throng of 2,000 Progressives greeted him enthusiastically when he took the stage. At one point, the crowd erupted into wild applause when someone shouted from the audience, "Our next President!"[63] In his lengthy speech that night, Roosevelt explained his unorthodox and unpopular endorsement of a Republican instead of a Progressive for governor of New York, extolled the virtue of the Monroe Doctrine, lambasted treaties as worthless, and abused the Payne-Aldrich Tariff, but never mentioned Panama.[64] Curiously, "the long-coveted canal . . . the dream and idealism of centuries," with its official opening had "at last become a tangible fact, a golden reality," went unnoticed by the Colonel.[65]

The following month, Roosevelt would use Panama to reinforce the importance of Monroe Doctrine vigilance when he wrote in

Image of an exhausted Roosevelt during his 1914 Progressive Party campaign, Library of Congress, 1914.

Outlook magazine that it was Belgium's neutrality in the Great War that caused the dire conditions of the German occupation. He cautioned readers that the same could befall the United States if it remained neutral. "If any old world military power were engaged in war and deemed such an action necessary and safe," wrote the former President, "it would at once seize the Panama Canal exactly as Belgium had Luxemburg have been overrun by Germany, as Korea has been seized by Japan.[66] But, on August 15, 1914 he was mute on the topic of the Panama Canal.

It is curious that after his elaborate political capital investment in creating a gleaming technological reality out of the remnants of the rusted-out, mud-covered, malaria infested ruins left by the bankrupt *Compagnie Universelle du Canal Interocéanique,* he completely

270

ignored the opening in his Hartford speech.[67] This should have been an occasion for crowing—his vindication after the shellacking he took from the *World* libel case—about the opening of the American eighth wonder of the world. Roosevelt himself referred to the project of as his crowning achievement in office. Why this uncharacteristic reticence about Panama? On the other hand, perhaps a better, more penetrating question to have asked Roosevelt—one that might have been asked by a cheeky reporter for *The World* in an earlier era—was why Panama in the first place? But then, as now, answers to that question would unsettle the status quo and disturb the reflection of self that most Americans saw in Theodore Roosevelt and the stunning achievement of the construction of the Panama Canal. Even though his personal stock was falling in 1914, his death five years later would rocket him to the zenith of popularity surpassing and outlasting any that he himself created in his long and successful career of manufacturing his own myth. In the twenty-first century, Roosevelt would enjoy a level of imperviousness to criticism that he fought so desperately to achieve in his lifetime.

One of the French dredges abandoned in Panama. Farnhum Bishop, Panama:n, Past and Present, 1916.

EPILOGUE

The More Things Change

One hundred years after the *SS Ancon* officially opened the Panama Canal, the question remains, "Who got the money?" There is little doubt where most of the money went. The sixteen signatories of William Nelson Cromwell's American Panama Canal syndicate agreement—including Theodore Roosevelt's brother-in-law Douglas Robinson, William Taft's brother Charles, and financier J.P. Morgan—benefited in the most straightforward way. The Consortium netted somewhere in the range of $24 million after paying the French receiver $16 million.[1] If the group split the proceeds evenly between all sixteen members, each man's share would be somewhere in the neighborhood of $1.5 million dollars, over $40 million each in today's terms. And as usual, Cromwell, the "Jesse James of Wall Street," realized huge profits on both sides of the deal. For negotiating the terms, the *San Francisco Call* reported that Cromwell's compensation was an astonishing, headline worthy, $2 million dollars, over $50 million in 2013 dollars. At the time, it was the largest legal fee received by any American lawyer in history.[2] Also to Cromwell's advantage, the sale also included seven million dollars' worth of Panama Railroad stock, which perhaps benefited Cromwell more than other syndicate members, because as well as being a director and legal counsel for the Railroad, he was also a major stockholder.

The indirect opportunities gained by the men associated with the American Panama Canal venture are incalculable. Cromwell was appointed sole fiscal commissioner for Panama by the government of Panama to manage the investment of the ten million dollars the United States paid to Panama for the concession to build the canal. Of the $10 million, $6 million was set aside by the Panama constitution strictly for real estate investments.[3] On Cromwell's direction, the Cromwell & Sullivan law firm funneled the investment into Manhattan properties, through the real estate firm of Douglas Robinson. Philippe Bunau-Varilla—who had been introduced to Roosevelt by Robinson's wife and Roosevelt's sister, Corinne—claimed that he suggested the mandate become a feature of the new Republic's constitution.[4] J.P. Morgan became the sole fiscal agent for transferring the $40 million and then afterward acted as the Republic of Panama's official banker. Douglas Robinson was also a director of J.P. Morgan's Astor National Bank, which had a hand in the real estate transfers.[5]

Additionally, as Special Fiscal Commissioner of Republic of Panama in the investment of the $10,000,000 received by them from the U.S., Cromwell invested $1,000,000 back into Panama Railroad bonds. He was the adviser for the Railroad $233,000 "emergency contracts" with the U.S. Isthmus Canal Commission, which he was awarded without competitive bidding, to the financial benefit of his holdings. And, Cromwell received $72,000 from government in payment for 270 railway shares reported secured from private stockholders. Cromwell also had other banking and corporate interests in Panama, including his stake in the American Trade Development Company which sold ice and electric power in Panama in direct competition with government plants. [6]

Under ordinary circumstances, given the market economy and political framework Americans function under and within, the response to Cromwell's orchestration of events might appear laudable; we might be expected to hear a bravo for the entrepreneurship skills exhibited by Cromwell and his "gang of rich Americans." However, the conditions under which the events surrounding the Panama Canal purchase transpired were not ordinary, market conditions. In this situation, the game was rigged. The Panama revolution and the purchase of the Panama Canal would not have—could not have—happened without the connivance and support of the President of the United States, Theodore Roosevelt.

Today, Panama and its Canal are going through another scandal, this time of its own making. In February of 2014, work on a massive

Canal expansion project, headed by the Spanish construction giant Sacyr, suddenly came to a halt. Sacyr and its other consortium members claimed to need an additional $1.6 billion from the Panama Canal Authority for unforeseen costs. Otherwise, Sacyr threatened, the work on the project would cease. Neither side would budge and true to their word, the construction syndicate sent their workers home. Panama's President Ricardo Martinelli escalated tensions when he announced that Panama would complete the project by itself if the syndicate did not resume construction.[7] During the dust-up over the unforeseen cost issues, newspaper and television journalists—much like Joseph Pulitzer's staff at *The World* in investigating Theodore Roosevelt's Panama Canal involvement in 1908—began to resurrect the long forgotten issue some had raised, that the bid by the syndicate had been ludicrously low in the first place. Many wondered if the agreement between Sacyr and Panama had been on the up-and-up.

After Martinelli assumed office in 2009, he organized and managed the bidding and contracting process for the construction of the new locks. According to the Spanish newspaper *El Confidencial*, Martinelli sent his confidant and tourism minister to Spain to discuss the contract with Sacyr. In the end, it was Sacyr's syndicate —which also included the Italian company Impregilo, Belgian dredging enterprise Jan de Nul, and Panamanian CUSA—a construction company held by the family of Alberto Alemán Zubieta who was at that time the Panama Canal Authority CEO—that offered the lowest bid.[8] It would be Panama's involvement with the Italian company Impregilo that would exposed Panama's President to charges of corruption. After months of investigations, the Italian Public Ministry announced that President Martinelli—who holds dual citizenship in Italy—would be indicted and prosecuted in Italy on extortion and corruption charges when he leaves office in June of 2014. Amongst other vice and corruption charges, the Italians believe Martinelli to be guilty of extorting kickbacks from Impregilo.[9] Martinelli is denying the charges.

The saga of the politics of greed of the government and business players in the Panama Canal has been endemic since its Count Ferdinand de Lesseps schemed to dig his sea-level canal across the

Isthmus. Networks of players seeking their fortunes found both ruin and success in the decades of death and recovery. Their survival was the result of having family, friends, and associates in high places in government and in the financial institutions of France, the United States and, ultimately in Panama. If the allegations against the Panamanian President are proven true it would match the nature of greed, corruption, deceit, and hubris of the French era and William Nelson Cromwell, Philippe Bunau-Varilla, and Theodore Roosevelt in the United States Panama Canal purchase. While the breadth of global business dealings in today's Panama Canal expansion may make the American experience in Panama pale in comparison, there is no doubt that vast fortunes were won and lost in international transactions like these. The formula is timeless: winning occurred often enough to encourage the gambling, the aligning of profiteers, and the amassing of enormous fortunes. These fortunes have been used, in part, to support further adventures such as the early twentieth century American Panama Canal construction and now its Panamanian twenty-first century expansion.

More villains emerge from the mire and muss of the acquisition of Panama Canal by the United States than do heroes. Even though historians are more likely to record his bigoted Confederate approach to matters of race than to note his uncompromising investigations of the Panama Canal purchase—Senator John Tyler Morgan is one such hero. He was relentless and fearless in his quest to uncover the truth behind Roosevelt's sudden pivot away from Nicaragua and toward Panama. Certainly Joseph Pulitzer, and his enterprising and audacious *World* staff demonstrated a daring determination to uphold the principle of speaking truth to power, and they shine as heroic models. Also later, as the canal project experienced times of crisis, we can point to the individual valiant acts of George Goethals and William Gorgas in implementation and management of the Canal. Yet, the long struggle for an Isthmusian Canal is more of a story of human misery and death that fed the appetites of those who sought power and loot, than it is a tale of heroes. The challenges faced today in Panama are but mere echoes of the manipulation, domination, and corruption spawned by Theodore Roosevelt and the clutch of power and money seekers he served in his Presidency.

NOTES

Introduction

1 United States, Charles M. Hough, and Albert B. Anderson. *The Roosevelt Panama Libel Case against the New York World and Indianapolis News: Decision of Charles M. Hough, Judge of the United States Court for the Southern District of New York, and Albert B. Anderson, Judge of the United States Court for the District of Indianapolis, Together with an Account of the Circumstances That Led to These Unprecedented Prosecutions on the Part of the United States Government, and a Stenographic Report of the Trial of the New York World.* ([S.l.]: Printed for the New York World, 1910), 5.

2 Henry Watterson, *Crittenden Press* (Marion, Ky.), 26 Feb. 1903, p. 1.

3 Julius Grigore, Jr. *First Presentation of All Stocks and Bonds Issued by the Compagnie Universelle du Canal Interoceanique de Panama, 1880 - 1889 and Compagnie Nouvelle du Canal de Panama, 1894*, W.G. Guy, Venice, Florida.

4 Joseph J. O'Brien, *Will the Panama Canal Fail?: The Blunders of De Lesseps and Their Significance to America* (Washington, D.C., s.n. 1911), 6-7.

5 Ibid.

6 Ibid.

7 C. E. Howard Vincent, *The Suez Canal, its Origin, Constitution, and Administration*, (London: Soulden & Co., 1905), 17.

8 O'Brien, 9.

9 Grigore, n.p.

10 "News by Telegraph," *San Francisco Bulletin.* (San Francisco, Ca.), 12 Sept 1883, p. 3.

11 "A Modern South Sea Bubble Bursting," *The Sunday Herald.* (Washington, D.C.), 01 Nov. 1885, p. 1.

12 Ernest Lambert, "The Story of Panama," *Review of Reviews*, Vol 7, (1889): 320.

13 Ibid.

14 Grigore, n.p.

15 Frank Lydston, Panama and the Sierras: *A Doctor's Wander Days.* Chicago: Riverton Press, 1900, 58.

16 R.H. Shepard, "The Count de Lesseps of Today," *McClure's Magazine* (June 1893): 89.

17 "The Great Trial Begun; Damaging Admissions Made by Charles De Lesseps," *New York Times*, (New York, N.Y.), 11 Jan 1893, p. 1.

18 Shepard, 89.

CHAPTER ONE

1   Richard Harding Davis, *Three Gringos in Venezuela and Central America*, (New York: Harper & Bros, 1896), 194.

2   Ibid., 194-197.

3   Ibid.

4   Theodor de Bry, "Balboa Throwing Indian Sodomites to the Dogs," 1594.

5   Samuel L Mitchill, and Edward Miller. *Medical Repository of Original Essays and Intelligence Relative to Physic, Surgery, Chemistry, and Natural History*, (New York: E. Bliss and E. White, 1797), 128.

6   Ibid., Mitchill reported, much amused at the Spanish response, 130.

7   *Daily Evening Star.* (Washington [D.C.]), 19 Sept. 1853, p. 1.

8   "The Panama Railroad," Society of Engineers. London: C. Whiting, (May 1869):46.

9   Ibid.

10 Ibid.

11 "The Construction of the Panama Railroad," *Popular Science Monthly*, (November 1874- April 1875): 256.

12 Wolford Nelson, *Five Years at Panama: the Transisthmian Canal.* London: Low, Marston, Searle & Rivington, 1891), 152.

13 "Panama Fever" North American, (Philadelphia, PA). September 13, 1853, p. 2.

14 Ibid, 150.

15 Ibid, 149.

16 Augustus Henry Keane and Clements R. Markham, *Central and South America.* (London: E. Stanford, 1901), 263.

17 Lindon Wallace Bates, *The Crisis at Panama* (New York: L.W. Bates,1906), 8.

18 Nelson, 151

19 Ibid., 151-152

20 Ulysses S. Grant, Personal Memoirs of U.S. Grant (New York: C.L. Webster & Co. 1885), 104.

21 Ibid.

22 Ibid.

23 Ibid.,

24 Ibid., 156.

25 Archibald Smith, "The Rise and Progress of Yellow fever in Peru," *The Edinburgh Medical and Surgical Journal* (1855):172.

26 Every presidential commission since Grant–including the 1902 Walker interoceanic commission preferred Nicaragua until just days before Roosevelt dragooned its members into revoking its original results.

27 War Department, Office of the Chief of Staff, War College Division, General Staff. (Washington: G.P.O., 1903), 19.

28 Harry C. Hale, *Notes on Panama* (Washington: Govt. Print. Off, 1903), 102.

29 Christopher Smart, et al. *The World Displayed ; or, A Curious Collection of Voyages and Travels* (Philadelphia: Dobelbower, Key, and Simpson, 1795), 115. <http://opac.newsbank.com/select/evans/29926>.

30 "Pizarro and the Conquest of Peru," *Hogg's Weekly Instructor*, Vol. 5-6 (1850):123.

31 In 1902, 150 of the 650 workers refused to leave their transport ship because of the rumor of yellow fever. Police, armed with guns and bayonets, went aboard and convinced 500 workers to disembark, but the presence of an armed force had no effect on 150 laborers who said they would rather die there than go ashore. After two hours of waiting, "the police then attacked the laborers with their batons, and scores of unfortunate men were felled to the deck, bleeding profusely. Many laborers took refuge in the rigging, and upwards of fifty jumped overboard into the sea to escape." C.H. Norman, "Letters to the Editor," *Liberty Review* Vol. 18, (1905):234.

32 Nelson, 149.

33 Edward Hobart Seymore, "The Present State of the Panama Canal," The *Nineteenth Century Review*, Vol. 176 (1892), 300 http://nrs.harvard.edu/urn-3:FHCL:1166941

34 H.C. Hale, *Notes on Panama*, (Washington: G.P.O. 1903), 19.

35 United States. 1902. *Hearings before the Senate Committee on Interoceanic Canals on H.R. 3110, first session Fifty-seventh Congress, March 14, 1902*, (Washington: G.P.O. 1903), 904.

36 Fessenden Nott Otis, *Isthmus of Panama: History of the Panama Railroad and of the Pacific Mail Steamship Company, Together with a Traveller's Guide and Business Man's Hand-Book for the Panama*

Railroad, and the Lines of Steamships Connecting It with Europe, the United States, the North and South Atlantic and Pacific Coasts, China, Australia, and Japan. (New York: Harper & Bros, 1867), vii.

37 Napoleon, Louis Bonaparte. *Canal of Nicaragua: or, a Project to Connect the Atlantic and Pacific Oceans by Means of a Canal.* (London: Mills & Son, 1846), 6.

38 Ibid., 9.

39 Theodore Roosevelt, *The Selected Letters of Theodore Roosevelt*, H.W. Brands, ed, (New York: Rowan &Littlefield, 2007), 132.

40 Otis, 21.

41 "For California," *Gallipolis Journal.* (Gallipolis, Ohio), 05 Feb. 1852, p. 2.

42 William V. Wells, *Walker's Expedition to Nicaragua: A History of the Central American War ... with a New and Accurate Map of Central America, and a Memoir and Portr. of William Walker.* (New York: Stringer and Townsend, 1856), 25.

43 "Gen. W.M. Walker and Nicaragua," *Raftsman's Journal.* (Clearfield, Pa.), 03 Dec. 1856.

44 "The Surrender of Walker," *Daily Nashville patriot.* (Nashville, Tenn.), 03 Oct. 1860, p.1.

45 "The Last of General Walker," *The Daily Dispatch.* (Richmond [Va.]), 01 Oct. 1860, p. 1.

46 "Operations of Mons. Belly," *The Daily Dispatch.* (Richmond [Va.]), 18 June 1858, p. 1.

47 "Inter-Oceanic Canal Project," *Evening Star.* (Washington, D.C.), 16 July 1879, p. 1.

48 James P. Boyd, *Military And Civil Life Of Gen. Ulysses S. Grant: Leading Soldier of the Age, President of The United States, Loved and Honored American Citizen, the World's Most Distinguished Man.* (Philadelphia, Pa: Scammell & Co., 1885), 584.

49 John H. Mitchell, *The Nicaragua Canal; The Only Feasible and Practical Route for An Inter-oceanic Canal; Speech ... In The Senate of the United States, Thursday June 5 and Saturday June 7, 1902.* (Washington: G.P.O. 1902), 20.

50 "The De Lesseps Canal Scheme," *Evening Star.* (Washington, D.C.), 28 July 1879, p.1.

51 Ibid.

52 Ibid.

53 "The Isthmus Canal," *Evening Star.* (Washington, D.C.), 28 July 1879, p.1.

54 "The Land of the Sun," *Belmont Chronicle.* (St. Clairsville, Ohio), 09 April 1885, p. 2.)
55 Ibid.
56 James Buchanan Eads, *Inter-oceanic Ship Railway: Address of James B. Eads Delivered to the San Francisco Chamber of Commerce.* (St. Louis, Mo.: Levison & Blythe Stationery Company, 1880), 6.
57 William Taylor, "The Panama Canal and the Merchant Marine," *Traffic World, Vol. 26, No. 15* (1915): 951.
58 "Work on Nicaragua Canal," *Evening Star.* (Washington, D.C.), 07 Feb. 1890, p.1.
59 "Conspirators Sentences," *Omaha Daily Bee.* (Omaha [Neb.]), 10 Feb. 1893, p.1.
60 "Caught a Minister," *St. Paul Daily Globe.* (Saint Paul, Minn.), 06 Jan 1893, p. 1; "Three are Challenged," *The Princeton Union.* (Princeton, Minn.), 24 Nov. 1892, p.1; "Another Scandal," *The Wheeling Daily Intelligencer.* (Wheeling, W. Va.), 23 June 1893, p. 1.
61 "The Panama Swindlers," *The Wheeling Daily Intelligencer.* (Wheeling, W. Va.), 10 Feb. 1893 p. 1.
62 "Its Faith Broken," *The Morning Call.* (San Francisco Ca.), 14 Jan. 1893., p.1.)
63 Merrill Edwards Gates, *Men of Mark in America; Ideals of American Life Told in Biographies of Eminent Living Americans* (Washington, D.C.: Men of Mark Pub. Co., 1905), 192.
64 Alexander S. Bacon, *The Woolly Horse,* (New York: n.p., 1909), 15.

CHAPTER 2

1 Thorstin Veblin, *Theory of the Leisure Class: An Economic Study of Institutions.* (New York: B.W. Huebsch, 1919), 209.
2 "Great Excitement at Stock Exchange," *The WheelingDdaily Intelligencer.* (Wheeling, W. Va.), 04 April 1877, p.1.
3 Ibid.
4 "Two of Our Leaders," *Concord: International Arbitration and Peace Association.* Vol 13-15 (364), 1898.
5 Royal Geographical Society (Great Britain). *Proceedings of the Royal Geographical Society and Monthly Record of Geography.* (London: Edward Stanford, 1879), 368.
6 Willis Fletcher Johnson, *Four Centuries of the Panama Canal.* (New York: H. Holt and Co, 1906), 76.

7   Colby Mitchell Chester, *The Panama Canal*. (Washington: National Geographic Society, 1905), 447.

8   "The Isthmusian Canal," *The New Orleans Daily Democrat*. (New Orleans, La.), 06 June 1879, p.1.

9   *"The Panama Canal'" Daily Los Angeles Herald*. (Los Angeles, Ca.), 09 Oct. 1880, p. 1.

10 "The Panama Canal Syndicate," *Sacramento Daily Record-Union*. (Sacramento, Calif.), 05 Oct. 1880, p. 2.

11 "Canal Conundrums," *The Salt Lake Herald*. (Salt Lake City, Utah), 05 Oct. 1880, p. 1.

12 Veblin, 230.

13 Panama Canal." *Evening Star*. (Washington, D.C.), 09 Sept. 1897, 1.

14 "Won't Buy the Panama Canal. No Negotiations with the United States" *Minneapolis Journal*. (Minneapolis MN.), 29 December, 1900, p.1.

15 "Pushing the Canal Bill," *The Evening Times*. (Washington, D.C.), 17 Dec. 1900, p. 1.

16 "Won't Buy the Panama Canal. No Negotiations with the United States," *Minneapolis Journal* 29 December 1900:1

17 "Duty of Congress," *Evening Star*. (Washington, D.C.), 7 Jan 1901, 1

18 Alexander S. Bacon, *The Woolly Horse*, (New York: n.p., 1909), 20.

19 "The Interoceanic Canal" *Macon Telegraph*, December 31, 1899: 8.

20 United States, Frank D. Pavey, William Nelson Cromwell, and Philippe Bunau-Varilla. *The Story of Panama. Hearings on the Rainey Resolution Before the Committee on Foreign Affairs of the House of Representatives*. (Washington: G.P.O., 1913), 691.

21 United States. *Investigation of Panama Canal Matters. Hearings Before the Committee on Interoceanic Canals of the United States Senate in the Matter of the Senate Resolution Adopted January 9, 1906, Providing for an Investigation of Matters Relating to the Panama Canal, Etc* (Washington: G.P.O., 1906), 3201.

22 "The French," *The Salt Lake Herald*. (Salt Lake City, Utah), 14 Dec. 1889, p.1.

23 *The Story of Panama. Hearings on the Rainey Resolution* , 630.

24 "The Week," *The Nation Vol. 70*. New York, N.Y.: J.H. Richards, (1900): 1.

25 "The Interoceanic Canal" *Macon Telegraph* (Macon Ga.), 31 Dec. 1899, p. 8.

26 "The Week," *The Nation Vol. 70* New York, N.Y.: J.H. Richards, (1900): 1.

27 "The New Panama Canal Company," *Engineering World; A Weekly Technical Journal of Civil, Mechanical, Electrical, Mining and Architectural Engineering and Construction, Vol 1-2.* Chicago: Engineering world Pub. Co., (1905): 353.

28 "Powerful Conspiracy to Defeat the Nicaragua Canal" *The St. Louis Republic.* (St. Louis, Mo.), 23 Dec. 1900, p. 1.

29 Ibid.

30 Ibid.

31 "The Hand of Colis. P. Huntington," *The San Francisco Call.* (San Francisco Calif.), 13 Nov. 1895, p. 1.

32 Joseph Nimmo, *The Nicaragua Canal: Investigate Before Investing,* Washington, D. C.: Rufus H. Darby, 6.

33 "The Hand of Colis. P. Huntington," *The San Francisco Call.* (San Francisco Calif.), 13 Nov. 1895, p. 1.

34 Ibid.

35 "Stops the Warfare," *The San Francisco Call.* (San Francisco, Ca.), 17 Dec. 1895 , p. 1.

36 "Panama Cana Scheme," *The Hawaiian Star.* (Honolulu, Oahu), 04 Jan. 1900, p.1.

37 William McKinley: "Second Annual Message," December 5, 1898. Online by Gerhard Peters and John T. Woolley, *The American Presidency Project.* http://www.presidency.ucsb.edu/ws/?pid=29539, n. p.

38 William McKinley: "Fourth Annual Message," December 3, 1900. Online by Gerhard Peters and John T. Woolley, *The American Presidency Project.* http://www.presidency.ucsb.edu/ws/?pid=29541, n.p.

39 "Opposition to Merry Remnders Rodrigues Persona Non Gratis," *Los Angles Herald*, 04 Jan. 1898, p.1. California Digital Newspaper Collection, Center for Bibliographic Studies and Research, University of California, Riverside, <http://cdnc.ucr.edu>.

40 "Wanted: A Canal." *The Hawaiian Gazette* (Honolulu , Hawaii]), 10 September 1897, p. 1.

41 "The New State Protests," *New-York Tribune.* (New York, N.Y.), 23 Jan. 1897, p.1.

42 "Senate Sensations, *Kansas City Daily Journal.* (Kansas City, Mo.), 23 Jan. 1897, p.1.

43 Corry M. Straddon, "Our Diplomatic Relations with Nicaragua," *The American Monthly Review of Reviews, Vol 20*, New York: Review of Reviews, (1897): 445.

44 "Congressional." *The Globe-Republican*, (Dodge City, Kan.), 28 January 1897, 6.

45 "The Canal Bill." *The San Francisco Call,* (San Francisco, Calif.), 22 January 1897, 3.

46 *Story of Panama* 98.

47 "Filibustering Tactics." *The San Francisco Call*, (San Francisco Calif.) January 23, 1897, 6.

48 "The Hand of Huntington." *The Riverside Daily Enterprise*, 8 November 1898, 1.

49 Henry T. Rainey, quoted in *The Story of Panama Hearings on the Rainey Resolution Before the Committee on Foreign Affairs of the House of Representatives.* (Washington: Govt. Print. Off, 1913) 61-62.

50 *Story of Panama*, 102.

51 William Nelson Cromwell quoted in *Story of Panama*, 149.

52 "Never Mind the Treaty," *The Minneapolis Journal.* (Minneapolis, Minn.), 02 Jan. 1901, p.1.

53 "The Canal Can Never be Finished." *The San Francisco Call*, (San Francisco Calif.) 4 December 1898, p. 1.

54 Ibid.

55 *Story of Panama*, 104.

56 Ibid, 224

57 Ibid.

58 "Canal Bill in the House," *The Times.* (Washington D.C.), 09 January 1899, 2.

59 Ibid.

60 *Story of Panama*, 224.

61 "Canal Project in Danger," *The Times.* (Washington D.C.), 14 January 1899, 3.

62 Ibid.

63 *Hearings Before the Committee on Interstate and Foreign Commerce of the House of Representatives on New Panama Canal Company, the Maritime Company, and the Nicaragua Canal Company, (Grace-Eyre-Craigan Syndicate.) Held January 17, 18, 19, 20, and 25, 1899.* (Washington: G.P.O., 1899) 9.

64 John Ely Briggs, *William Peters Hepburn.* (Iowa City, Ia: The State Historical Society of Iowa, 1919), 203.

65 "Reed in the Way." *Willmar Tribune,* (Wilmer Minn.), 10 May 1899, 2.

66 "Junket to Panama." *The Evening Times.* (Washington, D.C.), 15 March 1899, p. 3.

67 "Powerful Opposition to Nicaragua Canal." *San Francisco Call*, (San Francisco Calif.) 11 June 1999, p. 1.

68 Ibid.

69 *Story of Panama*, 224.

70 Isthmian Canal Commission (U.S.), and John Grimes Walker. *Report of the Isthmian Canal Commission, 1899-1901*. (Washington: G.O.P., 1904), 14.

71 "The Canal Commission," *The Anaconda Standard*. (Anaconda, Mont.), 02 Oct. 1899, p. 4.

72 John G. Walker, et al., *Report of the Isthmian Canal Commission*, (Washington: Govt. Pub. Off., 1899-1901), 20.

73 "Still Hve Faith in the Panama Canal," *The San Francisco Call*. (San Francisco, Calif.), 15 Oct. 1900, p.2.

74 Philippe Bunau-Varilla. *Panama; The Creation, Destruction, and Resurrection*. New York: R.M. McBride, 1920, 167.

75 William R. Grace and Joseph Pulitzer. *William R. Grace, Plaintiff, against Joseph Pulitzer, Defendant Summons, Complaint, Affidavits and Order. Miller, Peckham, & Dixon, Attorneys for Plaintiff*. New York: M.B. Brown, 1885. http://catalog.hathitrust.org/api/volumes/oclc/80614822.html, 14.

76 "Cragin-Eyre Concessions," *New-York Tribune*. (New York [N.Y.]), 10 Feb. 1900, 3.

77 *Hearings Before the Committee on Interstate and Foreign Commerce,* 135.

78 "The Isthmian Canal." *The Evening Times*. (Washington, D.C.), 29 Dec. 1899, 4.

79 "Morgan's Canal Report," *The Times*. (Washington, D.C.), 19 Jan. 1900, p. 1.

80 "Canal Bill Sure to Pass this Session, "*The San Francisco Call*. (San Francisco, Calif.), 23 Feb. 1900, p. 3.

81 "Canal Bill Passes," *The Hartford Republican*. (Hartford, Ky.), 11 May 1900, p. 1.

82 "Mr. Morgan's Plain Talk," *The Times*. (Washington, D.C.), 26 May 1900, p. 1.

83 Ibid.

84 Ibid.

85 "Favors Nicaragua Route," *New-York Tribune*. (New York, N.Y.), 05 Dec. 1900, p. 3.

86 "Business Notes." *Publishers Weekly*, (11 Aug 1906): 326.

87 Philippe Bunau-Varilla, *Panama; The Creation, Destruction, and Resurrection* (New York: R.M. McBride, 1920), 179.

88 Philippe Bunau-Varilla, *Nicaragua or Panama: The Substance of a Series of Conferences Made Before the Commercial Club of Cincinnati, [...] Before the Princeton University in New Jersey, Etc., Etc., and of a Formal Address to the Chamber of Commerce of the State of New York* (New York: Knickerbocker Press, 1901), 3.

89 Ibid., 28.

90 Ibid., 29.

91 Bunau-Varilla, *Panama,* 187.

92 Ibid., 186.

93 Ibid,. 188.

CHAPTER 3

1 Everett Marshall, *Complete Life of William McKinley and Story of His Assassination* (1901), 40.

2 "The Negro Who Thumped Czolgosz," *The Colored American.* (Washington, D.C.), 14 Sept. 1901, p.1.

3 "McKinley Lives!" *St. Albans Daily Messenger*, (St. Albans, Vt.), 07 Sept 1901, p. 5.

4 "Mob Sought to Kill Assassin," *The St. Louis Republic*, (St. Louis, Mo.), 7 Sept 1901, p. 2.

5 Ibid.

6 Ibid.

7 Pan-American Exposition. *Official Catalogue and Guide Book to the Pan-American Exposition: With Maps of Exposition and Illustrations*, Buffalo, N.Y., U.S.A., May 1st to Nov. 1st, 1901 (1901), 38.

8 "The Buffalo Specialists," *The Richmond Times*, (Richmond, Va.), 8 Sept 1901, p. 1.

9 "Platform Adopted by Republican State Convention," *The San Francisco Call*, (San Francisco, Calif.), 16 May1900, p. 1.

10 Lindley Keasbey, *The Nicaragua Canal And The Monroe Doctrine: A Political History Of Isthmus Transit, With Special Reference To The Nicaragua Canal Project And The Attitude Of The United States* (1896), p. 1.

11 "The People Want the Nicaragua Canal Built," *The San Diego News*, 21 Nov 1894, reprinted *Los Angles Herald*, 22 Nov. 1894, p.1.

12 "President Hayes Greatly Displeased with Secretary Thompson," *Las Vegas Morning Gazette.* (Las Vegas, N.M.), 15 Dec. 1880 , p. 1.

13 Ulysses S. Grant, quoted in Keasbey, 1.

14 "The Panama Canal Co.," *The Herald*, (Los Angeles Calif.), 30 Nov 1898, p. 9.

15 "Urges Immediate Canal Building," *The San Francisco Call*, 17 May 1900, 1.

16 Morgan, John Tyler. *An American Isthmian Canal and the Choice of Routes: Speech of Hon. John T. Morgan, of Alabama, in the Senate of the United States*, April 17, 1902 (1902), 11.

17 *The Successful American*, (Vol. 4, 1900): 308.

18 Ibid.

19 Rexmond Canning Cochrane, *Measures for Progress: A History of the National Bureau of Standards*, Issue 275 (1966), 2.

20 Pan-American Exposition. *Official Catalogue and Guide Book to the Pan-American Exposition With Maps of Exposition and Illustrations*, Buffalo, N.Y., U.S.A., May 1st to Nov. 1st, 1901. (Buffalo, N.Y.: Charles Ahrhart, 1901). n.p.

21 "Is Formally Opened," *The Billings Gazette*. (Billings, Mont.), 21 May 1901, p. 1.

22 Mark Bennitt, *The Pan-American Exposition and How to See It : With a Condensed Guide to Buffalo and Niagara Falls*. (Buffalo, N.Y.: Goff Co, 1901), n.p.

23 Mary Bronson Hartt, "How to See the Pan American Exposition," *Everybody's Magazine*, (Vol. 5, 1901): 394.

24 "A Weekly Review Of Current Progress In Electricity And Its Practical Applications," *The Electrical World And Engineer*, (Vol. 37, 1901): 827.

25 Bennitt, n.p.

26 *Scientific American: Supplement*, (Vol. 51, 1901): 21169.

27 Charles S Olcott, *The Life of William McKinley* (1916), 315.

28 "Was Warned," *Akron Daily Democrat*,(Akron Ohio), 7 Sept 1901, p. 1.

29 "Big Time," *Akron Daily Democrat*. (Akron, Ohio), 05 Sept. 1901, p.1

30 "President McKinley," *Ohio Farmer*, (Vol. 100, Sept 1901):186.

31 Everett Marshall, *Complete life of William McKinley and Story of His Assassination* (1901), 35.

32 Ibid.

33 "The Case of President McKinley," *Medical Record*, (Vol. 60, 1901): 603.

34 Ibid.

35 Murat Halstead, *The Illustrious Life of William McKinley: Our Martyred President* (1901), 60.

36 "President McKinley is Dying," *The San Francisco Call.* (San Francisco Calif.), 13 Sept 1901, p. 1.

37 "Condition Critical: President McKinley is Liable to Die at any Moment, " *The Houston Daily Post*, 13 Sept 1901, p. 1.

38 "Guides Hunted for Hours to Find President Roosevelt," *The St. Louis Republic.* (St. Louis, Mo.), 15 Sept 1901, p. 1.

39 "Exposition Temple of Music Scene of Dastardly Crime," *The San Francisco Call.* (San Francisco, Calif.), 07 Sept. 1901, p.1.

40 Murat Halsted, *The Life of Theodore Roosevelt the Twenty-Fifth President of the United States* (1903), 239.

41 "The Search for Roosevelt," *The Saint Paul Globe.* (St. Paul, Minn.), 15 Sept. 1901, p.1.

42 J. Martin Miller, *The Triumphant Life of Theodore Roosevelt, Citizen, Statesman, President.* Philadelphia: s.n, 1904, 135.

43 "Searching Now for Roosevelt," *The Evening World.* (New York, N.Y.), 13 Sept. 1901, p.1.

44 Ibid.

45 "Roosevelt's Exciting Ride," *The Indianapolis Journal.* (Indianapolis [Ind.]), 15 Sept. 1901, p.1.

46 Ibid., 240.

47 Alexander K. McClure and Charles Morris, *The Authentic Life of William McKinley ... Together with a Life Sketch of Theodore Roosevelt* (1901), 489.

48 Halstead, *The Life of Theodore Roosevelt*, 239.

49 "Search on a Mount," *The Indianapolis Journal.* (Indianapolis [Ind.]), 15 Sept. 1901, p. 1.

50 Norman Hall, quoted in Sandra Weber, *Adirondack Roots: Stories of Hiking, History, and Women* (2011), 27.

51 Halstead, *The Life of Theodore Roosevelt*, 240.

52 Quoted in Hermann Hagedorn, *The Roosevelt Family of Sagamore Hill* (1954), 118.

53 Theodore Roosevelt, *An Autobiography* (1923), 349.

54 Halstead, *The Life of Theodore Roosevelt*, 242.

55 Alfred L. Donaldson, *A History of the Adirondacks* (1921), 156.

56 "Theodore Roosevelt Has Taken Office," *The St. Louis Republic.* (St. Louis, Mo.), 15 Sept. 1901, p.1.

57 Theodore Roosevelt, quoted in Marshall Everett, *Complete Life of William McKinley and Story of His Assassination: An Authentic and*

Official Memorial Edition, Containing Every Incident in the Career of the Immortal Statesman, Soldier, Orator and Patriot (1901), 306.

58 "Guilty of Murder in the First-Degree," *The San Francisco Call.* (San Francisco [Calif.]), 25 Sept. 1901, p. 1.

59 "Seat in the Fatal Chair," *The Minneapolis Journal.* (Minneapolis, Minn.), 26 Sept. 1901, p.1.

60 "Observations," *The Courier.* (Lincoln, Neb.), 21 Sept. 1901, p.1.

CHAPTER 4

1 "His Final Address," *Crittenden Press.* (Marion, Ky.), 03 Oct. 1901, p.1.

2 "Isthmian Canal is Now a Certainty," *Honolulu Republican* (Honolulu, T.H.), 29 Oct 1901, p. 5.

3 Ibid.

4 Ibid.

5 "Reported discovery of an Isthmian Canal Route," *Congressional Serial Set, Monthly Bulletin of the Bureau of the American Republics,* (July 1901) 892-893.

6 "From Washington," *Alexandria Gazette* (Alexandria D.C.),, 16 Oct. 1901, p. 2.

7 United States, Frank D. Pavey, William Nelson Cromwell, and Philippe Bunau-Varilla. *The Story of Panama. Hearings on the Rainey Resolution Before the Committee on Foreign Affairs of the House of Representatives.* (Washington: Govt. Print. Off, 1913), 633.

8 *The Story of Panama*, 164.

9 Ibid.

10 Theodore Roosevelt, "Annual Address," 03 Dec, 1901, The American Presidency Project.

11 "Canal Treaty's Terms," *New-York Tribune*, 18 Oct. 1901, 1.

12 "The Senate," *Evening Star.* (Washington, D.C.), 17 Dec. 1901, p.1.

13 "Attempt to Kill Canal Treaty," *The Minneapolis Journal.* (Minneapolis, Minn.), 12 Dec. 1901, 1.

14 Ibid.

15 "Not a Menace to the Canal," *The Evening Times.* (Washington, D.C.), 12 Dec. 1901, p.1.

16 "Bought In By Speculators," *The Washington Times.* (Washington, D.C.), 11 Dec. 1901, p. 1. "Canal Treaty in Senate," *New York Tribune.* (New York, N.Y.), 05 Dec. 1901, p.1.

17 "A Canal Complication," *Omaha Daily Bee*. (Omaha, Neb.), 16 Dec. 1901. P. 1.

18 'Parisians in Uproar," *The Wichita Daily Eagle*. (Wichita, Kan.), 22 Dec. 1901p. 1.

19 Arthur Wellington Brayley, Arthur Wilson Tarbell, and Joe Mitchell Chapple, "Affairs at Washington," *National Magazine*, (Oct 1901): 618.

20 "Ready to Sell Out," *Evening Star* (Washington, D.C.), 21 Dec. 1901, 1.

21 "Chance for the Panama," *The Minneapolis Journal*. (Minneapolis, Minn.), 27 Dec. 1901, p. 1.

22 "An Isthmian Canal-Extraordinary Activity of the Panama Lobby," *Evening Star* (Washington, D.C.), 30 Dec 1901, 1.

23 "Canal Bill in Peril," *The Indianapolis Journal*. (Indianapolis, Ind.), 31 Dec. 1901, 1.

24 Ibid.

25 "Panama Offer Made," *New York Tribune* (New York, N.Y.), 5 Jan 1902, 1.

26 "Please Buy Our Nice Canal," *The Washington Times Star* (Washington, D.C.), 08 Jan. 1902, 1.

27 "Lively Debates on Canal Bill," *The St. Louis Republic*. (St. Louis, Mo.), 08 Jan. 1902, p, 1.

28 Ibid., 5.

29 "Panama Bill Debate," *The Indianapolis Journal*. (Indianapolis Ind.), 08 Jan. 1902, p. 2.

30 *The Evening World*. (New York, N.Y.), 20 Sept. 1901,1.

31 *The Evening World*. (New York, N.Y.), 02 Oct. 190, 1.

32 Theodore Roosevelt and Henry Cabot Lodge, *Selections from the Correspondence of Theodore Roosevelt and Henry Cabot Lodge, 1884-1918*, Vol. 1, (New York: Carles Schribner's Sons, 1925), 504.

33 Before the ratification of the 22nd Amendment in 1951 that limits Presidents to two terms in office, the unwritten rule that presidents would not seek a third term—thought to be inspired by George Washington's refusal to be nominated again after his second term—was honored until Franklin Roosevelt, became the first U.S. President to serve more than two terms. In all Franklin Roosevelt served four terms in office.

34 Roosevelt, *Selections from the Correspondence*, 434.

35 Ibid., 442.

36 David Magie. *Life of Garret Augustus Hobart: Twenty-Fourth Vice-President of the United States.* (New York: G.P. Putnam's Sons, 1910), 149.

37 "The Republican Convention," *The Outlook*, Vol. 65. (New York: Outlook Co, 1900) 489.

38 Roosevelt, *Selections from the Correspondence*, 432-440.

39 Arthur Wallace Dunn's account of a conversation he heard between Hanna and McKinley at the National convention of 1900. *From Harrison to Harding, a Personal Narrative, Covering a Third of a Century, 1888-1921.* (New York: G.P. Putnam's Sons, 1922).

40 Albert Shaw, *A Cartoon History of Roosevelt's Career: Illustrated by Six Hundred and Thirty Contemporary Cartoons and Many Other Pictures.* (New York: The Review of Reviews Company, 1910), 71.

41 United States. *Investigation of Panama Canal Matters. Hearings Before the Committee on Interoceanic Canals of the United States Senate in the Matter of the Senate Resolution Adopted January 9, 1906, Providing for an Investigation of Matters Relating to the Panama Canal, Etc. ... Jan. 11, 1906-Feb. 12, 1907.* Washington: Govt. Print. Off, 1907, 1147.

42 Theodore Roosevelt, *The Selected Letters of Theodore Roosevelt*, H.W. Brands, ed. (Maryland: Rowman and Littlefield, 2001), 93.

43 Ibid., 95.

44 Letter from Douglas Robinson to George B. Cortelyou. December 2, 1902 Theodore Roosevelt Papers, Manuscripts division. The Library of Congress. http://www.theodorerooseveltcenter.org/Research/Digital-Library/Record.aspx?libID=o39766. Theodore Roosevelt Digital Library. Dickinson State University.

45 Letter from Theodore Roosevelt to Douglas Robinson. January 7, 1904 Theodore Roosevelt Collection. MS Am 1785.9 (6). Houghton Library, Harvard University. http://www.theodorerooseveltcenter.org/Research/Digital-Library/Record.aspx?libID=o282215. Theodore Roosevelt Digital Library.

46 Letter from Douglas Robinson to Theodore Roosevelt. June 21, 1904. Theodore Roosevelt Papers, Manuscripts division. The Library of Congress. http://www.theodorerooseveltcenter.org/Research/Digital-Library/Record.aspx?libID=o45752. Theodore Roosevelt Digital Library. Dickinson State University.

47 Letter from Douglas Robinson to Theodore Roosevelt. February 15, 1902. Theodore Roosevelt Papers, Manuscripts division. The Library of Congress. http://www.theodorerooseveltcenter.org/Research/

Digital-Library/Record.aspx?libID=o283768. Theodore Roosevelt Digital Library. Dickinson State University.

48 "Panama Company Determined to Fight," *The St. Louis Republic*, 11 Jan. 1902, 1.

49 Ibid.

50 Ibid.

51 Report on Senator Hanna's telephone call. January 14, 1902 Theodore Roosevelt Papers, Manuscripts division. The Library of Congress. http://www.theodorerooseveltcenter.org/Research/Digital-Library/Record.aspx?libID=o283496. Theodore Roosevelt Digital Library. Dickinson State University.

52 Ibid.

53 "Mr. Morgan at White House," *The Evening Times*. (Washington, D.C.), 16 Jan. 1902, 1.

54 Letter from Theodore Roosevelt to John Grimes Walker. January 16, 1902. Theodore Roosevelt Papers, Manuscripts division. The Library of Congress. http://www.theodorerooseveltcenter.org/Research/Digital-Library/Record.aspx?libID=o181176. Theodore Roosevelt Digital Library. Dickinson State University.

55 Ibid.

56 John Hipple Mitchell, *The Nicaragua Canal; The Only Feasible and Practical Route for An Inter-oceanic Canal; Speech ... In The Senate of the United States, Thursday June 5 and Saturday June 7, 1902.* (Washington: G.P.O., 1902), 59

57 Ibid.

58 Ibid.

59 "Isthmian Canal," *Evening Star*. (Washington, D.C.), 16 Jan. 1902,1.

60 Earl Harding, *The Untold Story of Panama*, Athene Press: NY (1959), 13.

61 Ibid.

62 Ibid.

CHAPTER FIVE

1 Earl Harding, *The Untold Story of Panama,* (New York: Athene Press, 1959), 57.

2 Philippe Bunau-Varilla, *Panama: The Creation, Destruction, Resurrection*, (New York: McBride, Nast, and Co.), 124.

3 Philippe Bunau-Varilla quoted in "Volcanic Disturbances in Nicaragua," *Industrial Management; The Engineering Magazine Vol. 21, 1901):* 453.

4 Ibid., 191.

5 Ibid., 178.

6 Ibid. 228.

7 "Dead Body Litter All the Street," *San Francisco Call* (San Francisco Calif.), 15 May 1902, 1.

8 "Caribs Sacrificed to the Fire Gods," *Minneapolis Journal* (Minneapolis MN.), 15 May 1902, 1.

9 "The Earth Trembles," *The Indianapolis Journal.* (Indianapolis Ind.), 01 June 1902, p. 21.

10 Ibid.

11 "Canal Bill in Senate Next Week, *The Washington Times,* (Washington D.C.), 26 May 1902, p.1.

12 "Favors Panama Line," *The Wichita Daily Eagle,* (Wichita, Kan.), 07 June 1902, p. 1.

13 Bunau-Varilla, 263.

14 Herbert David Croly, *Marcus Alonzo Hanna; His Life and Work,* (New York: The Macmillan Company), 338. Also tellingly, in a brief given to the Rainey hearings, Cromwell asserted that he prepared the information for Hanna's famous earthquake speech, *The Story of Panama. Hearings on the Rainey Resolution Before the Committee on Foreign Affairs of the House of Representatives,*181.

15 Bunau-Varilla, *The Creation,* 246.

16 Ibid, 247.

17 "Reports of Plot to Pass Canal Bill," *The Washington times.* (Washington D.C.), 18 June 1902, p. 2.

18 Bunau-Varilla, *The Creation,* 247.

19 "Reports of a Plot to Pass Canal Bill," *The Washington Times,* (Washington D.C.), 18 June 1902, p. 1.

20 Bunau-Varilla, *The Creation,* 247.

21 Feeling Favors Canal," *San Francisco Call,* (San Francisco Calif.) 21 June 1902, p. 1.

22 "Panama's Friends," *The Saint Louis Republic,* (Saint Louis, Mo.) 20 June, 1902, p. 1.

23 "Feeling in Favor of Canal," *The San Francisco Call,* (San Francisco Calif.), 21 June 1902, p.1.

24 "Morgan's Canal Resolution," *The San Francisco Call.* (San Francisco Calif.), 29 June 1902, p. 1.

25 Ibid.

26 Ibid.

27 "Messers Beverage and Bailey Clash," *The Washington Times,*

(Washington D.C.), 1 July 1902, p. 1.

28 "Must Not Bombard Panama City," *The Washington Times.* (Washington D.C.), 22 July 1902, p. 1.

29 "Canal Negotiations," *Evening Star.* (Washington, D.C.), 29 Aug. 1902, p. 1.

30 "Flaws in the Panama Canal Company Concession," *The Washington Times,* (Washington D.C.), 14 Sept. 1902, p. 1.

31 "Government Will Not Delay," *The Stark County Democrat.* (Canton, Ohio), 31 Oct. 1902, p.1.

32 "To Build the Canal Despite Columbia," *The Evening Times.* (Washington, D.C.), 30 Oct. 1902 p. 1.

33 "Would Wage War on the Columbians, *The San Francisco Call.* (San Francisco Calif.), 29 Nov. 1902, p. 1.

34 "The Administration Fears that Columbia Schemes," *The San Francisco Call.* (San Francisco Calif.), 26 Nov. 1902, p. 1.

35 "Scandal in Panama Canal Commission," *The Saint Paul Globe.* (St. Paul, Minn.), 27 Dec. 1902, p.1.

36 "First Scandal Out," *The Minneapolis Journal.* (Minneapolis, Minn.), 26 Dec. 1902 p.1.

37 The United States, Frank D. Pavey, William Nelson Cromwell, and Philippe Bunau-Varilla. *The Story of Panama. Hearings on the Rainey Resolution Before the Committee on Foreign Affairs of the House of Representatives.* (Washington: G.P.O., 1913), 664.

38 "Canal Treaty Soon," *Evening Star.* (Washington, D.C.), 03 Jan. 1903 p.1.

39 "For Canal Treaty," *Evening Star,* (Washington, D.C.), 27 June 1903, p. 1.

40 "Senator Morgan," *The Wichita Daily Eagle.* (Wichita, Kan.), 11 March 1903, p.1.

41 Theodore Roosevelt, *The Letters Selected of Theodore Roosevelt,* vol, 3, ed. by Elting E. Morison, (Cambridge ,Mass.: Harvard University Press, 1951), 567.

42 Ibid., 318.

43 Arthur Wellington Brayley, Arthur Wilson Tarbell, and Joe Mitchell Chapple, "Affairs at Washington," *National Magazine,* (Oct 1901): 619.

44 Ibid., 618

45 Ibid.

46 Ibid.

47 "Civilization's Right of Domain," *The Minneapolis Journal.* (Minneapolis, Minn.), 18 June 1903, p. 1.

48 Ibid.

49 Ibid.

50 Ibid.

51 "Columbia's Treatment of the Treaty," *Literary Digest*, (29 Aug 1903): 246.

52 "Horrible Atrocities by Turks," *The Daily Journal.* (Salem, Or.), 02 Dec. 1902, p.1.

53 "Little Time Needed," *Evening Star.* (Washington, D.C.), 15 June 1903, p. 1.

54 *Correspondence Concerning the Convention between the United States and Colombia for the Construction of an Interoceanic Canal Across the Isthmus of Panama. Message from the President of the United States, Transmitting a Report from the Secretary of State, with Accompanying Papers ... December 19, 1903.--Read; Referred to the Committee on Foreign Relations and Ordered to Be Printed* (Washington: Gov't Print. Off., 1903), 25-36.

55 Annie Riley, *Bull Moose Trails Supplement to "Rooseveltian Fact and Fable,"* (New York: The author, 1912), 37.

56 *Correspondence Concerning the Convention,* 16.

57 Ibid.

58 "Panama Fight in House," *New-York Tribune,* 12 Dec. 1903, p. 2.

59 *"I Took the Isthmus": Ex-President Roosevelt's Confession, Colombia's Protest, and an Editorial Comment by American Newspapers on "How the United States Acquired the Right to Build the Panama Canal,"* New York: M.B. Brown Print. Co., 1911, 5.

60 "Hay's Notes Stirs Wrath of Senators," *San Francisco Call*, 1 Sept., 1903, p. 1.

61 *"I Took the Isthmus,"* 5.

62 Ibid.

63 *The Story of Panama,* 369.

64 "Inside a Revolution," *The Saint Paul Globe.* (St. Paul, Minn.), 27 Nov. 1903, p. 4.

65 Ibid.

66 Ibid.

67 Ibid.

68 *The Story of Panama,* 53.

69 "As They Tell It 'Way Down in Panama," *The Minneapolis Journal.* (Minneapolis, Minn.), 26 Dec. 1903, p.1.

70 *The Story of Panama,* 362.

71 Ibid.

72 Ibid., 365.

73 Ibid., 700.

74 Ibid., 446.

75 Ibid., 714.

76 Bunau-Varilla afterward referred to Cromwell as "the lawyer Cromwell," and portrayed him as frazzled by the complexities of the Panama revolutions and of abandoning the insurrectionists "to their fate," Bunau-Varilla, 222.

CHAPTER SIX

1 "Shots Smash Isthmusian Town," *The Butte Inter Mountain.* (Butte, Mont.), 04 Nov 1903, p.1.

2 "Revolution Spreads On Isthmus," *The Washington Times*, 04 Nov. 1903, p. 1.

3 "Inside Facts of a Revolution," St. *Paul Globe*, 27 Nov 1903, p. 4.

4 Ibid.

5 "The Panama Canal," *Arizona republican.* (Phoenix, Ariz.), 08 Oct. 1903, p. 1.

6 "Nicaragua Now Holds Attention," *The San Francisco Call.* (San Francisco Calif.), 19 Aug. 1903, p.1.

7 Ibid.

8 "Gigantic Boodle Game," *The Evening Statesman*, (Walla Walla, Wash.) 29 Sept 1903, p. 4.

9 "Nicaragua Now Holds Attention," *The San Francisco Call*, 19 August 1903, p. 1.

10 "Nashville at Colon," *Washington Evening Star,* (Washington, D.C.), 03 Nov. 1903 , p. 6.

11 "Panama Shelled," *Washington Evening Star*, (Washington, D.C.), 04 Nov. 1903 , p. 7.

12 "Ready for a Revolt United States Expects an Uprising in Colombia," *Montgomery Advertiser,* 29 Oct, 1903, p. 7.

13 "Proclamation of Independence Follows Uprising," *San Francisco Call*, 3 Nov 1903, p. 3.

14 Annie Riley, *Bull Moose Trails Supplement to "Rooseveltian Fact and Fable,"* (New York: The author, 1912), 103.

15 "Warships Parade," *The Daily Pioneer* (Minn.), 19 Aug. 1903, p. 1.

16 "Current Topics," *The Commoner,* (Lincoln, Neb.), 13 Nov. 1903, p. 1.

17 The United States. *Papers Relating to the Foreign Relations of the United States.* (Washington: G.P.O., 1904), 250.

18 Ibid., 231.

19 Ibid., 250.

20 Ibid.

21 Ibid.

22 Ibid., 271.

23 Philippe Bunau-Varilla, *Panama: The Creation, Destruction, Resurrection*, (New York: McBride, Nast, and Co.), 332.

24 "The Panama Question," reprint of the *Milwaukee Daily News* in *The Public: a Journal of Democracy*, Vols. 262-313, (Chicago: The Public, 1903), 568-569.

25 "Asked for Facts," *The St. Louis Republic* (St. Louis, Mo.), January 08, 1904, p. 5.

26 Daniel Henry Chamberlain, *The Panama Affair of 1903: Roosevelt--Hay Diplomacy: Open Letter to John Hay*, (S.l: s.n, 1904), 5.

27 "State Department Besieged," *The Daily Pioneer* (Bemidji, Beltrami Co., Minn.), 6 Nov. 1903, p.1.

28 Ibid.

29 "The Panama Dishonor," *The Nation* 77 (July 1903-December 1904): 374.

30 Daniel Henry Chamberlain, 14.

31 Ibid., 14-15.

32 "Brief News Items," *The Forest Republican,* (Tionesta, Pa.), 23 Dec. 1903, p. 2.

33 "Dems in the Dark," *The Minneapolis Journal* (Minneapolis, Minn.), 11 Nov. 1903, p. 1.

34 Ibid.

35 Ibid.

36 Ibid.

37 "The Newest Example of American Imperialism," *The Intermountain Catholic,* 21 Nov 1903, p. 1.

38 "Mission of Gen. Reyes," *Evening Star.* (Washington, D.C.), 27 Nov. 1903, p.15.

39 Ibid.

40 Ibid.

41 "Columbian Women Would Sell Gems," *The Stark County Democrat* (Canton, Ohio), 01 Dec 1903, p. 7.

42 "Panama Question," *The Evening Bulletin*, 23 Dec 1903, p. 1.

43 Chamberlain qtd. in Annie Riley Hale, *Bull Moose Trails Supplement to "Rooseveltian Fact and Fable."* New York: The author, 1912), 38.

44 "Germany Suspects America," *Frankfurt Zeitung* reprinted in *San Francisco Call*, 6 Nov 1903, p. 1.

45 "The Panama Question," *Toronto Weekly Sun,* reprinted in *Public; A Journal of Democracy* (Chicago: The Public Pub. Co., 1903), 569.

46 Ibid.

47 Frederick Remington, "A Rodeo at Los Ojos," *Harper's New Monthly Magazine* 88 (December 1893): 524.

48 Theodore Roosevelt, *Selected Letters of Theodore Roosevelt,* H.W. Brands, ed., (Maryland: Rowman and Littlefield, 2007), p. 347.

49 "Panama Incident Most Disgraceful Episode In All Annals Of America," *The St. Louis Republic.* (St. Louis, Mo.), 11 Jan. 1904, p. 1.

50 Ibid.

51 "Disgraceful Episode, He Says," *Bisbee Daily Review* (Bisbee, Ariz.), 15 Jan. 1904, p. 01.

52 "Morgan's Disgust," *Arizona Republican,* 21 Jan. 1904, p. 1.

53 "From Washington," *Clarke Courier.* (Berryville, Va.), 06 Jan. 1904, p. 1.

54 "Senate and House," *The Salt Lake Tribune.* (Salt Lake City, Utah), 20 Jan. 1904, p.1.

55 "Gorman's Folly," *The Minneapolis Journal* (Minneapolis, Minn.), 23 Dec1903, p. 4.

56 Edward Garstin Smith, *The Real Roosevelt*, (London: C.F. Cazenove, 1910), 114.

57 Annie Riley Hale, *Bull Moose Trails Supplement to "Rooseveltian Fact and Fable".* New York: The author, 1912), 92.

58 "The Panama Filibuster," *The Public: a Journal of Democracy, Vols. 262-313*, (Chicago: The Public, 1903) 532.

59 Earl Harding, *The Untold Story of Panama,* (New York: Athene Press, 1959), 47.

60 *The Story of Panama. Hearings on the Rainey Resolution Before the Committee on Foreign Affairs of the House of Representatives.* (Washington: G.P.O., 1913), 10.

61 Ibid.

62 Ibid., 38-39.

63 Roosevelt had an innate, almost genius, understanding of the power of images. When Roosevelt set out for Cuba aboard a dangerously overcrowded ship, he shrewdly squeezed two "moving picture" cameramen onto the troop transport. Earlier, when his editors suggested that a photograph would enhance his story of the pursuit of thieves who stole a boat from his Dakota ranch, Roosevelt used

two of his hired-hands to stage a reenactment of the event. *Theodore Roosevelt and the Boat Thieves*. 1886. Theodore Roosevelt Birthplace National Historic Site. http://www.theodorerooseveltcenter.org/en/Research/Digital-Library/Record.aspx?libID=o284916. Theodore Roosevelt Digital Library. Dickinson State University.

64 "See With His Own Eyes," *The National Tribune* (Washington, D.C.), 15 Nov. 1906, p. 01.

65 "The President Off to Panama," *The Sun*. (New York N.Y.), 09 Nov. 1906, 01.

CHAPTER SEVEN

1 John Langdon Heaton, *The Story of a Page; Thirty Years of Public Service and Public Discussion in the Editorial Columns of the New York World*. (New York: Harper & Brothers, 1913), 269.

2 Earl Harding, *The Untold Story of Panama* (New York: Athene Press, 1959), 89.

3 "Trusts Favor Taft," *The Marion Daily Mirror*. (Marion, Ohio), 03 Oct. 1908, p.1.

4 Ibid.

5 "Still Happening on Haskell Republican Plea of No Funds," *The Daily Ardmoreite*. (Ardmore, Okla.), 12 Oct. 1908, p.1.

6 "Money Paid in Paris," *Omaha Daily Bee*, 9 Dec. 1908, p. 1.

7 "Panama Canal Scandal," *Monroe City Democrat*. (Monroe City, Mo.), 29 Oct. 1908.

8 United States, Charles M. Hough, and Albert B. Anderson. *The Roosevelt Panama Libel Case against the New York World and Indianapolis News: Decision of Charles M. Hough, Judge of the United States Court for the Southern District of New York, and Albert B. Anderson, Judge of the United States Court for the District of Indians. Together with an Account of the Circumstances That Led to These Unprecedented Prosecutions on the Part of the United States Government, and a Stenographic Report of the Trial of the New York World*. (S.l.: Printed for the New York World, 1910), 2-3.

9 Ibid.

10 J.C. Welliver, "Democrats Knew of Panama Charge," *The Washington Times* (Washington D.C.), 03 October 1908, p.1, 2.

11 *The Roosevelt Panama Libel Case*, 11.

12 Ibid. 7.

13 Ibid.

14 "More Canal Graft," *The Salt Lake Herald*. (Salt Lake City Utah), 27 Oct. 1908, p.1.

15 Ibid.

16 Ibid.

17 Ibid.

18 "Panama Scandal," *Chicago Journal*, reprint *The New Ulm Review*, (New Ulm, Minn.), 4 Nov, 1908, p.4.

19 "Who got the $40,000,000?" *The Seattle Star*. (Seattle, Wash.), 14 Oct. 1908, p.1.

20 "Some Political Gossip," *The Iola Register*. (Iola, Kan.), 27 June 1902, p. 11.

21 "Roosevelt Plotted to Ruin Me," *New York Times*, 24 March1907, p. 1. http://query.nytimes.com/mem/archivefree/pdf?res=F00C12FF3C5C 15738DDDAD0A94DB405B878CF1D3

22 Heaton, 269.

23 Irving C. Norwood "Exit—Roosevelt the Dominant," *The Outing Magazine*,Vol. 53, (1909): 725.

24 David Graham Phillips, "The Treason of the Senate," *Cosmopolitan*, Vol 42 (1906): 77.

25 "Cautic Letter from President Scores Editors," *Los Angles Herald*, 07 Dec, 1908, p.1. California Digital Newspaper Collection, Center for Bibliographic Studies and Research, University of California, Riverside, <http://cdnc.ucr.edu>.

26 Letter from William Dudley Foulke to Theodore Roosevelt. April 14, 1903. Theodore Roosevelt Papers, Manuscripts division. Library of Congress. http://www.theodorerooseveltcenter.org/Research/Digital-Library/Record.aspx?libID=o40738. Theodore Roosevelt Digital Library. Dickinson State University.

27 "Cautic Letter from President Scores Editors," *Los Angles Herald*, 07 Dec, 1908, p.1. California Digital Newspaper Collection, Center for Bibliographic Studies and Research, University of California, Riverside, <http://cdnc.ucr.edu>.

28 John Langdon Heaton, 2.

29 "The President Replies," *New York Times*, 02 Dec. 1908.http://query. nytimes.com/gst/abstract.html?res=F3091FFB3C5D16738DDDAE08 94DA415B888CF1D3

30 William McMurtrie Speer, Editorial. Reprinted in *The Roosevelt Panama Libel Case*, 14.

31 Ibid.

32 Ibid.

33 Theodore Roosevelt, "Special Message to Congress" December 15, 1908. Eds, Gerhard Peters and John T. Woolley, *The American Presidency Project.* http://www.presidency.ucsb.edu/ws/?pid=69678

34 Ibid.

35 Ibid.

36 Ibid.

37 Theodore Roosevelt, *Selected Letters of Theodore Roosevelt,* H.W. Brands, ed., (Maryland: Rowman and Littlefield, 2007), 504.

38 Heaton, 2.

39 "World Case to Grand Jury, *The Sun* (New York, N.Y.), 19 Jan 1909, p.4.

40 "More Hot Stuff," *The Times and Democrat.* (Orangeburg, S.C.), 18 Dec. 1908, p 1.

41 "Vicious Attack" *Daily Missiolian*, 19 Jan 1909, 1.

42 "How it Appears Abroad," *London Globe*, reprint *Auburn Citizen*, 21 Dec 1908, p.4. http://fultonhistory.com/newspaper%202/ Auburn%20NY%20Citizen/Auburn%20NY%20Citizen%201908.pdf/ Newspaper%20Auburn%20NY%20Citizen%201908%20-%201856. PDF

43 "President Calls for Justice," *The San Francisco Call*, 16 Dec 1908, p 1.

44 District of Columbia, Charles Moore, Edwin C. Brandenburg, and Daniel E. Garges. *The Code of Law for the District of Columbia: Enacted March 3, 1901, Amended by the Acts Approved January 31 and June 30, 1902, and Amended by Further Acts of Congress to and Including March 3, 1905.* (Washington: G.P.O., 1906), 172.

45 "U.S. Government Suing for Libel," *Spokane Review*, 19 Jan 1909. http://news.google.com/newspapers?nid=1314&dat=19090119&id=2 65XAAAAIBAJ&sjid=nfMDAAAAIBAJ&pg=4366,541464

46 *The Story of Panama*, 307.

47 *The Roosevelt Panama Libel Case*, 19.

48 Ibid.

49 Ibid., 86-87.

50 "Pushing Suit," *The Billings Gazette.* (Billings, Mont.), 09 April 1909, 1.

51 "Resigns Rather than Act in Panama Cases," *The Evening World.* (New York, N.Y.), 05 March 1909, p. 1.

52 Ibid.

53 Ibid.

54 Ibid.

55 "Joseph Kealing Moral Coward," *The Seattle Republican.* (Seattle, Wash.), 19 March 1909, p.1.

56 "Current Topics," *The Commoner.* (Lincoln, Neb.), 12 March 1909., 7.

57 "Editors Fight Venue Change," *Los Angeles Herald.* (Los Angeles, Calif.), 02 June 1909, p. 3.

58 "Canal Libel Hearing," *New-York Tribune.* (New York, N.Y.), 02 June 1909, 2.

59 "Editors Fight Venue Change," *Los Angeles Herald.* (Los Angeles, Calif.), 02 June 1909, p. 3.

60 "The Panama Libel Case," *The World Almanac and Book of Facts*, New York: Press Pub. Co., 1909: 20.

61 "Court Quashes Libel Charge," *Los Angeles Herald* (Los Angeles, Calif.), 27 Jan. 1910, p.1.

62 Ibid.

63 *The Roosevelt Panama Libel Case*, 109.

64 Ibid. 311.

65 "U.S. Supreme Court Quashes Panama Suit Against The World," *The Evening World.* (New York, N.Y.), 03 Jan. 1911, p.1.

66 "The Panama Libel Suit is Dead," *Watsons' Magazine*, Vol. 4, edited Thomas Edward Watson (Jan, 1910): 216.

67 "The World Will Present Panama Case to Congress," *The Evening World.* (New York, N.Y.), 04 Jan. 1911, p. 2.

68 Earl Harding, 55-62.

69 "May Look Into Purchase of Panama Canal," *Daily Capital Journal.* (Salem, Or.), 06 April 1911, p.1.

70 "House May Hear the Panama Story," *The Salt Lake Tribune.* (Salt Lake City, Utah), 04 Jan. 1912, p.1.

71 *The Roosevelt Panama Libel Case*, 3.

72 "Panama Canal Builder Comes to See Taft," *The Day Book.* (Chicago, Ill.), 08 Feb. 1912, p. 12.

73 "Crossroads of the Pacific Ready," *The San Francisco Call.* (San Francisco Calif.), 14 Aug. 1912, p. 9.

74 "The Gates at Panama," *The San Francisco Call.* (San Francisco Calif.), 04 Feb. 1912, p. 21.

75 Ibid.

76 "What are Your Preparations for 1915?" *Aberdeen Herald.* (Aberdeen, Chehalis County, W.T.), 19 Aug. 1912, p. 2.

77 "Says Country Can Get Along Without T.R.," *The Salt Lake Tribune.* (Salt Lake City, Utah), 24 May 1912. , p.1.

78 Ibid.

79 "Roosevelt Draws Immense Crowds," Ibid.

80 Ibid., p.4.

81 "Governor Wilson Discusses Tariff," Ibid.

82 "Panama Canal Builder Comes to See Taft," *The Day Book*. (Chicago, Ill.), 08 Feb. 1912, p. 12.

CHAPTER EIGHT

1 "Hartford Will Hear Roosevelt," *The Daily Missoulian*. (Missoula, Mont.), 15 Aug. 1914, p. 2. Bird's classic good looks and his position in society made him along with his sister the subject of *Charles Sumner Bird and His Sister Edith Bird Bass*, 1907.
Cecilia Beaux, American, 1855–1942. Boston Museum of Fine Arts, http://www.mfa.org/collections/object/brother-and-sister-charles-sumner-bird-and-his-sister-edith-bird-mrs-robert-bass-34473

2 "Roosevelt Will Be Progressive Candidate for President, 1916," *The Day Book*. (Chicago, Ill.), 23 May 1914, p. 2.

3 "Shout and Make Your Voice Strong," *The Ogden Standard*. (Ogden City, Utah), 31 Dec. 1914, p. 5.

4 Ibid.

5 "They Can't Fool the People About Teddy, *The Daily Missoulian*. (Missoula, Mont.), 14 April 1912, p. 16.

6 "Striking a Man Who is Down," T*he Pensacola Journal*. (Pensacola, Fla.), 24 Sept. 1908,4.

7 "Congress Vs. The President," *The National Tribune*. (Washington, D.C.), 20 Dec. 1906, p. 1.

8 Irving C. Norwood, "Exit—Roosevelt the Dominant," *The Outing Magazine*, Vol. 53, (1909): 730.

9 "Senator Foraker and Brownsville, *Evening Star*. (Washington, D.C.), 20 June 1907 p. 1.

10 "T.R. Digs a Hole," *The Times and Democrat*. (Orangeburg, S.C.), 29 Sept. 1908, p.1.

11 "Roosevelt Has Evidence and is Getting Ready," *Rock Island Argus*. (Rock Island, Ill.), 18 Dec. 1908, p.1.

12 Edwin Garstin Smith. *The Real Roosevelt*, (London: Cazanova,1910), p. 78.

13 Irving C. Norwood, "Exit—Roosevelt the Dominant," *The Outing Magazine*, Vol. 53, (1909): 730.

14 "Mr. Long Strikes Back," *The Literary Digest*, Vol.34, (1907): 967.

15 Annie Riley Hale, *"Rooseveltian Fact and Fable.* (New York: Hale, 1912), 87.

16 Irving C. Norwood "Exit—Roosevelt the Dominant," *The Outing Magazine,*Vol. 53, (1909): 722.

17 Ibid.

18 "The Nation Welcomes Col Roosevelt as Conquering Hero," *The Salt Lake Herald-Republican.* (Salt Lake City, Utah), 19 June 1910, p.1.

19 Hermann Hagedon, *The Roosevelt Family of Sagamore Hill,* (New York: McMillina, 1954), 308.

20 "T.R. Tells of River, *Harrisburg Telegraph.* (Harrisburg, Pa.), 27 May 1914, p.12.

21 "Exit Roosevelt—the Dominant," *The Outing Magazine*, Vol. 53, (1909): 722.

22 Theodore Roosevelt, *Through the Brazilian Wilderness* (New York: C. Scribner's Sons, 1914), 304.

23 Ibid.

24 Oscar K. Davis, *Released For Publication; Some Inside Political History Of Theodore Roosevelt And His Times, 1898-1918* (Boston: Houghton Mifflin Company, 1925), 434.

25 Ibid.

26 "Roosevelt Will Be Progressive Candidate for President, 1916," *The Day Book.* (Chicago, Ill.), 23 May 1914, p.1.

27 "Weather Report," *New York Tribune* (New York :N.Y.) 14 August 1915, p. 1.

28 "Roosevelt Marches Among Strange People," *The Day Book.* (Chicago, Ill.), 07 April 1914, p. 11.

29 Roosevelt, *Through the Brazilian Wilderness*, 5.

30 "President Near Death," *New York Tribune* (New York:N.Y.) 4 Sept. 1902, p. 1.

31 "Thrilling Story of Trolley Accident Which Nearly Killed the President," *The Evening World* (New York, NY) 3 Sept. 1902, p. 1.

32 Theodore Roosevelt Digital Library. *Letter from Theodore Roosevelt to Henry Cabot Lodge.* September 25, 1902 Theodore Roosevelt Papers, Manuscripts division. The Library of Congress. http://www.theodorerooseveltcenter.org/Research/Digital-Library/Record.aspx?libID=o183130

33 Michael Joseph Donovan, *The Roosevelt That I Know; Ten Years of Boxing with The President--And Other Memories Of Famous Fighting Men* (New York, B.W. Dodge & Company, 1909), 16.

34 Roosevelt, Theodore. 1913. *An Autobiography* (New York: Charles

Scribner's Sons), 41.

35 "Shrank's Trial Opens," *The Evening Standard*. (Ogden City, Utah), 12 Nov. 1912, p. 1.

36 "Roosevelt Blames Shooting on Newspapers," Salt Lake Tribune 15 October 1912), 2.

37 Ibid.

38 W. J. Foley "A Bullet and a Bull Moose" JAMA. 1969 Sep. 29; 209(13): 2035-8.

39 Edward Wagenknecht, *The Seven Worlds of Theodore Roosevelt* (Guilford, Conn: Lyons Press, 2009), 32.

40 "The Colonel's Health," *Montgomery Advisor*, 29 June 1914, www.genealogy.com (accessed 2 May 2012), 4.

41 Anthony Fiala, photographer. *The River of Doubt,* Washington, D.C. 35 mm film. United States: Roosevelt Memorial Association,1928. From Library of Congress, *Early Motion Pictures, 1897-1920*. RealMedia, MPEG, Quick Time, http://hdl.loc.gov/loc.mbrsmi/lcmp002.m2a25469 (accessed 13 Feb 2012), part 7.

42 Rudolf Marx, *The Health Of The President: Theodore Roosevelt*, http://www.archive.org (accessed 23 April 2012), n.p.

43 "Wilson to Apology to Columbia?" *New York Times*, 09 April 1914, p.1. 1914http://query.nytimes.com/gst/abstract.html?res=F00613FB3 D5E13738DDDA00894DC405B848DF1D3

44 "Columbian Payment Blackmail T.R. Says," *El Paso Herald*. (El Paso, Tex.), 03 July 1914. , p.1.

45 Annie Riley Hale, *Bull Moose Trails Supplement to "Rooseveltian Fact and Fable."* New York: The author, 1912, 24.

46 "National Press Club Stages War in Three Acts—Based on Roosevelt's Discovery," *The Washington Herald*. (Washington, D.C.), 17 June 1914."Roosevelt Made King Dodo of Doubtdom Washington Scientists Build Shores Around His Celebrated River," *Idaho Statesman*, June 11, 1914 (accessed 14 May 2012), 7.

47 Thomas Herbert, Russell. *Theodore Roosevelt, Typical American: His Life and Work : Patriot, Orator, Historian, Sportsman, Soldier, Statesman and President.* S.l: s.n.], 1919, describes an "ignorant and hostile " press reaction to Roosevelt's discovery. "Roosevelt Made King Dodo of Doubtdom Washington Scientists Build Shores Around His Celebrated River," *Idaho Statesman*, June 11, 1914, p. 7, describes one farce based on the River of Doubt claims, can be found on the subscription data base www.genealogy.com.

48 "Roosevelt to Speak at Louisiana Campaign," *The Democratic Banner.* (Mt. Vernon, Ohio), 07 July 1914, p.1. Additionally, accusations were made that the Panama purchase was "a sordid commercial conspiracy backed by the Roosevelt Administration," and Roosevelt possessed an "insatiable ambition and contempt for lawful methods [that] made him a party to the conspiracy of the Panama Canal lobby," "Roosevelt and Panama," *Jonesboro Weekly Sun,* July 29, 1914, p.1., and can be found on the subscription data base www.genealogy.com.

49 "Roosevelt V. Pinchot," *The Denison Review.* (Denison, Iowa), 01 July 1914., p.1.

50 *"I Took The Isthmus": Ex-President Roosevelt's Confession, Colombia's Protest, and an Editorial Comment by American Newspapers on "How The United States Acquired the Right to Build the Panama Canal,"* 1911, (New York: M.B. Brown Print. Co), 39.

51 "Big Ditch Open on Aug 15," *The Anderson Daily Intelligencer.* (Anderson, S.C.), 24 July 1914.

52 Canal Zone. *The Panama Canal Record: Official Publication of the Panama Canal, Vol 23,* Balboa Heights, C.Z.: The Canal (1920): 737.

53 *The Tacoma Times.* (Tacoma, Wash.), 15 Aug. 1914. P. 1. *East Oregonian* (Pendleton, Umatilla Co., Or.), 15 Aug. 1914, p.1. *The Times Dispatch.* (Richmond, Va.), 16 Aug. 1914, p.1.

54 "Panama Canal Is Opened to the World," *New-York Tribune.* (New York, N.Y.), 16 August 1914, p. 1.

55 John Barrett, "The Opening of the Panama Canal," *Bulletin of the Pan American Union,* 1914 (Vol. 39):345.

56 "The Panama Canal Officially Opened," *New York Times,* 16 Aug. 1914, p.1. http://query.nytimes.com/gst/abstract.html?res=F00F10F 9385916738DDDAF0994D0405B848DF1D3 (accessed 13 Feb 2012), n.p.

57 "Anna Roosevelt," *National Park Service,* accessed 17 April 2012, http://www.nps.gov/thrb/historyculture/annaroosevelt.htm

58 Barrett, "The Opening of the Panama Canal," *Bulletin of the Pan American Union,* 1914 (Vol. 39), 352.

59 ibid.

60 ibid.

61 ibid. 355.

62 Ibid.

63 "The Col. Tells Why He is For Hinman," *New York Times,* Aug 16 1914, p.10. http://chroniclingamerica.loc.gov/lccn/sn83030214/1914-08-16/ed-1/seq-9/

64 Payne-Aldrich tariff of 1909: The first successful tariff bill since 1897 Payne-Aldrich. Roosevelt used the bill's unpopularity to bludgeon his former protégé, William Taft, in Roosevelt's Bull Moose bid for the Presidency.

65 George A. Talley. *The Panama Canal; An Elucidation of Its Governmental Features As Prescribed by Treaties; a Discussion of Toll Exemption and the Repeal Bill of 1914; and Other Pertinent Chapters.* (Wilmington, Del: Star Pub. Co, 1915), 47.

66 "See Lesson in Belgium Plight," *Bismarck daily tribune.* (Bismarck, N.D.), 25 Sept. 1914, p.1.

67 "Colonel Tell Why he is for Hinnman," *New York Times*, 16 Aug 1914, p.10. http://query.nytimes.com/gst/abstract.html?res=F00D13F93859 16738DDDAF0994D0405B848DF1D3

Epilogue

1 United States. *Investigation of Panama Canal Matters. Hearings Before the Committee on Interoceanic Canals of the United States Senate in the Matter of the Senate Resolution Adopted January 9, 1906, Providing for an Investigation of Matters Relating to the Panama Canal, Etc. ...* [Jan. 11, 1906-Feb. 12, 1907], Vol 2. (Washington: G. P. O., 1907), 1100.

2 "Two Million Dollars This Lawyer's Fee," *The San Francisco Call.* (San Francisco, Calif.), 14 March 1903, p.1.

3 "Panama Money in New York," *The Washington Times.* (Washington, D.C.), 02 Sept. 1904, p. 12.

4 Ibid.

5 "New York," *Trust Companies*, Vol 4 (1907): 186.

6 "Mr. Cromwell's Diversity of Holdings," *Engineering World*, Vols. 3-5, (1906), 442.

7 "Panama President to Face Corruption Charges," *Newsmax*, http://www.newsmax.com/Newsfront/Panama-Canal-Ricardo-Martinelli-Italy/2014/04/15/id/565764/

8 Panama Canal Authority, press release, (27 Mar 2014) https://www.pancanal.com/eng/pr/press-releases/2014/03/20/pr508.html

9 Ibid.

INDEX

K

BIBLIOGRAPHY

Primary Sources

Newspapers

Library of Congress, *Chronicling America: Historic American Newspapers* http://chroniclingamerica.loc.gov/

Aberdeen Herald. (Aberdeen, Wa.), 19 Aug. 1912.

Akron Daily Democrat. (Akron Ohio), 7 Sept 1901.

Akron Daily Democrat. (Akron, Ohio), 05 Sept. 1901.

Alexandria Gazette. (Alexandria D.C.), 16 Oct. 1901.

Arizona Republican, 21 Jan. 1904.

Arizona Republican. (Phoenix, Ariz.), 08 Oct. 1903.

Belmont Chronicle. (St. Clairsville, Ohio), 09 April 1885.

Bisbee Daily Review. (Bisbee, Ariz.), 15 Jan. 1904.

Bismarck Daily Tribune. (Bismarck, N.D.), 25 Sept. 1914.

Clarke Courier. (Berryville, Va.), 06 Jan. 1904.

Crittenden Press (Marion, Ky.), 26 Feb. 1903.

Crittenden Press. (Marion, Ky.), 03 Oct. 1901.

Daily Capital Journal. (Salem, Or.), 06 April 1911.

Daily Dispatch. (Richmond Va.), 01 Oct. 1860.

Daily Dispatch. (Richmond Va.), 18 June 1858.

Daily Evening Star. (Washington D.C.), 19 Sept. 1853

Daily Los Angeles Herald. (Los Angeles Calif.), 09 Oct. 1880.

Daily Missiolian. (Missoula Mont.), 19 Jan 1909

Daily Nashville Patriot. (Nashville, Tenn.), 03 Oct. 1860

East Oregonian. (Pendleton, Umatilla Co., Or.), 15 Aug. 1914

El Paso Herald. (El Paso, Tex.), 03 July 1914.

Evening Star. (Washington, D.C.), 27 June 1903

Evening Star. (Washington, D.C.), 30 Dec 1901

Evening star. (Washington, D.C.), 03 Jan. 1903

Evening star. (Washington, D.C.), 07 Feb. 1890.

Evening Star. (Washington, D.C.), 09 Sept. 1897.

Evening Star. (Washington, D.C.), 12 Dec. 1898.

Evening Star. (Washington, D.C.), 15 June 1903.

Evening Star. (Washington, D.C.), 16 Jan. 1902.

Evening Star. (Washington, D.C.), 16 July 1879.

Evening Star. (Washington, D.C.), 17 Dec. 1901.

Evening Star. (Washington, D.C.), 20 June 1907.

Evening Star. (Washington, D.C.), 21 Dec. 1901.

Evening Star. (Washington, D.C.), 27 Nov. 1903.

Evening star. (Washington, D.C.), 28 July 1879.

Evening Star. (Washington, D.C.), 29 Aug. 1902

Evening Times, The. (Washington, D.C.), 29 Dec. 1899.

Gallipolis Journal. (Gallipolis, Ohio), 05 Feb. 1852.

Harrisburg Telegraph. (Harrisburg, Pa.), 27 May 1914.

Hartford Republican, The. (Hartford, Ky.), 11 May 1900.

Honolulu Republican. (Honolulu, T.H.), 29 Oct 1901.

Houston Daily Post, The. (Houston Tx), 13 Sept 1901.

Indianapolis Journal, The. (Indianapolis Ind.), 15 Sept. 1901.

Kansas City Daily Journal. (Kansas City, Mo.), 23 Jan. 1897

Las Vegas Morning Gazette. (Las Vegas, N.M.), 15 Dec. 1880.

Los Angeles Herald (Los Angeles Calif.), 27 Jan. 1910.

Los Angeles Herald. (Los Angeles Calif.), 02 June 1909.

Los Angeles Herald. (Los Angeles Calif.), 19 June 1910.

Las Vegas Morning gazette. (Las Vegas, N.M.), 15 Dec. 1880.

Macon Telegraph. (Macon Ga.), December 31, 1899.

Minneapolis Journal The, (Minneapolis MN.), 15 May 1902.

Minneapolis Journal, The, (Minneapolis MN.), 29 Dec. 1900.

Minneapolis Journal, The. (Minneapolis, MN.), 02 Jan. 1901.

Minneapolis Journal, The. (Minneapolis, MN.), 26 Sept. 1901

Monroe City Democrat. (Monroe City, Mo.), 29 Oct. 1908.

Morning Call, The. (San Francisco Calif.), 14 Jan. 1893.

New Orleans Daily Democrat, The. (New Orleans, La.), 06 June 1879.

New York Tribune. (New York :N.Y.) 14 August 1915

New York Tribune. (New York: N.Y.) 4 Sept. 1902

New-York Tribune. (New York, N.Y.), 16 August 1914.

New-York Tribune. (New York :N.Y.), 12 Dec. 1903.

New-York Tribune. (New York :N.Y.), 18 Oct. 1901.

New-York Tribune. (New York :N.Y.), 5 Jan 1902.

New-York Tribune. (New York N.Y.), 02 June 1909.

New-York Tribune. (New York N.Y.), 05 Dec. 1900.

New-York Tribune. (New York N.Y.), 10 Feb. 1900.

New-York tribune. (New York N.Y.), 23 Jan. 1897

New-York Tribune. (New York, N.Y.), 05 Dec. 1901.

North American (Philadelphia, PA) Sept. 13, 1853.

Omaha Daily Bee, (Omaha Neb.), 9 Dec. 1908.

Omaha daily bee. (Omaha Neb.), 10 Feb. 1893.

Omaha Daily Bee. (Omaha, Neb.), 16 Dec. 1901.

Raftsman's Journal. (Clearfield, Pa.), 03 Dec. 1860.

Rock Island Argus. (Rock Island, Ill.), 18 Dec. 1908.

Sacramento Daily Record-Union. (Sacramento, Calif.), 05 Oct. 1880.

Saint Paul Globe, The. (St. Paul, Minn.), 15 Sept. 1901.

Salt Lake Herald, The. (Salt Lake City Utah), 05 Oct. 1880.

Salt Lake Herald, The. (Salt Lake City, Utah), 15 Oct. 1900.

Salt Lake Tribune, The. (Salt Lake City, Utah), 15 October 1912.

San Francisco Bulletin (San Francisco, Ca.), 12 Sept. 1883.

San Francisco Call, The, (San Francisco Calif.), 16 May 1900.

San Francisco Call, The. (San Francisco Calif.), 21 June 1902

San Francisco Call, The. (San Francisco Calif.), 07 Sept. 1901.

San Francisco Call, The. (San Francisco Calif.), 13 Nov. 1895.

San Francisco Call, The. (San Francisco Calif.), 13 Sept 1901.

San Francisco Call, The. (San Francisco Calif.), 13 Sept 1901.

San Francisco Call, The. (San Francisco Calif.), 17 Dec. 1895.

San Francisco Call, The. (San Francisco Calif.), 21 June 1902

San Francisco Call, The. (San Francisco Calif.), 23 Feb. 1900.

San Francisco Call, The. (San Francisco Calif.), 15 Oct. 1900.

San Francisco Call, The. (San Francisco Calif.), 25 Sept. 1901

San Francisco Call, The. (San Francisco Calif.), 26 Nov. 1902

San Francisco Call, The. (San Francisco Calif.), 29 June 1902
San Francisco Call, The. (San Francisco Calif.), 29 Nov. 1902.
San Francisco Call, The. (San Francisco, Calif.), 3 Nov 1903.
San Francisco Call, The. (San Francisco, Calif.), 19 Aug. 1903
San Francisco Call, The. (San Francisco, Calif.), 19 August 1903.
San Francisco Call, The. (San Francisco Calif.), 11 June 1999.
San Francisco Call, The. (San Francisco Calif.), 15 May 1902.
San Francisco Call, The. (San Francisco Calif.), January 23, 1897, 6.
San Francisco Call, The. (San Francisco Calif.), 22 January 1897.
San Francisco Call, The. (San Francisco Calif.), 4 December 1898.
San Francisco Call, The. (San Francisco, Calif.), 14 March 1903.
San Francisco Call, The. (San Francisco Calif.), 16 Dec 1908.
San Francisco Call, The. (San Francisco Calif.), 14 Aug. 1912.
Spokane Review, (Spokane Wa.). 19 Jan 1909.
St. Louis Republic, The. (St. Louis Mo.), 7 Sept 1901.
St. Louis Republic, The. (St. Louis, Mo.), 15 Sept 1901.
St. Louis Republic, The. (St. Louis, Mo.), 15 Sept 1901.
St. Louis Republic, The. (St. Louis, Mo.), 15 Sept. 1901
St. Louis Republic, The. (St. Louis, Mo.), 23 Dec. 1900.
St. Paul Daily Globe. (St. Paul, Minn.), 06 Jan 1893.
St. Paul Globe. (St. Paul, Minn.,) 27 Nov 1903.
Sunday Herald (Washington, D.C.), 01 Nov 1885.
The Anaconda Standard. (Anaconda, Mont.), 02 Oct. 1899.
The Anderson Daily Intelligencer. (Anderson, S.C.), 24 July 1914.
The Billings Gazette. (Billings, Mont.), 09 April 1909.
The Billings Gazette. (Billings, Mont.), 21 May 1901.
The Butte Inter Mountain. (Butte, Mont.), 04 Nov 1903.
The Colored American. (Washington, D.C.), 14 Sept. 1901.
The Commoner, (Lincoln, Neb.), 13 Nov. 1903.
The Commoner. (Lincoln, Neb.), 12 March 1909.
The Courier. (Lincoln, Neb.), 21 Sept. 1901.
The Daily Ardmoreite. (Ardmore, Okla.), 12 Oct. 1908.
The Daily Gate City. (Keokuk, Iowa), 07 April 1914Ohio), 07 July
1914.
The Daily Journal. (Salem, Or.), 02 Dec. 1902
The Daily Missoulian. (Missoula, Mont.), 14 April 1912.
The Daily Missoulian. (Missoula, Mont.), 15 Aug. 1914.

The Daily Pioneer (Bemidji, Beltrami Co., Minn.), 19 Aug. 1903.

The Daily Pioneer (Bemidji, Beltrami Co., Minn.), 6 Nov. 1903.

The Day Book. (Chicago, Ill.), 07 April 1914

The Day Book. (Chicago, Ill.), 08 Feb. 1912.

The Day Book. (Chicago, Ill.), 23 May 1914.

The Denison Review. (Denison, Iowa), 01 July 1914.

The Evening Bulletin, (Maysville, Ky.), 23 Dec 1903.

The Evening Standard. (Ogden City, Utah), 12 Nov. 1912.

The Evening Statesman, (Walla Walla, Wash.) 29 Sept 1903.

The Evening Times. (Washington, D.C.), 12 Dec. 1901.

The Evening Times. (Washington, D.C.), 15 March 1899.

The Evening Times. (Washington, D.C.), 16 Jan. 1902.

The Evening Times. (Washington, D.C.), 30 Oct. 1902.

The Evening World. (New York, NY) 3 Sept. 1902.

The Evening World. (New York, N.Y.), 02 Oct. 190, 1.

The Evening World. (New York, N.Y.), 03 Jan. 1911.

The Evening World. (New York, N.Y.), 05 March 1909.

The Evening World. (New York, N.Y.), 05 March1909.

The Evening World. (New York, N.Y.), 20 Sept. 1901

The Forest Republican. (Tionesta, Pa.), 23 Dec. 1903.

The Globe-Republican (Dodge City, Kan.), 28 January 1897.

The Hawaiian Gazette (Honolulu [Oahu, Hawaii]), 10 Sept. 1897.

The Hawaiian Star. (Honolulu Oahu), 04 Jan. 1900.

The Herald. (Los Angeles Calif.), 04 Jan. 1898.

The Herald, (Los Angeles Calif.), 30 Nov 1898.

The Independent, (Honolulu, H.I.), 15 Jan. 1904.

The Indianapolis journal. (Indianapolis Ind.), 30 Oct. 1903

The Indianapolis Journal. (Indianapolis Ind.), 31 Dec. 1901.

The Indianapolis Journal. (Indianapolis, Ind.), 01 June 1902.

The Intermountain Catholic. (Salt Lake City, Utah), 21 Nov 1903.

The Iola Register. (Iola, Kan.), 27 June 1902.

The Marion Daily Mirror. (Marion, Ohio), 03 Oct. 1908.

The Minneapolis Journal (Minneapolis, Minn.), 11 Nov. 1903.

The Minneapolis Journal (Minneapolis, Minn.), 23 Dec1903.

The Minneapolis Journal. (Minneapolis, Minn.), 12 Dec. 1901.

The Minneapolis Journal. (Minneapolis, Minn.), 18 June 1903

The Minneapolis journal. (Minneapolis, Minn.), 26 Dec. 1902

The Minneapolis Journal. (Minneapolis, Minn.), 26 Dec. 1903.

The Minneapolis Journal. (Minneapolis, Minn.), 27 Dec. 1901.

The National Tribune (Washington, D.C.), 15 Nov. 1906.

The National Tribune (Washington, D.C.), 15 Nov. 1906.

The National Tribune. (Washington, D.C.), 20 Dec. 1906.

The New Ulm Review. (New Ulm, Minn.), 4 Nov, 1908.

The Ogden Standard. (Ogden City, Utah), 31 Dec. 1914.

The Pensacola Journal. (Pensacola, Fla.), 24 Sept. 1908.

The Princeton union. (Princeton, Minn.), 24 Nov. 1892.

The Richmond Times, (Richmond, Va.), 8 Sept 1901.

The Roanoke Daily Times. (Roanoke, Va.), 23 Jan. 1897

The Saint Louis Republic, (Saint Louis, Mo.) 20 June, 1902

The Saint Paul Globe. (St. Paul, Minn.), 27 Dec. 1902.

The Saint Paul Globe. (St. Paul, Minn.), 27 Nov. 1903.

The Salt Lake Herald-Republican. (Salt Lake City, Utah), 19 June 1910

The Salt Lake Herald. (Salt Lake City Utah), 27 Oct. 1908.

The Salt Lake Tribune. (Salt Lake City, Utah), 04 Jan. 1912.

The Salt Lake Tribune. (Salt Lake City, Utah), 20 Jan. 1904

The Salt Lake Tribune. (Salt Lake City, Utah), 24 May 1912.

The Seattle Republican. (Seattle, Wash.), 19 March 1909.

The Seattle Star. (Seattle, Wash.), 14 Oct. 1908.

The Seattle Star. (Seattle, Wash.), 18 June 1910.

St. Albans Daily Messenger, (St. Albans, Vt.), 07 Sept 1901.

The St. Louis Republic, (St. Louis, Mo.), 11 Jan. 1902.

The St. Louis Republic. (St. Louis, Mo.), 08 Jan. 1902.

The St. Louis Republic. (St. Louis, Mo.), 11 Jan. 1904.

The Stark County Democrat (Canton, Ohio), 01 Dec 1903.

The Stark County Democrat. (Canton, Ohio), 31 Oct. 1902

The Sun (New York, N.Y.), 19 Jan 1909.

The Sun. (New York, N.Y.), 09 Nov. 1906.

The Tacoma Times. (Tacoma, Wash.), 15 Aug. 1914

The Democratic Banner. (Mt. Vernon, Ohio), 07 July 1914.

The Times (Richmond, Va.), 8 Sept 1901.

The Times (Washington D.C.), 14 January 1899

The Times and Democrat. (Orangeburg, S.C.), 18 Dec. 1908.

The Times and Democrat. (Orangeburg, S.C.), 29 Sept. 1908.

The Times Dispatch. (Richmond, Va.), 16 Aug. 1914.
The Times, (Washington, D.C.), 09 January 1899.
The Times. (Washington, D.C.), 19 Jan. 1900.
The Times. (Washington, D.C.), 26 May 1900.
The Washington Times (Washington, D.C.), 03 October 1908.
The Washington Times. (Washington, D.C.), 04 Nov. 1903.
The Washington Times. (Washington D.C.), 1 July 1902.
The Washington Times. (Washington D.C.), 14 Sept. 1902
The Washington Times. (Washington D.C.), 26 May 1902.
The Washington Times. (Washington, D.C.), 08 Jan. 1902.
The Washington Times. (Washington, D.C.), 02 Sept. 1904
The Washington Times. (Washington D.C.), 18 June 1902.
The Washington Times. (Washington D.C.), 22 July 1902
The Washington Times. (Washington, D.C.), 11 Dec. 1901.
The Wichita Daily Eagle. (Wichita, Kan.), 07 June 1902.
The Wichita Daily Eagle. (Wichita, Kan.), 11 March 1903
The Wichita Daily Eagle. (Wichita, Kan.), 22 Dec. 1901.
Washington Evening Star, (Washington, D.C.), 03 Nov. 1903.
Washington Evening Star, (Washington, D.C.), 04 Nov. 1903.
Washington Evening Star, (Washington, D.C.), 7 Jan 1901.
Wheeling Daily Intelligencer, The. (Wheeling, W. Va.), 04 April 1877.
Wheeling Daily Intelligencer, The. (Wheeling, W. Va.), 10 Feb. 1893.
Wheeling Daily Intelligencer, The. (Wheeling, W. Va.), 23 June 1893.
Willmar Tribune (Wilmer Minn.), 10 May 1899.

Other Newspapers

London Globe, reprint *Auburn Citizen,* 21 Dec 1908, p.4
http://fultonhistory.com/newspaper%202/Auburn%20NY%20
Citizen/Auburn%20NY%20Citizen%201908.pdf/Newspaper%20
Auburn%20NY%20Citizen%201908%20-%201856.PDF

Los Angles Herald, 07 Dec, 1908, p.1. California Digital Newspaper
Collection, Center for Bibliographic Studies and Research,
University of California, Riverside, <http://cdnc.ucr.edu>.

Los Angles Herald, 04 Jan. 1898, p.1. California Digital Newspaper Collection, Center for Bibliographic Studies and Research, University of California, Riverside, <http://cdnc.ucr.edu>.

Los Angles Herald, 22 Nov. 1894. California Digital Newspaper Collection, Center for Bibliographic Studies and Research, University of California, Riverside, <http://cdnc.ucr.edu>.

New York Times, 02 Dec. 1908.
http://query.nytimes.com/gst/abstract.html?res=F3091FFB3C5D16 738DDDAE0894DA415B888CF1D3

The New York Times, 11 Jan 1893.
http://query.nytimes.com/mem/archive-free/pdf?res=F40910FE3C 5515738DDDA80994D9405B8385F0D3

New York Times, 24 March1907.
http://query.nytimes.com/mem/archivefree/pdf?res=F00C12FF3C5 C15738DDDAD0A94DB405B878CF1D3

New York Times, 09 April 1914. 1914.
http://query.nytimes.com/gst/abstract.html?res=F00613FB3D5E13 738DDDA00894DC405B848DF1D3

New York Times, 16 Aug. 1914.
http://query.nytimes.com/gst/abstract.html?res=F00F10F93859167 38DDDAF0994D0405B848DF1D3

Books

Bacon, Alexander S. *The Woolly Horse*, New York: n.p., 1909.

Bates, Lindon Wallace. *The Crisis at Panama*. New York: L.W. Bates,1906.

Bennitt, Mark. *The Pan-American Exposition and How to See It: With a Condensed Guide to Buffalo and Niagara Falls*. Buffalo, N.Y.: Goff Co, 1901.

Bunau-Varilla, Philippe. *Nicaragua or Panama: The Substance of a Series of Conferences Made Before the Commercial Club of Cincinnati, ... Before the Princeton University in New Jersey, Etc., Etc., and of a Formal Address to the Chamber of Commerce of the State of New York*. New York: Knickerbocker Press, 1901.

———. *Panama; The Creation, Destruction, and Resurrection*. New York: R.M. McBride, 1920.

Chamberlain, Daniel Henry. *The Panama Affair of 1903: Roosevelt--Hay Diplomacy: Open Letter to John Hay*, S.l: s.n, 1904.

Colby Mitchell Chester . *The Panama Canal*. Washington: National Geographic Society, 1905.

Davis, Oscar K. *Released For Publication; Some Inside Political History Of Theodore Roosevelt And His Times, 1898-1918*. Boston: Houghton Mifflin Company, 1925.

Davis, Richard Harding. *Three Gringos in Venezuela and Central America*, New York: Harper & Bros, 1896.

Donovan, Michael Joseph. *The Roosevelt That I Know; Ten Years Of Boxing With The President--And Other Memories Of Famous Fighting Men*. New York, B.W. Dodge & Company, 1909.

Dunn, Arthur Wallace. *From Harrison to Harding, a Personal Narrative, Covering a Third of a Century, 1888-1921*. New York: G.P. Putnam's Sons, 1922.

Eads, James Buchanan. *Inter-oceanic Ship Railway: Address of James B. Eads Delivered to the San Francisco Chamber of Commerce*. St. Louis, Mo.: Levison & Blythe Stationery Company, 1880.

Everett, Marshall. *Complete Life of William McKinley and Story of His Assassination: An Authentic and Official Memorial Edition, Containing Every Incident in the Career of the Immortal Statesman, Soldier, Orator and Patriot*. S.l.: The Author, 1901.

Gates, Merrill Edwards. *Men of Mark in America; Ideals of American Life Told in Biographies of Eminent Living Americans* (Washington, D.C.: Men of Mark Pub. Co., 1905.

Grace, William R. and Joseph Pulitzer. *William R. Grace, Plaintiff, against Joseph Pulitzer, Defendant Summons, Complaint, Affidavits and Order. Miller, Peckham, & Dixon, Attorneys for Plaintiff.* New York: M.B. Brown, 1885.

Grant, Ulysses S. *Personal Memoirs of U.S. Grant.* New York: C.L. Webster & Co. 1885.

Halstead, Murat. *The Illustrious Life of William McKinley: Our Martyred President.* Lansing, MI: P.A. Stone, 1901.

———. *The Life of Theodore Roosevelt, Twenty-Fifth President of the United States.* Akron, O.: The Saalfield publishing co, 1902.

Hale, Annie Riley. *Bull Moose Trails Supplement to "Rooseveltian Fact and Fable,"* New York: The author, 1912.

———. *"Rooseveltian Fact and Fable.* New York: Hale, 1912.

Harding, Earl. *The Untold Story of Panama*, Athene Press: NY, 1959.

Heaton, John Langdon. *The Story of a Page; Thirty Years of Public Service and Public Discussion in the Editorial Columns of the New York World.* New York: Harper & Brothers, 1913.

"I Took the Isthmus": Ex-President Roosevelt's Confession, Colombia's Protest, and an Editorial Comment by American Newspapers on "How the United States Acquired the Right to Build the Panama Canal," New York: M.B. Brown Print. Co., 1911.

Keasbey, Lindley *The Nicaragua Canal And The Monroe Doctrine: A Political History Of Isthmus Transit, With Special Reference To The Nicaragua Canal Project And The Attitude Of The United States,* New York: G. P. Putnam's Sons, 1896.

Keane, Augustus Henry and Clements R. Markham, *Central and South America*. London: E. Stanford, 1901.

Lydston, G. Frank. *Panama and the Sierras: A Doctor's Wander Days*. Chicago: Riverton Press, 1900.

McClure, Alexander K., and Charles Morris. *The Authentic Life of William McKinley ... Together with a Life Sketch of Theodore Roosevelt*. Philadelphia: s.n.,1901.

Miller, J. Martin. *The Triumphant Life of Theodore Roosevelt, Citizen, Statesman, President*. Philadelphia: s.n, 1904.

Mitchill, Samuel L and Edward Miller. *Medical Repository of Original Essays and Intelligence Relative to Physic, Surgery, Chemistry, and Natural History*, New York: E. Bliss and E. White, 1797.

Napoleon, Louis Bonaparte. *Canal of Nicaragua: or, a Project to Connect the Atlantic and Pacific Oceans by Means of a Canal*. London: Mills & Son, 1846.

Nelson, Wolford. *Five Years at Panama: the Transisthmian Canal*. London: Low, Marston, Searle & Rivington, 1891.

Nimmo, Joseph. *The Nicaragua Canal: Investigate Before Investing*, Washington, D. C.: Rufus H. Darby, 1898.

O'Brien, Joseph J. *Will the Panama Canal Fail?: the Blunders of De Lesseps and Their Significance to America*. Washington, D.C., s.n., 1911.

Otis, Fessenden Nott. *Isthmus of Panama: History of the Panama Railroad and of the Pacific Mail Steamship Company, Together with a Traveller's Guide and Business Man's Hand-Book for the Panama Railroad, and the Lines of Steamships Connecting It with Europe, the United States, the North and South Atlantic and Pacific Coasts, China, Australia, and Japan*. New York: Harper & Bros, 1867.
Pan-American Exposition. *Official Catalogue and Guide Book to the*

Pan-American Exposition With Maps of Exposition and Illustrations, Buffalo, N.Y., U.S.A., May 1st to Nov. 1st, 1901. Buffalo, N.Y.: Charles Ahrhart, 1901.

Roosevelt, Theodore . *The Selected Letters of Theodore Roosevelt,* H.W. Brands, ed, New York: Rowan &Littlefield, 2007.

——— and Henry Cabot Lodge, *Selections from the Correspondence of Theodore Roosevelt and Henry Cabot Lodge, 1884-1918,* Vol. 1., New York: Carles Schribner's Sons, 1925.

———. *Selected Letters of Theodore Roosevelt,* H.W. Brands, ed., Maryland: Rowman and Littlefield, 2001.

———. *The Letters Selected of Theodore Roosevelt,* vol, 3, ed. by Elting E. Morison, (Cambridge ,Mass.: Harvard University Press, 1951.

———. *Theodore Roosevelt; An Autobiography.* New York: The Macmillan Company, 1913.

———. *Through the Brazilian Wilderness* , New York: C. Scribner's Sons, 1914.

Shaw, Albert. *A Cartoon History of Roosevelt's Career: Illustrated by Six Hundred and Thirty Contemporary Cartoons and Many Other Pictures.* New York: The Review of Reviews Company, 1910.

Smart, Christopher and et al. *The World Displayed ; or, A Curious Collection of Voyages and Travels.* Philadelphia: Dobelbower, Key, and Simpson, 1795. <http://opac.newsbank.com/select/evans/29926>

Smith, Edward Garstin. *The Real Roosevelt.* London, Eng: C.F. Cazenove, 1910.

Talley, George A. .*The Panama Canal; An Elucidation of Its Governmental Features As Prescribed by Treaties; a Discussion of Toll Exemption and the Repeal Bill of 1914; and Other Pertinent Chapters.* Wilmington, Del: Star Pub. Co, 1915.

United States, Charles M. Hough, and Albert B. Anderson. *The Roosevelt Panama Libel Case against the New York World and Indianapolis News: Decision of Charles M. Hough, Judge of the United States Court for the Southern District of New York, and Albert B. Anderson, Judge of the United States Court for the District of Indianapolis, Together with an Account of the Circumstances That Led to These Unprecedented Prosecutions on the Part of the United States Government, and a Stenographic Report of the Trial of the New York World.* S.l.: Printed for the New York World, 1910.

Veblin, Thorstin. *Theory of the Leisure Class: An Economic Study of Institutions.* New York: B.W. Huebsch, 1919.

Wells, William V. *Walker's Expedition to Nicaragua: A History of the Central American War ... with a New and Accurate Map of Central America, and a Memoir and Portr. of William Walker.* (New York: Stringer and Townsend, 1856.

Journals and Magazines

Barrett, John. "The Opening of the Panama Canal," *Bulletin of the Pan American Union,* Vol. 39, 1914.

Brayley, Arthur Wellington, Arthur Wilson Tarbell, and Joe Mitchell Chapple, "Affairs at Washington," *National Magazine,* Oct 1901.

"Business Notes." *Publishers Weekly,* 11 Aug 1906.

"Columbia's Treatment of the Treaty," *Literary Digest,* 29 Aug 1903.

Cullen, Edward. "The Panama Railroad," *Society of Engineers,* May 1869.

Everybody's Magazine, Vol. 5, 1901.

Lambert, Ernest. "The Story of Panama," *Review of Reviews,* Vol 7, 1889.

"Mr. Cromwell's Diversity of Holdings," *Engineering World,* Vols. 3-5, (1906): 442.

"Mr. Long Strikes Back," *The Literary Digest*, Vol.34, 1907.

"New York," *Trust Companies,* Vol 4, 1907.

Norman, C.H. "Letters to the Editor," *Liberty Review: A Magazine of Politics, Economics, and Sociology,* Vol. 18, 1905.
Medical Record, Vol. 60, 1901.

Norwood, Irving C. "Exit—Roosevelt the Dominant," *The Outing Magazine,* Vol. 53, 1909.

"Old Fashioned Fourth," *The Successful American*, Vol. 4, 1900.

Phillips, David Graham. "The Treason of the Senate," *Cosmopolitan, Vol 42* (1906.

Remington, Frederick. "A Rodeo at Los Ojos," *Harper's New Monthly Magazine* Vol. 88, December 1893.

"Pizarro and the Conquest of Peru," *Hogg's Weekly Instructor*, Vol. 5-6, 1850.

Royal Geographical Society (Great Britain). *Proceedings of the Royal Geographical Society and Monthly Record of Geography*, 1879.

Scientific American: Supplement, Vol. 51, 1901.

Seymore, Edward Hobart. "The Present State of the Panama Canal," The *Nineteenth Century Review*, Vol. 176 (1892), 300.
http://nrs.harvard.edu/urn-3:FHCL:1166941

Shepard, R.H. "The Count de Lesseps of Today," *McClure's Magazine*, June 1893.

Smith, Archibald "The Rise and Progress of Yellow fever in Peru," *The Edinburgh Medical and Surgical Journal*, 1855.

Straddon, Corry M. "Our Diplomatic Relations with Nicaragua," *The American Monthly Review of Reviews, Vol 20*, New York: Review of Reviews, 1897.

Taylor, William. "The Panama Canal and the Merchant Marine," *Traffic World, Vol. 26, No. 15*, 1915.

"The Construction of the Panama Railroad," *Popular Science Monthly*, Nov1874-April 1875.

"The New Panama Canal Company," *Engineering World; A Weekly Technical Journal of Civil, Mechanical, Electrical, Mining and Architectural Engineering and Construction, Vol 1-2*. 1905.

"The Panama Dishonor," *The Nation* Vol. 77. July 1903-December 1904.

"The Panama Filibuster," *The Public: a Journal of Democracy*, Vols. 262-313. 1903.

"The Panama Libel Case," *The World Almanac and Book of Facts*, 1909.

"The Pan American Exposition," *The Electrical World And Engineer*, Vol. 37, 1901.

"The Republican Convention," *The Outlook* Vol. 65, 1900.

"The Week," *The Nation* Vol. 70, 1900.

"Two of Our Leaders," *Concord: International Arbitration and Peace Association*. Vol 13-15, 1898.

"Volcanic Disturbances in Nicaragua," *Industrial Management; The Engineering Magazine Vol. 21*, 1901.

Miscellaneous

Fiala, Anthony. Photographer. *The River of Doubt*, Washington, D.C. 35 mm film, part 7..United States: Roosevelt Memorial

Association,1928. From Library of Congress, *Early Motion Pictures, 1897-1920*. RealMedia, MPEG, Quick Time, http://hdl.loc.gov/loc. mbrsmi/lcmp002.m2a25469

McKinley, William, "Second Annual Message," December 5, 1898. Online by Gerhard Peters and John T. Woolley, *The American Presidency Project*. http://www.presidency.ucsb.edu/ws/?pid=29539

———. "Fourth Annual Message," December 3, 1900. Online by Gerhard Peters and John T. Woolley, *The American Presidency Project*. http://www.presidency.ucsb.edu/ws/?pid=29541

Pan-American Exposition. *Official Catalogue and Guide Book to the Pan-American Exposition: With Maps of Exposition and Illustrations, Buffalo, N.Y., U.S.A., May 1st to Nov. 1st, 1901* , S.l.:s.p., 1901.

Roosevelt, Theodore. Annual Address, Dec3, 1901, Online by Gerhard Peters and John T. Woolley, *The American Presidency Project*. http://www.presidency.ucsb.edu/ws/?pid=29541

———. "Special Message to Congress" December 15, 1908. Eds, Gerhard Peters and John T. Woolley, *The American Presidency Project*. http://www.presidency.ucsb.edu/ws/?pid=69678

Theodore Roosevelt Center Dickinson State University
http://www.theodorerooseveltcenter.org/

Letter from Douglas Robinson to George B. Cortelyou. December 2, 1902 Theodore Roosevelt Papers, Manuscripts division. The Library of Congress. http://www.theodorerooseveltcenter.org/Research/ Digital Library/Record.aspx?libID=o39766.

Letter from Douglas Robinson to Theodore Roosevelt. February 15, 1902. Theodore Roosevelt Papers, Manuscripts division. The Library of Congress. http://www.theodorerooseveltcenter.org/ Research/Digital-Library/Record.aspx?libID=o283768

Letter from Douglas Robinson to Theodore Roosevelt. June 21, 1904. Theodore Roosevelt Papers, Manuscripts division. The Library of Congress. http://www.theodorerooseveltcenter.org/Research/Digital-Library/Record.aspx?libID=o45752

Letter from Theodore Roosevelt to Douglas Robinson. January 7, 1904 Theodore Roosevelt Collection. MS Am 1785.9 (6). Houghton Library, Harvard University. http://www.theodorerooseveltcenter.org/Research/Digital-Library/Record.aspx?libID=o282215

Letter from Theodore Roosevelt to Henry Cabot Lodge. September 25, 1902 Theodore Roosevelt Papers, Manuscripts division. The Library of Congress. http://www.theodorerooseveltcenter.org/Research/Digital-Library/Record.aspx?libID=o183130

Letter from Theodore Roosevelt to John Grimes Walker. January 16, 1902. Theodore Roosevelt Papers, Manuscripts division. The Library of Congress. http://www.theodorerooseveltcenter.org/Research/Digital-Library/Record.aspx?libID=o181176

Letter from William Dudley Foulke to Theodore Roosevelt. April 14, 1903. Theodore Roosevelt Papers, Manuscripts division. Library of Congress. http://www.theodorerooseveltcenter.org/Research/Digital-Library/Record.aspx?libID=o40738

Report on Senator Hanna's telephone call. January 14, 1902 Theodore Roosevelt Papers, Manuscripts division. The Library of Congress. http://www.theodorerooseveltcenter.org/Research/Digital-Library/Record.aspx?libID=o283496

Theodore Roosevelt and the Boat Thieves. 1886. Theodore Roosevelt Birthplace National Historic Site. http://www.theodorerooseveltcenter.org/en/Research/Digital-Library/Record.aspx?libID=o284916.

Government Publications

"Reported discovery of an Isthmian Canal Route," Congressional Serial Set, Monthly Bulletin of the Bureau of the American Republics, Washington: G.P.O., July 1901.

Correspondence Concerning the Convention between the United States and Colombia for the Construction of an Interoceanic Canal Across the Isthmus of Panama. Message from the President of the United States, Transmitting a Report from the Secretary of State, with Accompanying Papers ... December 19, 1903.--Read; Referred to the Committee on Foreign Relations and Ordered to Be Printed, Washington: G.P.O., 1903.

Hale, Harry C. *Notes on Panama.* Washington: G.O.P., 1903.

Hearings Before the Committee on Interstate and Foreign Commerce of the House of Representatives on New Panama Canal Company, the Maritime Company, and the Nicaragua Canal Company, (Grace-Eyre-Craigan Syndicate.) Held January 17, 18, 19, 20, and 25, 1899. Washington: G.P.O., 1899.

Isthmian Canal Commission (U.S.), and John Grimes Walker. *Report of the Isthmian Canal Commission, 1899-1901.* Washington: G.P.O., 1904.

Mitchell, John H. *The Nicaragua Canal; The Only Feasible and Practical Route for An Inter-oceanic Canal; Speech ... In The Senate of the United States, Thursday June 5 and Saturday June 7, 1902.* Washington: G.P.O., 1902.

United States, Frank D. Pavey, William Nelson Cromwell, and Philippe Bunau-Varilla. *The Story of Panama. Hearings on the Rainey Resolution Before the Committee on Foreign Affairs of the House of Representatives.* (Washington: G.P.O., 1913.

United States. 1902. *Hearings before the Senate Committee on Interoceanic Canals on H.R. 3110, first session Fifty-seventh Congress, March 14, 1902,* Washington: G.P.O., 1903.

United States. *Investigation of Panama Canal Matters. Hearings Before the Committee on Interoceanic Canals of the United States Senate in the Matter of the Senate Resolution Adopted January 9, 1906, Providing for an Investigation of Matters Relating to the Panama Canal, Etc.* Washington: G.P.O., 1906.

War Department, Office of the Chief of Staff, War College Division, General Staff. Washington: G.P.O., 1903.

Secondary Sources

Books

Ainslie, Helen . *One Hundred Famous Americans*. New York: G. Routledge and Sons, 1889.

Boyd, James P. *Military And Civil Life Of Gen. Ulysses S. Grant: Leading Soldier of the Age, President of The United States, Loved and Honored American Citizen, the World's Most Distinguished Man.* (Philadelphia, Pa: Scammell & Co., 1885.

Croly, Herbert David. *Marcus Alonzo Hanna; His Life and Work*, (New York: The Macmillan Company, 1912.
Briggs, John Ely. *William Peters Hepburn*. (Iowa City, Ia: The State Historical Society of Iowa, 1919.

Cochrane, Rexmond C. *Measures for Progress: A History of the National Bureau of Standards*. New York: Arno Press, 1976.

Donaldson, Alfred L. *A History of the Adirondacks*. New York: Century Co, 1921.

Grigore, Julius, Jr. *First Presentation of All Stocks and Bonds Issued by the Compagnie Universelle du Canal Interoceanique de Panama, 1880 - 1889 and Compagnie Nouvelle du Canal de Panama, 1894*, W.G. Guy, Venice, Florida, 1997.

Hagedorn, Hermann. *The Roosevelt Family of Sagamore Hill*. New York: Macmillan, 1954.

Magie, David . *Life of Garret Augustus Hobart: Twenty-Fourth Vice-President of the United States*. (New York: G.P. Putnam's Sons, 1910

Olcott, Charles S. *The Life of William McKinley*. Boston: Houghton Mifflin Company, 1916.

Russell, Thomas Herbert. *Theodore Roosevelt, Typical American: His Life and Work : Patriot, Orator, Historian, Sportsman, Soldier, Statesman and President.* S.l: s.n., 1919.

Weber, Sandra. *Adirondack Roots: Stories of Hiking, History, and Women.* Charleston, SC: History Press, 2011.

Miscellaneous

"Anna Roosevelt," *National Park Service,* accessed 17 April 2012, http://www.nps.gov/thrb/historyculture/annaroosevelt.htm

Canal Zone. *The Panama Canal Record: Official Publication of the Panama Canal, Vol 23,* Balboa Heights, C.Z.: The Canal, 1920. Foley, W. J. "A Bullet and a Bull Moose" JAMA. 1969 Sep. 29 *JAMA.* 1969.

Marx, Rudolf. *The Health Of The President: Theodore Roosevelt,* http://www.healthguidance.org/entry/8931/1/The-Health-Of-The-President-Theodore-Roosevelt.html

Theodore Roosevelt to Frederick Courteney Selous, quoted in Edward Wagenknecht, *The Seven Worlds of Theodore Roosevelt,* Guilford, Conn: Lyons Press, 2009.

"Panama President to Face Corruption Charges," *Newsmax, http:// www.newsmax.com/Newsfront/Panama-Canal-Ricardo-Martinelli-Italy/2014/04/15/id/565764/*

Panama Canal Authority, press release, (27 Mar 2014) https://www.pancanal.com/eng/pr/press-releases/2014/03/20/pr508.html

ILLUSTRATIONS

Library of Congress

"Admiral John Grimes Walker," Photographic print. Library of Congress, 1904.

"Col. Theo. Roosevelt and his brother-in-law Douglas Robinson." Photographic print. Library of Congress, 1910.

"General William Walker." Photographic print. Library of Congress, circa 1855.

"Joseph Gurney Cannon," Photographic print. Library of Congress, 1903.

"President Roosevelt and Vice-President Charles Fairbanks," Photographic print. Library of Congress, 1904.

"President Roosevelt pointing at a map of South American…" Photographic print. Library of Congress, c. 1913.

"Roosevelt at the controls of a giant canal digger in Panama." Photographic print. Library of Congress, 1906.

"Senator John Tyler Morgan." Photographic print. Library of Congress, Library of Congress, 1880.

"Walter Wellman." Photographic print. Library of Congress, 1910.

Arnold, Charles Dudley. "[McKinley] Delivering the Address-President's Day." Photographic print. Library of Congress, 5 September 1901.

Bains News Service. "Elbert Martin and Bullet Pierced Speech." Photographic print. Library of Congress, October 1912.

———. "Roosevelt at Oyster Bay." Negative, glass. Library of Congress, 22 October 1912.

———. "T.R. on Tour." Negative, glass. Library of Congress, 1914.

Dalrymple, Louis. "A New Uniform and New Responsibilities." Photomechanical print: offset, color. *Puck*, Library of Congress, 2 October 1901.

J. Ottmann Lith. Co. "Roosevelt's Rough Diggers." Photomechanical print: offset, color. *Puck*, Library of Congress, 1906.

Keppler, Udo. "A Revelation in Revolutions." Photomechanical print: offset, color. *Puck*, Library of Congress, 25 November 1903.

———. "Christmas on the Isthmus." Photomechanical print: offset, color. *Puck*, Library of Congress, 23 December, 1903.

———. "Stop, Look, Listen!!! " Photomechanical print: offset, color. *Puck*, Library of Congress, 7 March 1912.

———. "The Isthmian Canal Game." Photomechanical print: offset, color. *Puck*, Library of Congress, 23 April 1902.

———. "Waiting." Photomechanical print: offset, color. *Puck*, Library of Congress, 22 June 1904.

Underwood & Underwood. "President Theodore Roosevelt and Senator Henry Cabot Lodge leaving the Hotel." Photographic print on stereo card. Library of Congress, 1902.

Books

Andrews, Elisha Benjamin. Photograph. *History of the United States Vol. 5*. New York: C. Scribner's, 1912.

Bishop, Farnham. Photograph.*Panama, Past and Present*. New York: Century Co, 1916.

Briggs, John Ely. Photograph. *William Peters Hepburn*. Iowa City, IA: The State Historical Society of Iowa, 1919.

Barrett, John. Drawing. *Panama Canal: What It Is, What It Means*. Washington, D.C.: Pan American Union, 1913.

Bunau-Varilla, Philippe. Nicaragua stamp. *Panama; The Creation, Destruction, and Resurrection*. London: Constable & Company, 1913.

Corthell, E. L. Photomechanical print of Ead's Ship Railway. *The Atlantic & Pacific Ship-Railway Across the Isthmus of Tehuantepec, in Mexico: Considered Commercially, Politically & Constructively*, New York: s.n.,1886.

Davis, Oscar King and John Kimberly Mumford. *William McKinley with his first Vice-President Garret Hobart. Photograph. The Life of William McKinley: Including a Genealogical Record of the McKinley Family and Copious Extracts from the Late President's Public Speeches, Messages to Congress, Proclamations, and Other State Papers : Illustrated with Nearly Two Hundred Photographs and Four Full Pages in Color.* New York: P.F. Collier & Son, 1901.

Garland, Hamlin. Photograph. *Ulysses S. Grant; His Life and Character.* New York: Doubleday & McClure Co, 1898.

Gros, Raymond. *T.R. in Cartoon.* Reprint "Back in the Old Place," "The Calebra Cut." New York: Saalfield Pub. Co, 1910.

Pan-American Exposition: Its Plan and Purpose. Cover art. Buffalo N.Y., 1901.

Sears, Lorenzo. John Hay, Author and Statesman. *Secretary of State John Hay.* New York: Dodd, Mead and Co, 1914.

Shaw, Albert. "The Man Behind the Egg!" "Senator Gorman fires a shotgun at Roosevelt." *A Cartoon History of Roosevelt's Career: Illustrated by Six Hundred and Thirty Contemporary Cartoons and Many Other Pictures.* New York: The Review of Reviews Company, 1910.

Trowbridge, Francis Bacon. *The Hoadley Genealogy: A History of the Descendants of William Hoadley of Branford, Connecticut Together with Some Account of Other Families of the Name.* New Haven, Conn: Printed for the author by Tuttle, Morehouse & Taylor, 1894.

Magazines/Journals

American Monthly Review of Reviews, Vol. 25. Reprints. "Uncle Sam stands at the doors of the U.S. Congress," "Members of the Isthmusian Canal," "The Isthmian Canal Commission," "In which will he sink his wallet, " "Uncle Sam swing Monroe Doctrine stick." *Cartoons.* January-June, 1902.

Arnold, C.D. Photo of operating room where doctors preformed McKinley's surgery. *The Trained Nurse and Hospital Review*, Vol. 27, No. 1, July, 1901.

Barrett, John. Guests aboard the S.S. "The Opening of the Panama Canal," *Bulletin of the Pan American Union*, Vol. 39, 1914.

Creeland, Joseph. "Joseph Pulitzer, Master Journalist," *Pearson's Magazine*, Vol. 21, 1909.

Harper's Weekly, Vol. 49, "The First Mountain to be Removed." Cartoon. July 1905.

Ireland, Alleyne. "A Modern Superman: A character Study of the Late Joseph Pulitzer," *The American Magazine*, Vol. 73, 1912.

Norwood, Irving. A disfigured Roosevelt. "Exit— Roosevelt, The Dominant," Outing Magazine, Vol. 53, 1909.

Newspapers

Goodwin's Weekly: A Thinking Paper for Thinking People (Salt Lake City, Utah), "Wandamere the Great." Advertisement. 01 June 1912.

Minneapolis Journal, " Mt. Hanna Volcano." Cartoon. 07 June 1902.

Seattle Star, "Nations Greets its Foremost Citizen." Front page. 18 June 1910.

The Washington Times Star, "Please Buy Our Nice Canal." Cartoon. 08 Jan. 1902.

Miscellaneous

Jackman, W.G. "Cornelius Vanderbilt." Engraving. *Hunt's Merchants Magazine*, (before 1877), Wikimedia Commons. http://commons.wikimedia.org/wiki/Cornelius_ Vanderbilt#mediaviewer/File:Cornelius_Vanderbilt_three-quarter_ view.jpg

"Ferdinand Marie Vicomte de Lesseps," Photographic print. 1880, Wikimedia Commons. http://commons.wikimedia.org/wiki/File:Lesseps_Ferdinand_de.JPG

"Letter from Corinne Roosevelt Robinson to Theodore Roosevelt." Theodore Roosevelt Center. January 22, 1902. http://www.theodorerooseveltcenter.org/

"William Nelson Cromwell," Photographic print. *Frank Leslie's Illustrated Newspaper*, Vol. 58, May 1904, WikimediaCommons. http://commons.wikimedia.org/wiki/File:William_Nelson_Cromwell_I.jpg

www.ingramcontent.com/pod-product-compliance
Lightning Source LLC
Chambersburg PA
CBHW031234090426
42742CB00007B/189